THE FINAL QUEST

ELFQUEST®

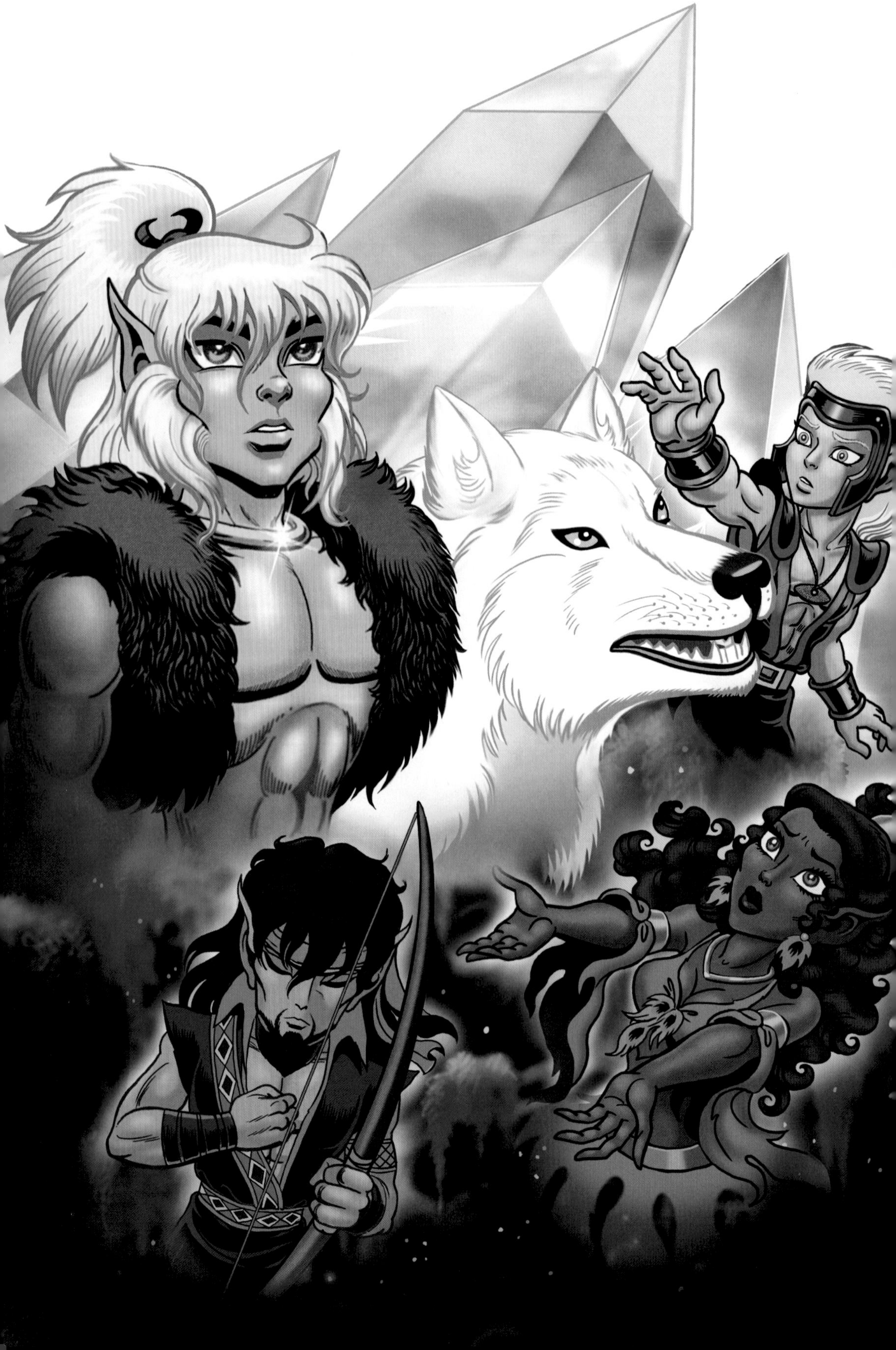

THE FINAL QUEST
ELFQUEST®

VOLUME TWO

BY WENDY AND RICHARD PINI

COLORS BY
SONNY STRAIT

LETTERS BY
NATE PIEKOS OF BLAMBOT®

DARK HORSE BOOKS

President & Publisher MIKE RICHARDSON

Editor SPENCER CUSHING

Designer SARAH TERRY

Digital Art Technician ALLYSON HALLER

NEIL HANKERSON Executive Vice President - TOM WEDDLE Chief Financial Officer - RANDY STRADLEY Vice President
of Publishing - MICHAEL MARTENS Vice President of Book Trade Sales - MATT PARKINSON Vice President of Marketing
DAVID SCROGGY Vice President of Product Development - DALE LaFOUNTAIN Vice President of Information Technology
CARA NIECE Vice President of Production and Scheduling - KEN LIZZI General Counsel DAVEY ESTRADA Editorial Director
DAVE MARSHALL Editor in Chief - SCOTT ALLIE Executive Senior Editor - CHRIS WARNER Senior Books Editor - CARY
GRAZZINI Director of Print and Development - LIA RIBACCHI Art Director - MARK BERNARDI Director of Digital Publishing

Published by Dark Horse Books
A division of Dark Horse Comics, Inc.
10956 SE Main Street
Milwaukie, OR 97222

First edition: April 2016
ISBN 978-1-61655-410-1
1 3 5 7 9 10 8 6 4 2
Printed in China

International Licensing: (503) 905-2377
Comic Shop Locator Service: (888) 266-4226

ELFQUEST: THE FINAL QUEST VOLUME 2

This volume collects and reprints the comic books ElfQuest: The Final Quest #7–#12.

LIBRARY OF CONGRESS CATALOGING-IN-PUBLICATION DATA

Names: Pini, Wendy, author, illustrator. | Pini, Richard, author,
illustrator. | Strait, Sonny, illustrator. | Piekos, Nate, illustrator.
Title: ElfQuest, the final quest, Volume two / by Wendy and Richard Pini ;
colors by Sonny Strait ; letters by Nate Piekos of Blambot.
Description: First edition. | Milwaukie, OR : Dark Horse Books, 2016. | This
volume collects and reprints the comic books ElfQuest: The Final Quest
#7-#12. | Description based on print version record and CIP data provided
by publisher; resource not viewed.
Identifiers: LCCN 2015050837 (print) | LCCN 2015045160 (ebook) | ISBN
9781630083342 () | ISBN 9781616554101 (paperback)
Subjects: LCSH: Elves–Comic books, strips, etc. | Graphic novels. | BISAC:
COMICS & GRAPHIC NOVELS / Fantasy. | GSAFD: Comic books, strips, etc.
Classification: LCC PN6728.E45 (print) | LCC PN6728.E45 P56393 2016 (ebook) |
DDC 741.5/973–dc23
LC record available at http://lccn.loc.gov/2015050837

A DISASTROUS THREAT grows with every
passing day. As the human warlord Grohmul
Djun strives to eradicate the entire race of
elves, his massive war fleet is poised to
overrun lands that have known only peace for
generations. Meanwhile, the Wolfriders feel
the subtle but ever-growing effects of living
near the Palace of the High Ones. There are
fateful, perhaps irreversible changes in the
wind. Cutter Kinseeker, Blood of Ten Chiefs,
realizes the time has come for a decision to
be made—one that will affect the life of every
elf living on the World of Two Moons.

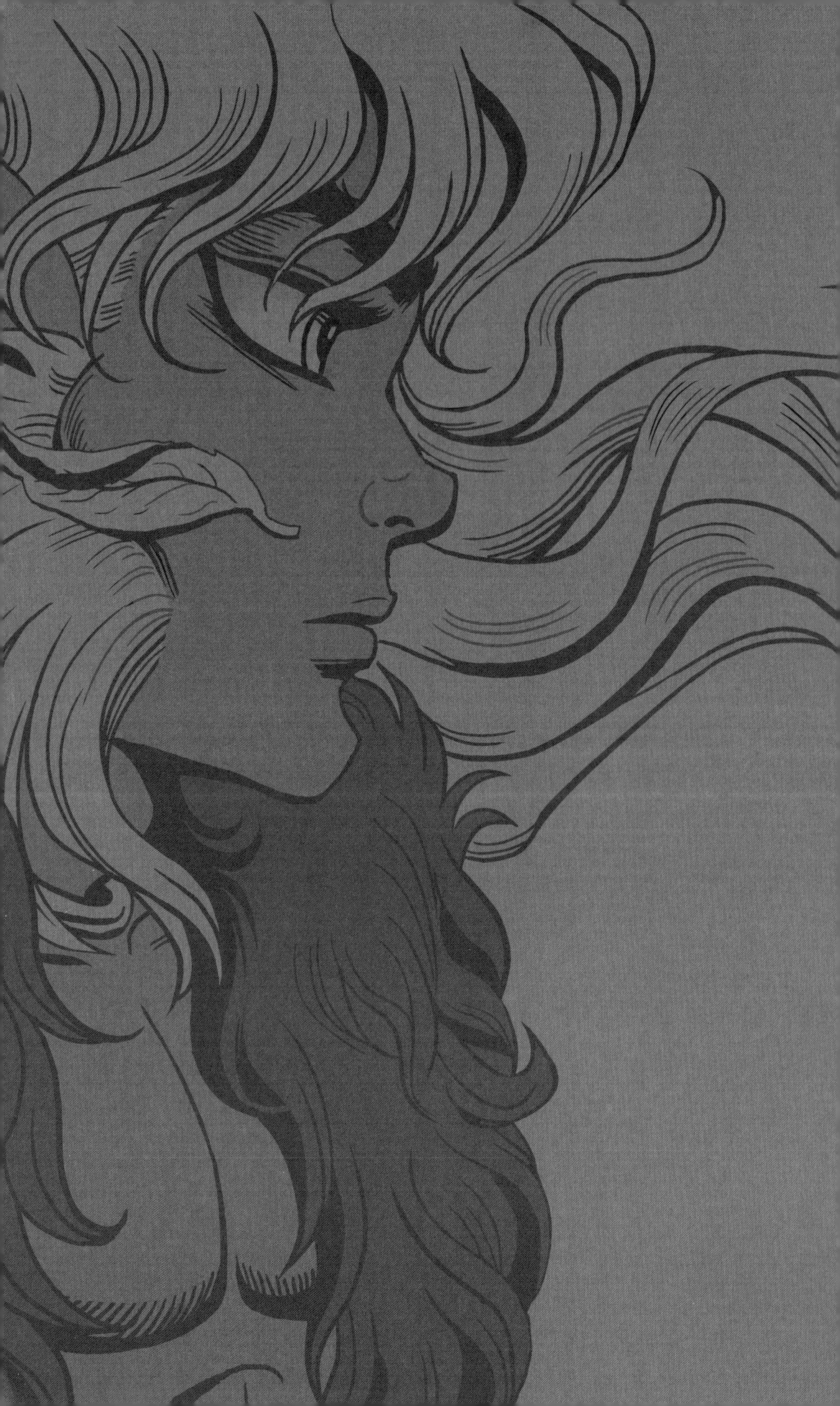

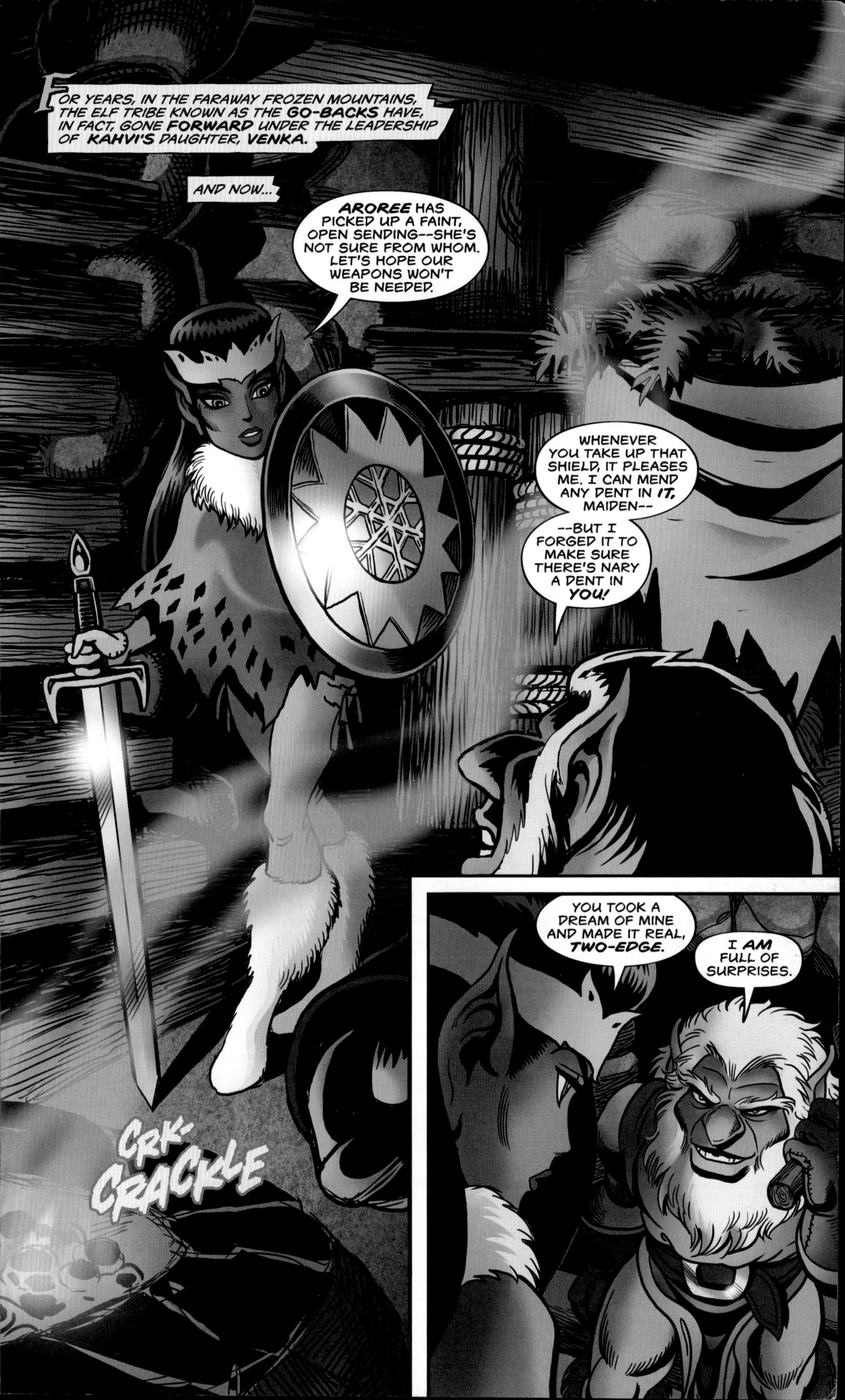
FOR YEARS, IN THE FARAWAY FROZEN MOUNTAINS, THE ELF TRIBE KNOWN AS THE GO-BACKS HAVE, IN FACT, GONE FORWARD UNDER THE LEADERSHIP OF KAHVI'S DAUGHTER, VENKA.
AND NOW...
AROREE HAS PICKED UP A FAINT, OPEN SENDING--SHE'S NOT SURE FROM WHOM. LET'S HOPE OUR WEAPONS WON'T BE NEEDED.
WHENEVER YOU TAKE UP THAT SHIELD, IT PLEASES ME. I CAN MEND ANY DENT IN IT, MAIDEN--
--BUT I FORGED IT TO MAKE SURE THERE'S NARY A DENT IN YOU!
CRK-CRACKLE
YOU TOOK A DREAM OF MINE AND MADE IT REAL, TWO-EDGE.
I AM FULL OF SURPRISES.

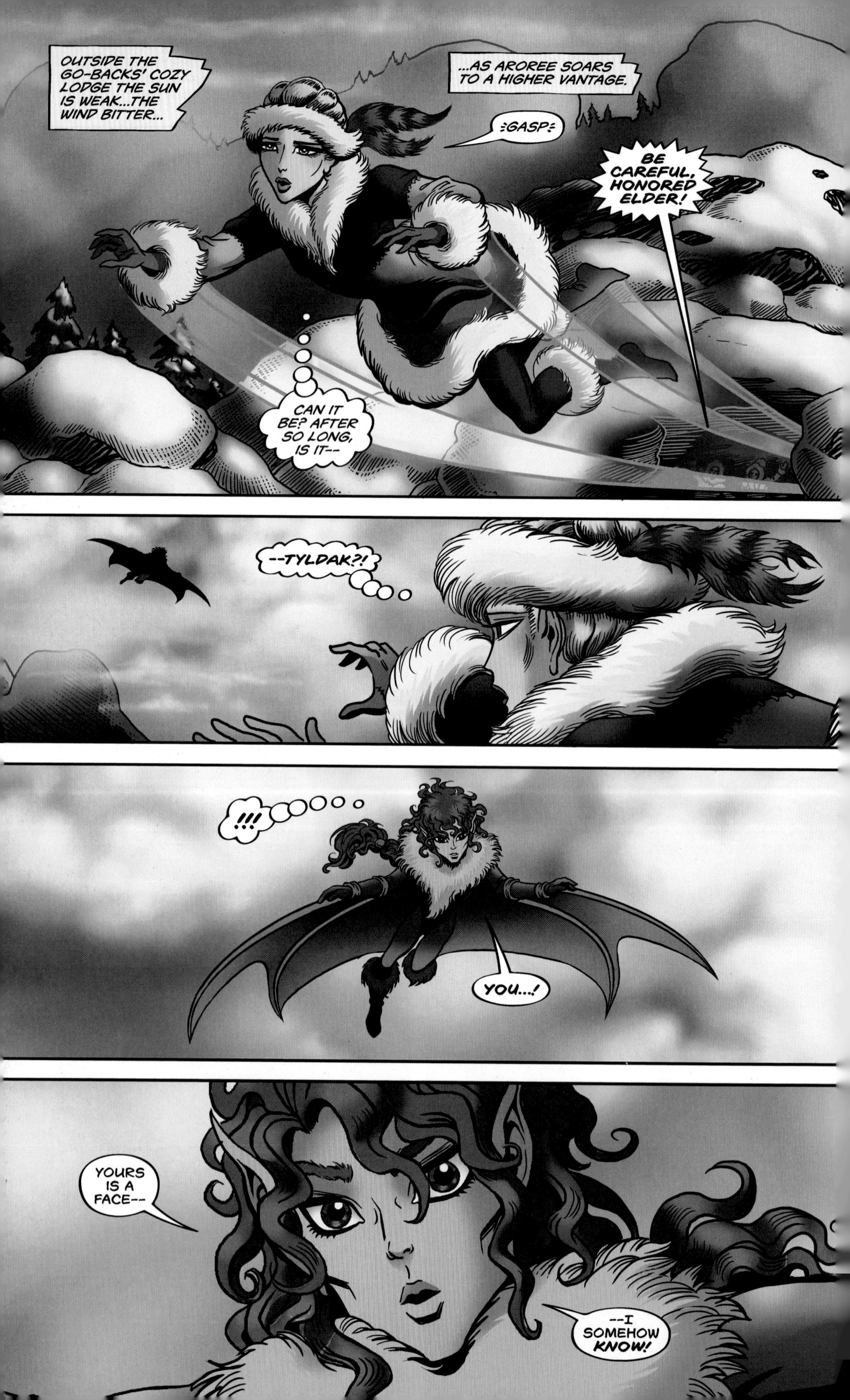
OUTSIDE THE GO-BACKS' COZY LODGE THE SUN IS WEAK...THE WIND BITTER...
...AS AROREE SOARS TO A HIGHER VANTAGE.
:GASP:
BE CAREFUL, HONORED ELDER!
CAN IT BE? AFTER SO LONG, IS IT--
--TYLDAK?!
!!!
YOU...!
YOURS IS A FACE--
--I SOMEHOW KNOW!

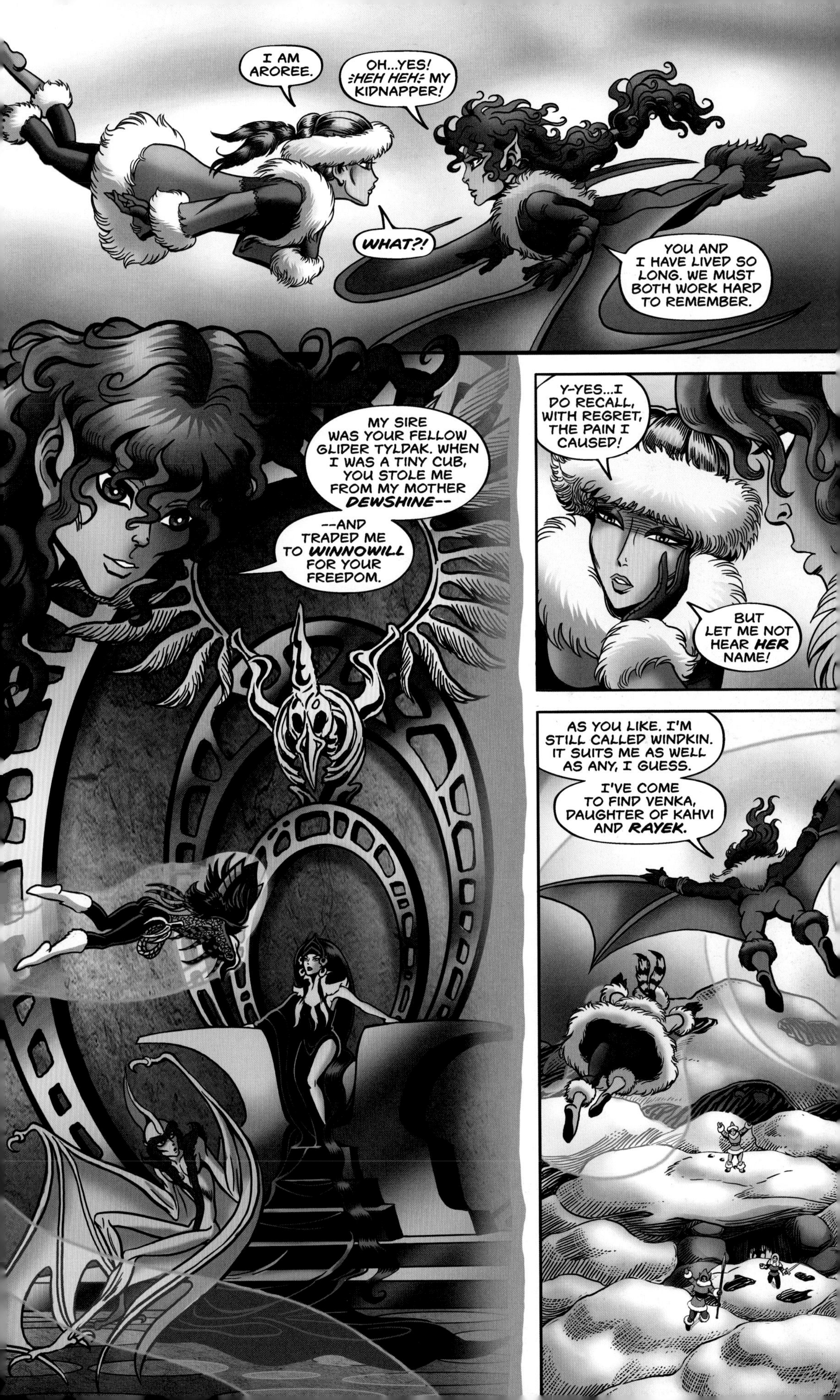
I AM AROREE.
OH...YES! HEH HEH MY KIDNAPPER!
WHAT?!
YOU AND I HAVE LIVED SO LONG. WE MUST BOTH WORK HARD TO REMEMBER.
MY SIRE WAS YOUR FELLOW GLIDER TYLDAK. WHEN I WAS A TINY CUB, YOU STOLE ME FROM MY MOTHER DEWSHINE--
--AND TRADED ME TO WINNOWILL FOR YOUR FREEDOM.
Y-YES...I DO RECALL, WITH REGRET, THE PAIN I CAUSED!
BUT LET ME NOT HEAR HER NAME!
AS YOU LIKE. I'M STILL CALLED WINDKIN. IT SUITS ME AS WELL AS ANY, I GUESS.
I'VE COME TO FIND VENKA, DAUGHTER OF KAHVI AND RAYEK.

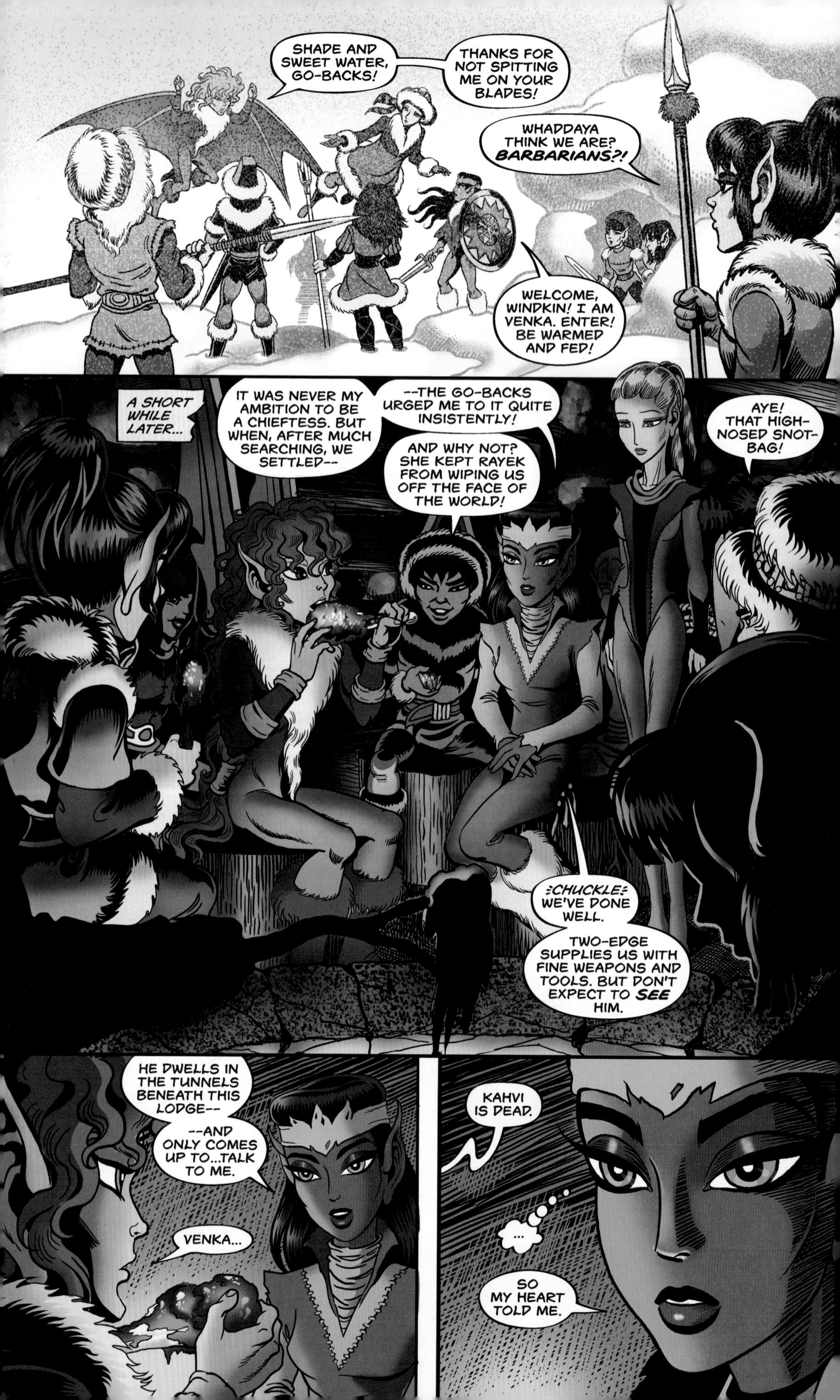
SHADE AND SWEET WATER, GO-BACKS!
THANKS FOR NOT SPITTING ME ON YOUR BLADES!
WHADDAYA THINK WE ARE? ***BARBARIANS?!***
WELCOME, WINDKIN! I AM VENKA. ENTER! BE WARMED AND FED!
A SHORT WHILE LATER...
IT WAS NEVER MY AMBITION TO BE A CHIEFTESS. BUT WHEN, AFTER MUCH SEARCHING, WE SETTLED--
--THE GO-BACKS URGED ME TO IT QUITE INSISTENTLY!
AND WHY NOT? SHE KEPT RAYEK FROM WIPING US OFF THE FACE OF THE WORLD!
AYE! THAT HIGH-NOSED SNOT-BAG!
:CHUCKLE: WE'VE DONE WELL.
TWO-EDGE SUPPLIES US WITH FINE WEAPONS AND TOOLS. BUT DON'T EXPECT TO ***SEE*** HIM.
HE DWELLS IN THE TUNNELS BENEATH THIS LODGE--
--AND ONLY COMES UP TO...TALK TO ME.
VENKA...
KAHVI IS DEAD.
...
SO MY HEART TOLD ME.

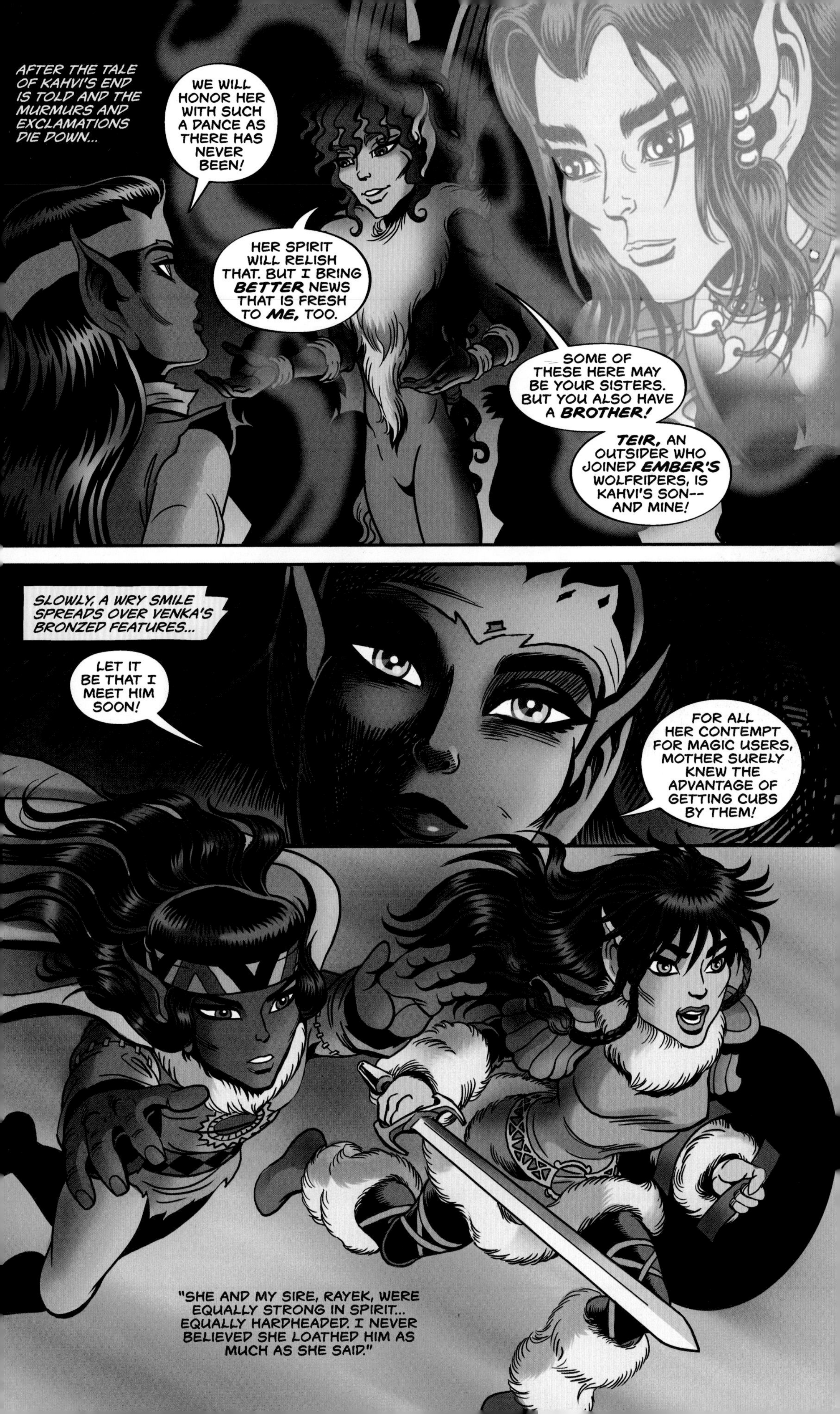

AFTER THE TALE OF KAHVI'S END IS TOLD AND THE MURMURS AND EXCLAMATIONS DIE DOWN...
WE WILL HONOR HER WITH SUCH A DANCE AS THERE HAS NEVER BEEN!
HER SPIRIT WILL RELISH THAT. BUT I BRING BETTER NEWS THAT IS FRESH TO ME, TOO.
SOME OF THESE HERE MAY BE YOUR SISTERS. BUT YOU ALSO HAVE A BROTHER!
TEIR, AN OUTSIDER WHO JOINED EMBER'S WOLFRIDERS, IS KAHVI'S SON--AND MINE!
SLOWLY, A WRY SMILE SPREADS OVER VENKA'S BRONZED FEATURES...
LET IT BE THAT I MEET HIM SOON!
FOR ALL HER CONTEMPT FOR MAGIC USERS, MOTHER SURELY KNEW THE ADVANTAGE OF GETTING CUBS BY THEM!
"SHE AND MY SIRE, RAYEK, WERE EQUALLY STRONG IN SPIRIT... EQUALLY HARDHEADED. I NEVER BELIEVED SHE LOATHED HIM AS MUCH AS SHE SAID."

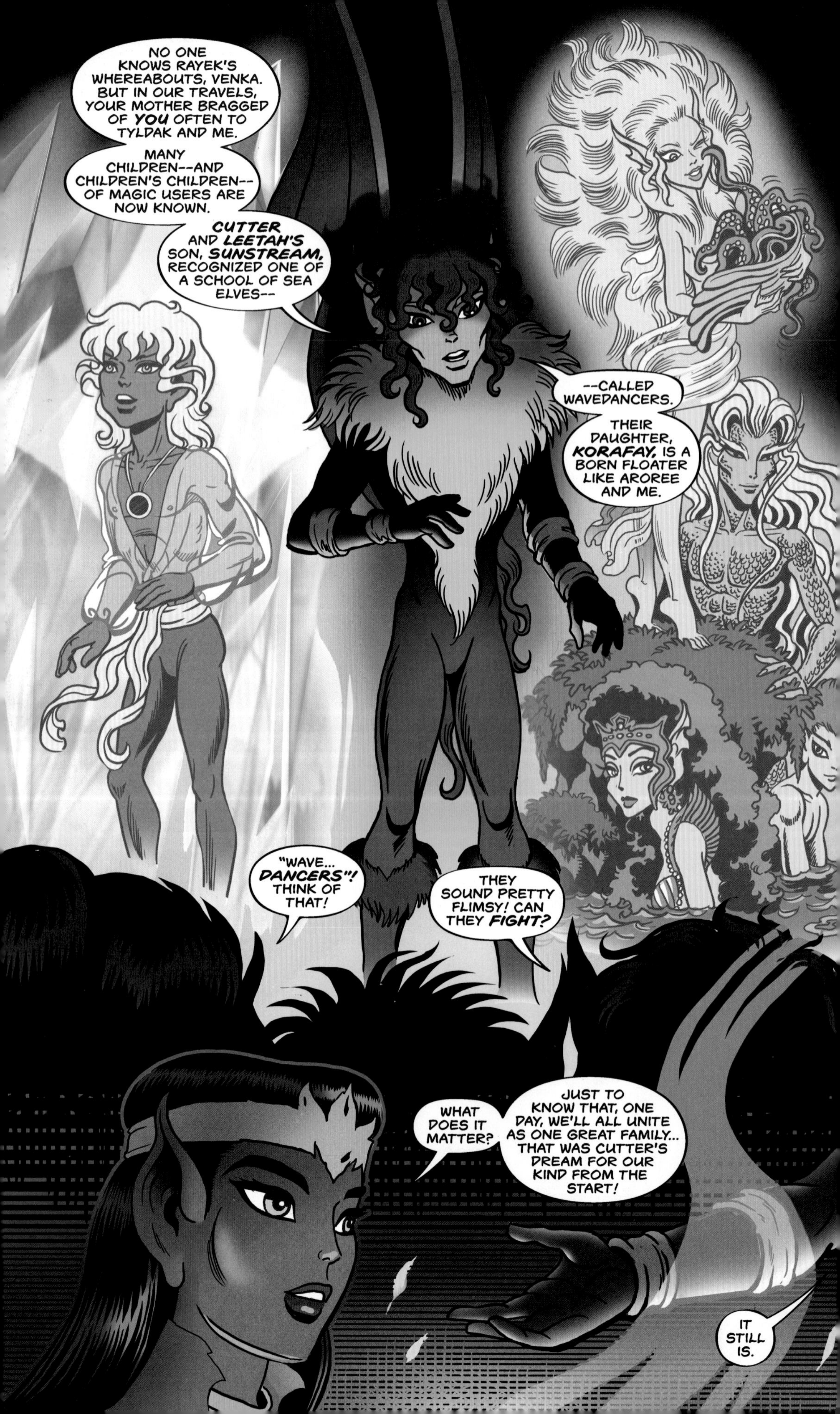

NO ONE KNOWS RAYEK'S WHEREABOUTS, VENKA. BUT IN OUR TRAVELS, YOUR MOTHER BRAGGED OF YOU OFTEN TO TYLDAK AND ME.
MANY CHILDREN--AND CHILDREN'S CHILDREN--OF MAGIC USERS ARE NOW KNOWN.
CUTTER AND LEETAH'S SON, SUNSTREAM, RECOGNIZED ONE OF A SCHOOL OF SEA ELVES--
--CALLED WAVEDANCERS.
THEIR DAUGHTER, KORAFAY, IS A BORN FLOATER LIKE AROREE AND ME.
"WAVE... DANCERS"! THINK OF THAT!
THEY SOUND PRETTY FLIMSY! CAN THEY FIGHT?
WHAT DOES IT MATTER?
JUST TO KNOW THAT, ONE DAY, WE'LL ALL UNITE AS ONE GREAT FAMILY... THAT WAS CUTTER'S DREAM FOR OUR KIND FROM THE START!
IT STILL IS.

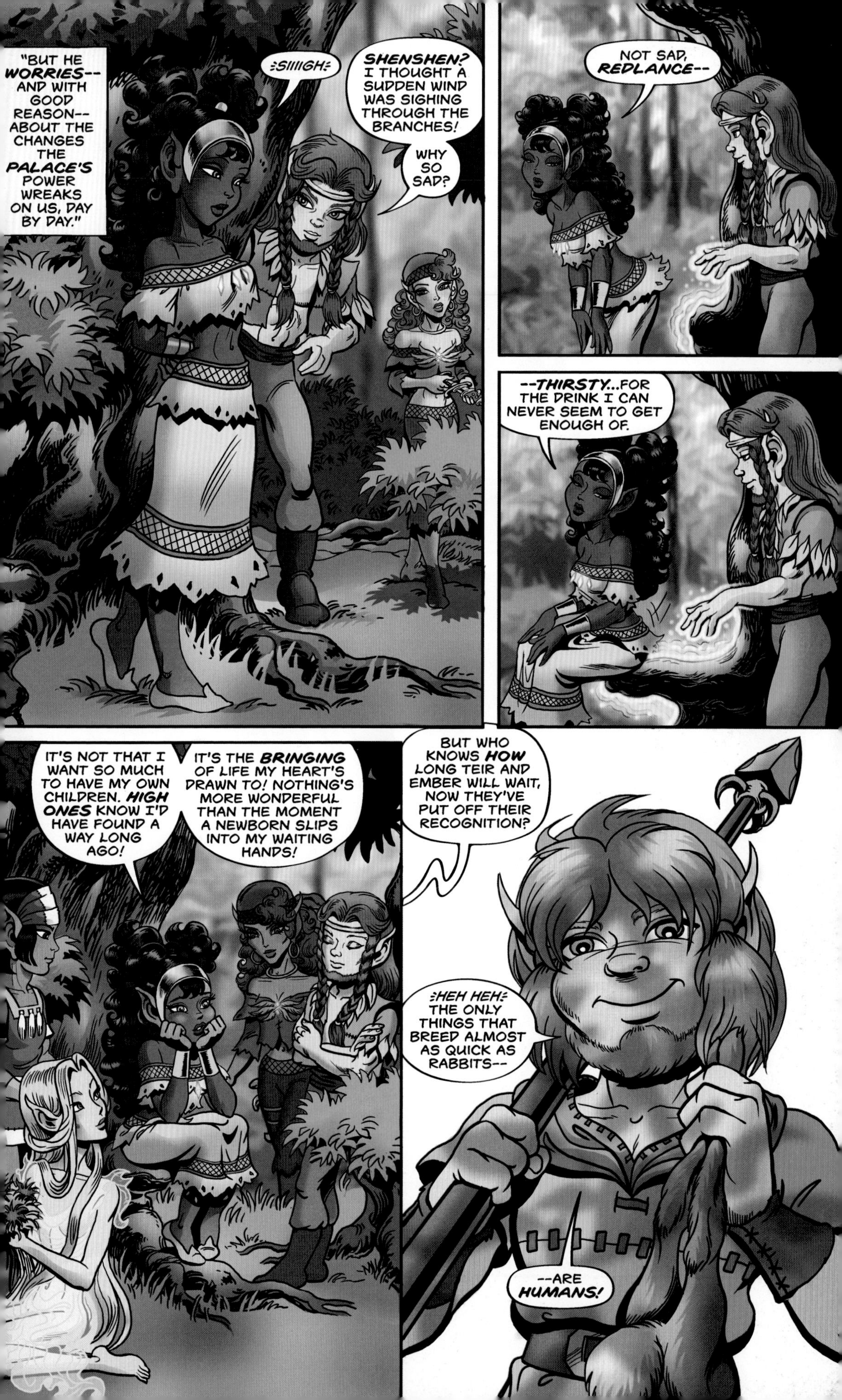
"BUT HE WORRIES-- AND WITH GOOD REASON-- ABOUT THE CHANGES THE PALACE'S POWER WREAKS ON US, DAY BY DAY."
SIIIIGH
SHENSHEN? I THOUGHT A SUDDEN WIND WAS SIGHING THROUGH THE BRANCHES!
WHY SO SAD?
NOT SAD, REDLANCE--
--THIRSTY...FOR THE DRINK I CAN NEVER SEEM TO GET ENOUGH OF.
IT'S NOT THAT I WANT SO MUCH TO HAVE MY OWN CHILDREN. HIGH ONES KNOW I'D HAVE FOUND A WAY LONG AGO!
IT'S THE BRINGING OF LIFE MY HEART'S DRAWN TO! NOTHING'S MORE WONDERFUL THAN THE MOMENT A NEWBORN SLIPS INTO MY WAITING HANDS!
BUT WHO KNOWS HOW LONG TEIR AND EMBER WILL WAIT, NOW THEY'VE PUT OFF THEIR RECOGNITION?
HEH HEH THE ONLY THINGS THAT BREED ALMOST AS QUICK AS RABBITS--
--ARE HUMANS!

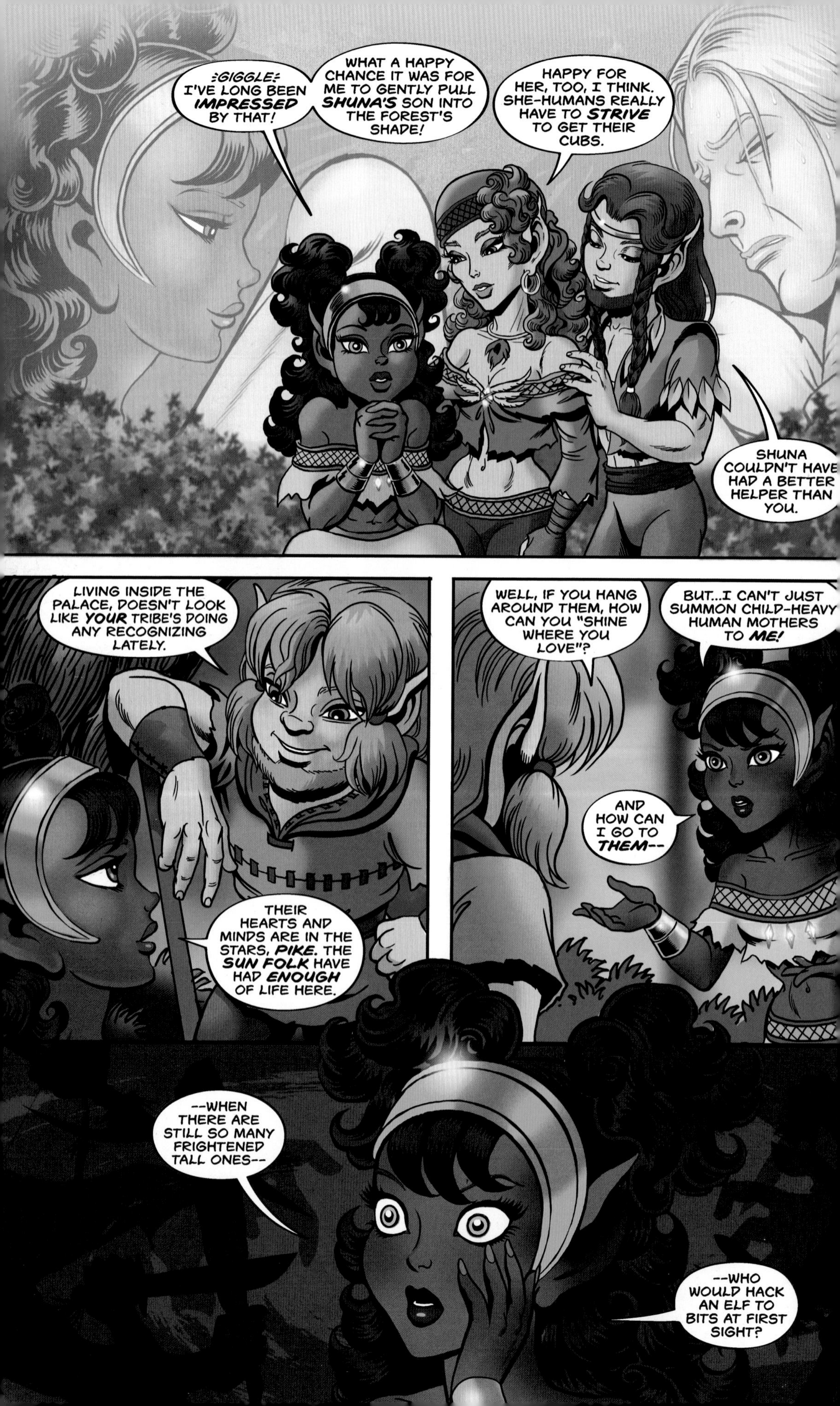

:GIGGLE: I'VE LONG BEEN IMPRESSED BY THAT!
WHAT A HAPPY CHANCE IT WAS FOR ME TO GENTLY PULL SHUNA'S SON INTO THE FOREST'S SHADE!
HAPPY FOR HER, TOO, I THINK. SHE-HUMANS REALLY HAVE TO STRIVE TO GET THEIR CUBS.
SHUNA COULDN'T HAVE HAD A BETTER HELPER THAN YOU.
LIVING INSIDE THE PALACE, DOESN'T LOOK LIKE YOUR TRIBE'S DOING ANY RECOGNIZING LATELY.
THEIR HEARTS AND MINDS ARE IN THE STARS, PIKE. THE SUN FOLK HAVE HAD ENOUGH OF LIFE HERE.
WELL, IF YOU HANG AROUND THEM, HOW CAN YOU "SHINE WHERE YOU LOVE"?
BUT...I CAN'T JUST SUMMON CHILD-HEAVY HUMAN MOTHERS TO ME!
AND HOW CAN I GO TO THEM--
--WHEN THERE ARE STILL SO MANY FRIGHTENED TALL ONES--
--WHO WOULD HACK AN ELF TO BITS AT FIRST SIGHT?

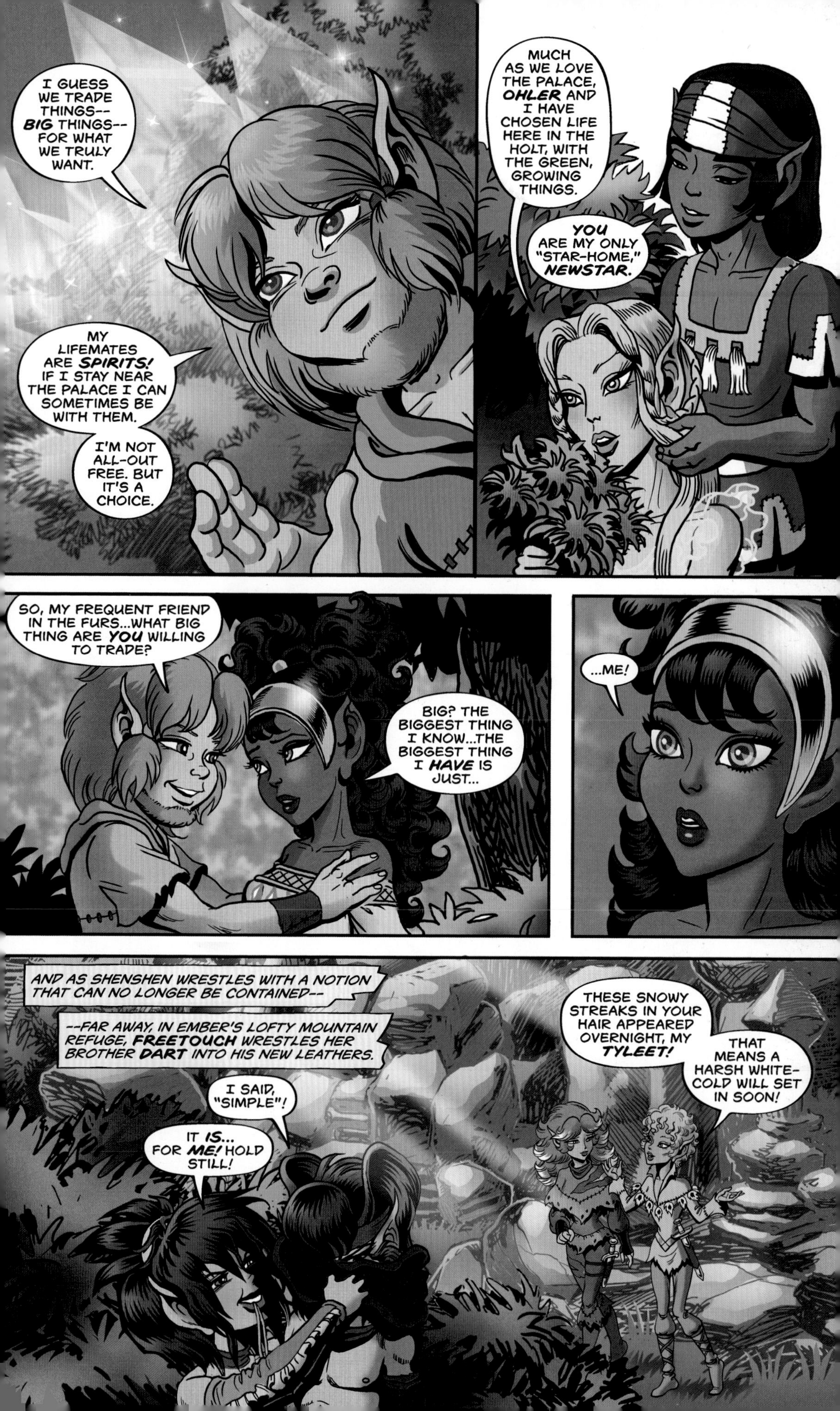
I GUESS WE TRADE THINGS-- BIG THINGS-- FOR WHAT WE TRULY WANT.
MY LIFEMATES ARE SPIRITS! IF I STAY NEAR THE PALACE I CAN SOMETIMES BE WITH THEM.
I'M NOT ALL-OUT FREE. BUT IT'S A CHOICE.
MUCH AS WE LOVE THE PALACE, OHLER AND I HAVE CHOSEN LIFE HERE IN THE HOLT, WITH THE GREEN, GROWING THINGS.
YOU ARE MY ONLY "STAR-HOME," NEWSTAR.
SO, MY FREQUENT FRIEND IN THE FURS...WHAT BIG THING ARE YOU WILLING TO TRADE?
BIG? THE BIGGEST THING I KNOW...THE BIGGEST THING I HAVE IS JUST...
...ME!
AND AS SHENSHEN WRESTLES WITH A NOTION THAT CAN NO LONGER BE CONTAINED--
--FAR AWAY, IN EMBER'S LOFTY MOUNTAIN REFUGE, FREETOUCH WRESTLES HER BROTHER DART INTO HIS NEW LEATHERS.
I SAID, "SIMPLE"!
IT IS... FOR ME! HOLD STILL!
THESE SNOWY STREAKS IN YOUR HAIR APPEARED OVERNIGHT, MY TYLEET!
THAT MEANS A HARSH WHITE-COLD WILL SET IN SOON!

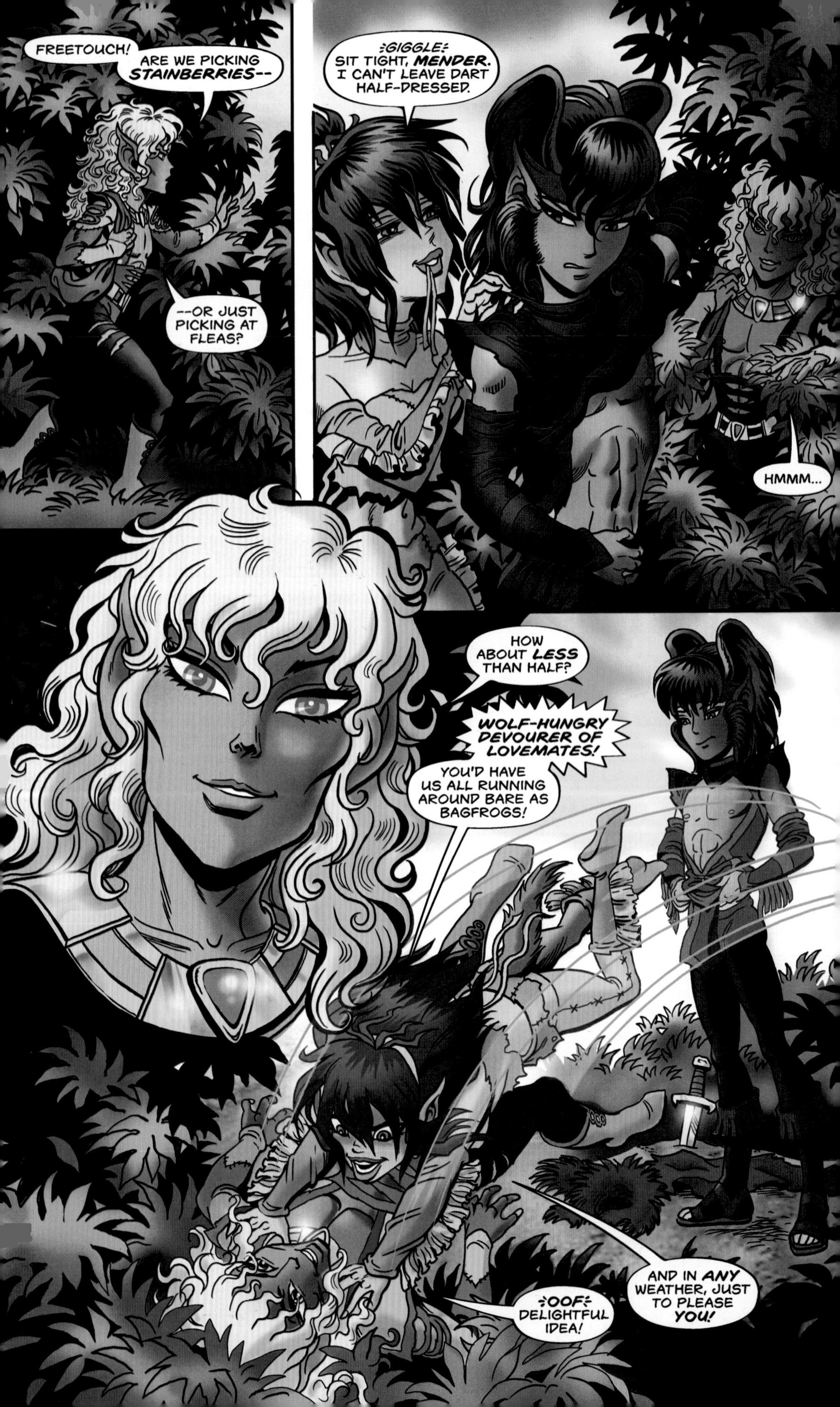
FREETOUCH!
ARE WE PICKING STAINBERRIES--
--OR JUST PICKING AT FLEAS?
:GIGGLE: SIT TIGHT, MENDER. I CAN'T LEAVE DART HALF-DRESSED.
HMMM...
HOW ABOUT LESS THAN HALF?
WOLF-HUNGRY DEVOURER OF LOVEMATES!
YOU'D HAVE US ALL RUNNING AROUND BARE AS BAGFROGS!
AND IN ANY WEATHER, JUST TO PLEASE YOU!
:OOF: DELIGHTFUL IDEA!

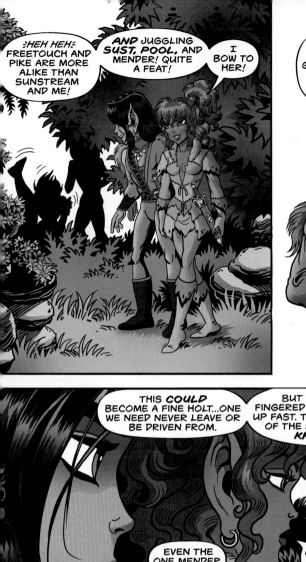

:HEH HEH: FREETOUCH AND PIKE ARE MORE ALIKE THAN SUNSTREAM AND ME!

AND JUGGLING SUST, POOL, AND MENDER! QUITE A FEAT!

I BOW TO HER!

SHE AND DART CAME TO US WITH SO MANY GIFTS! FOOD...CLOTHES... AND THESE FROM TREESTUMP AND CLEARBROOK!

"TWIN FLAMES"! THEY KNOW US WELL, DON'T THEY, BELOVED?

THIS COULD BECOME A FINE HOLT...ONE WE NEED NEVER LEAVE OR BE DRIVEN FROM.

BUT THOSE FIVE-FINGERED CUBS WILL GROW UP FAST. THEY'RE NOT MADE OF THE SAME STUFF AS KHORBASI.

EVEN THE ONE MENDER HEALED?

TINGEH? SHE'S LIKE MY SISTER, SHUNA. SEEMS ONCE AN ELF HEALER WORKS ON A HUMAN--

--THEY CARRY A BIT OF OUR MAGIC WITH THEM FOR LIFE.

"BUT WHAT OF THE OTHERS?"

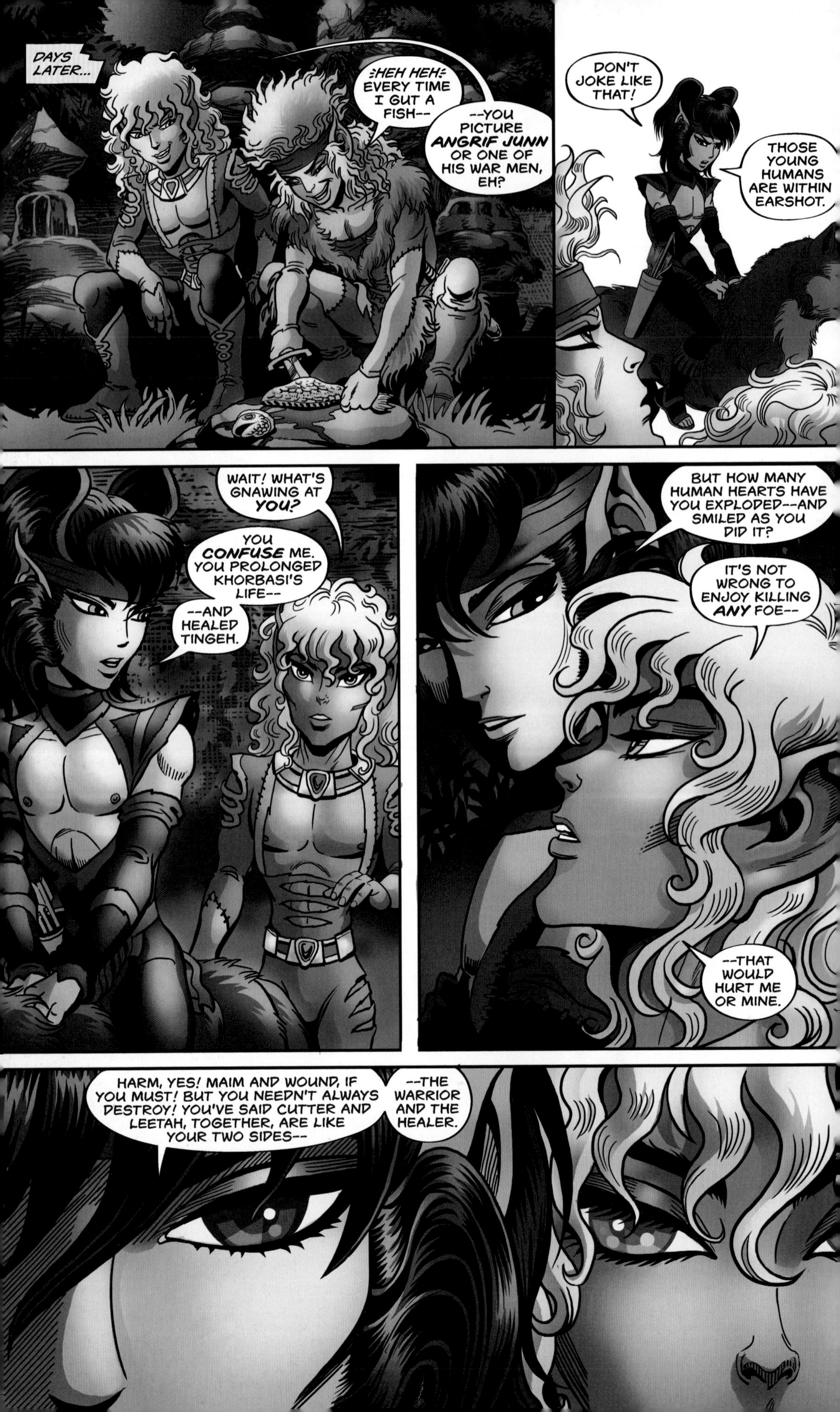
DAYS LATER...
HEH HEH EVERY TIME I GUT A FISH--
--YOU PICTURE ANGRIF JUNN OR ONE OF HIS WAR MEN, EH?
DON'T JOKE LIKE THAT!
THOSE YOUNG HUMANS ARE WITHIN EARSHOT.
WAIT! WHAT'S GNAWING AT YOU?
YOU CONFUSE ME. YOU PROLONGED KHORBASI'S LIFE--
--AND HEALED TINGEH.
BUT HOW MANY HUMAN HEARTS HAVE YOU EXPLODED--AND SMILED AS YOU DID IT?
IT'S NOT WRONG TO ENJOY KILLING ANY FOE--
--THAT WOULD HURT ME OR MINE.
HARM, YES! MAIM AND WOUND, IF YOU MUST! BUT YOU NEEDN'T ALWAYS DESTROY! YOU'VE SAID CUTTER AND LEETAH, TOGETHER, ARE LIKE YOUR TWO SIDES--
--THE WARRIOR AND THE HEALER.

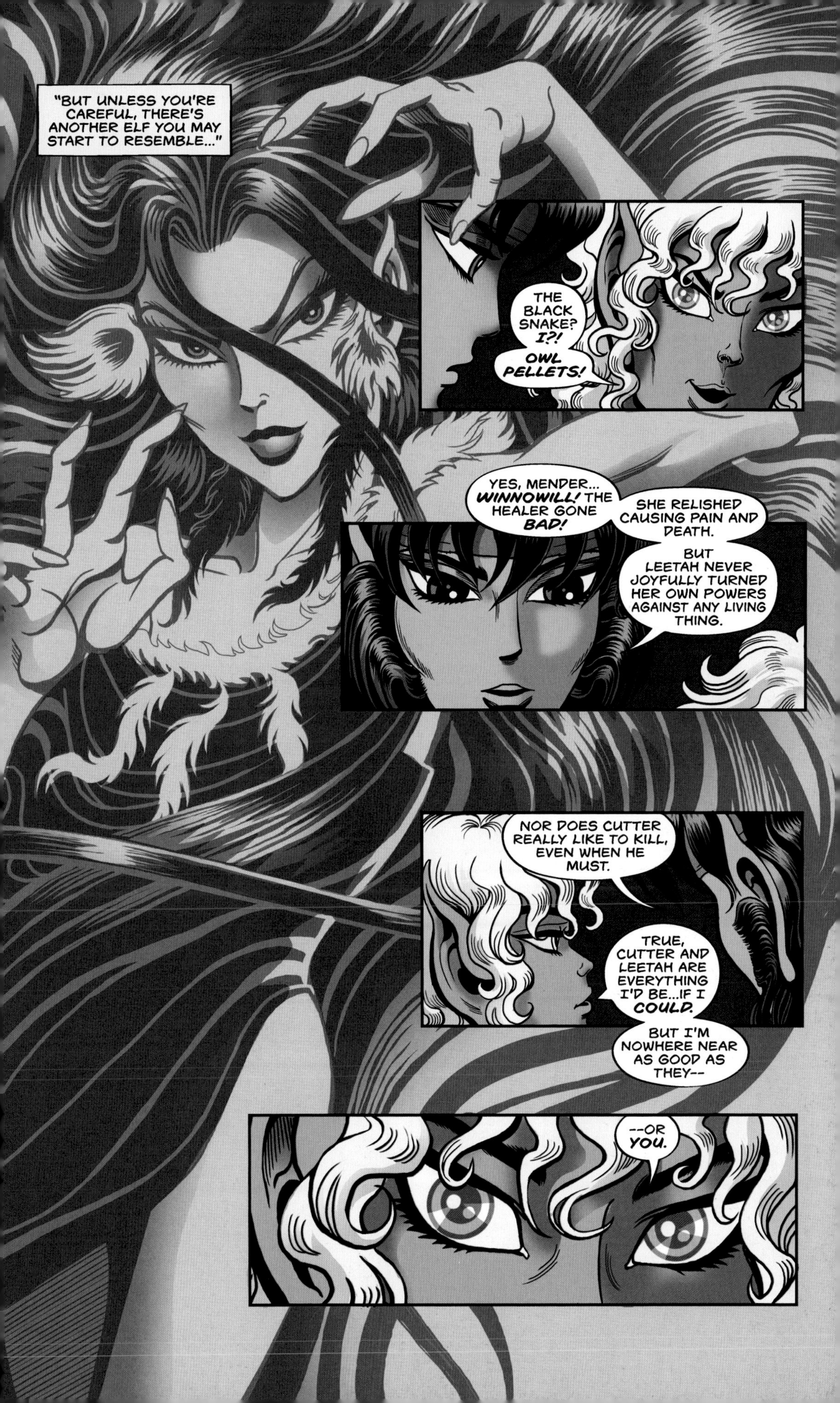
"BUT UNLESS YOU'RE CAREFUL, THERE'S ANOTHER ELF YOU MAY START TO RESEMBLE..."
THE BLACK SNAKE? I?!
OWL PELLETS!
YES, MENDER... WINNOWILL! THE HEALER GONE BAD!
SHE RELISHED CAUSING PAIN AND DEATH.
BUT LEETAH NEVER JOYFULLY TURNED HER OWN POWERS AGAINST ANY LIVING THING.
NOR DOES CUTTER REALLY LIKE TO KILL, EVEN WHEN HE MUST.
TRUE, CUTTER AND LEETAH ARE EVERYTHING I'D BE...IF I COULD.
BUT I'M NOWHERE NEAR AS GOOD AS THEY--
--OR YOU.

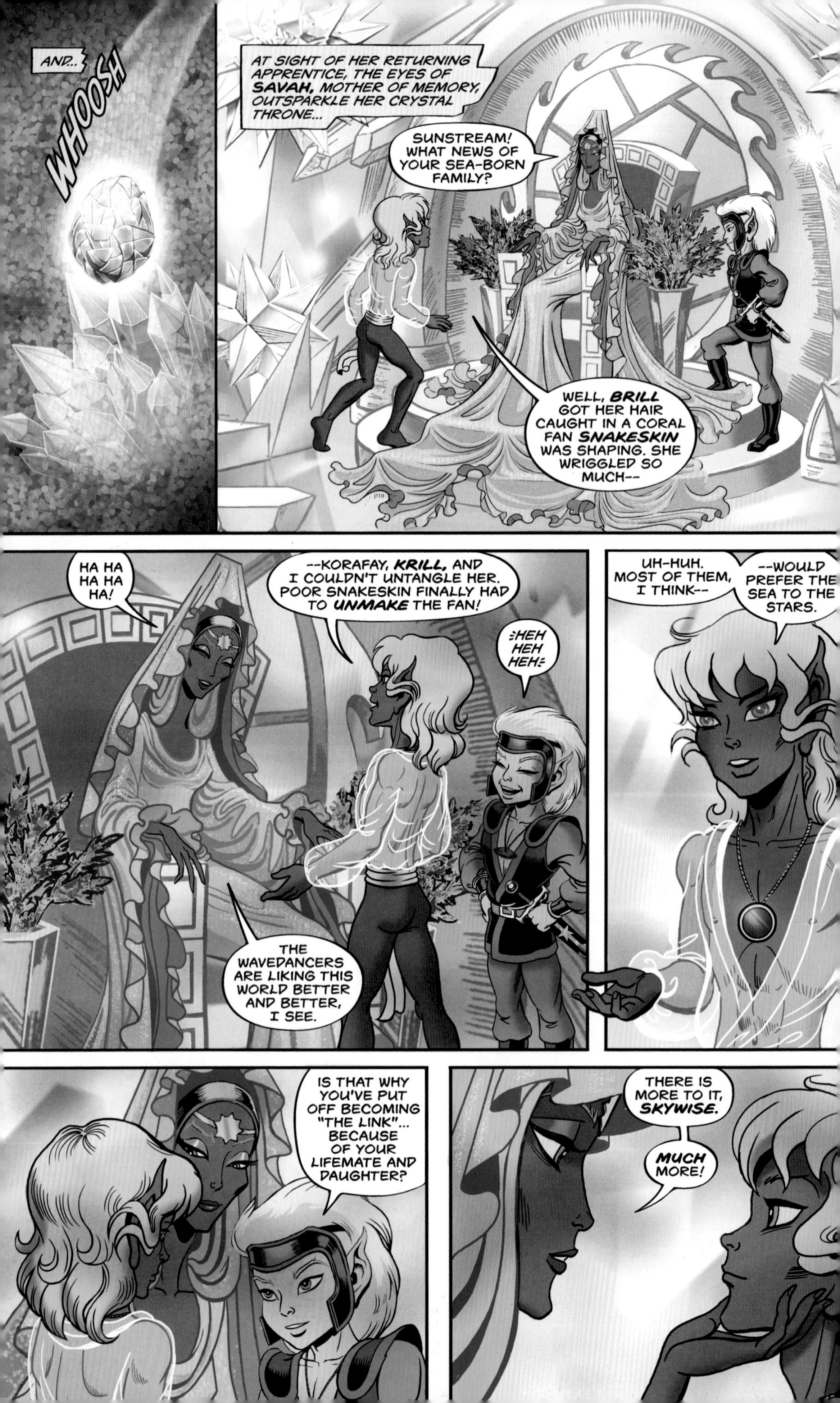
AND...
WHOOSH
AT SIGHT OF HER RETURNING APPRENTICE, THE EYES OF SAVAH, MOTHER OF MEMORY, OUTSPARKLE HER CRYSTAL THRONE...
SUNSTREAM! WHAT NEWS OF YOUR SEA-BORN FAMILY?
WELL, BRILL GOT HER HAIR CAUGHT IN A CORAL FAN SNAKESKIN WAS SHAPING. SHE WRIGGLED SO MUCH--
HA HA HA HA HA!
--KORAFAY, KRILL, AND I COULDN'T UNTANGLE HER. POOR SNAKESKIN FINALLY HAD TO UNMAKE THE FAN!
HEH HEH HEH
THE WAVEDANCERS ARE LIKING THIS WORLD BETTER AND BETTER, I SEE.
UH-HUH. MOST OF THEM, I THINK--
--WOULD PREFER THE SEA TO THE STARS.
IS THAT WHY YOU'VE PUT OFF BECOMING "THE LINK"... BECAUSE OF YOUR LIFEMATE AND DAUGHTER?
THERE IS MORE TO IT, SKYWISE.
MUCH MORE!

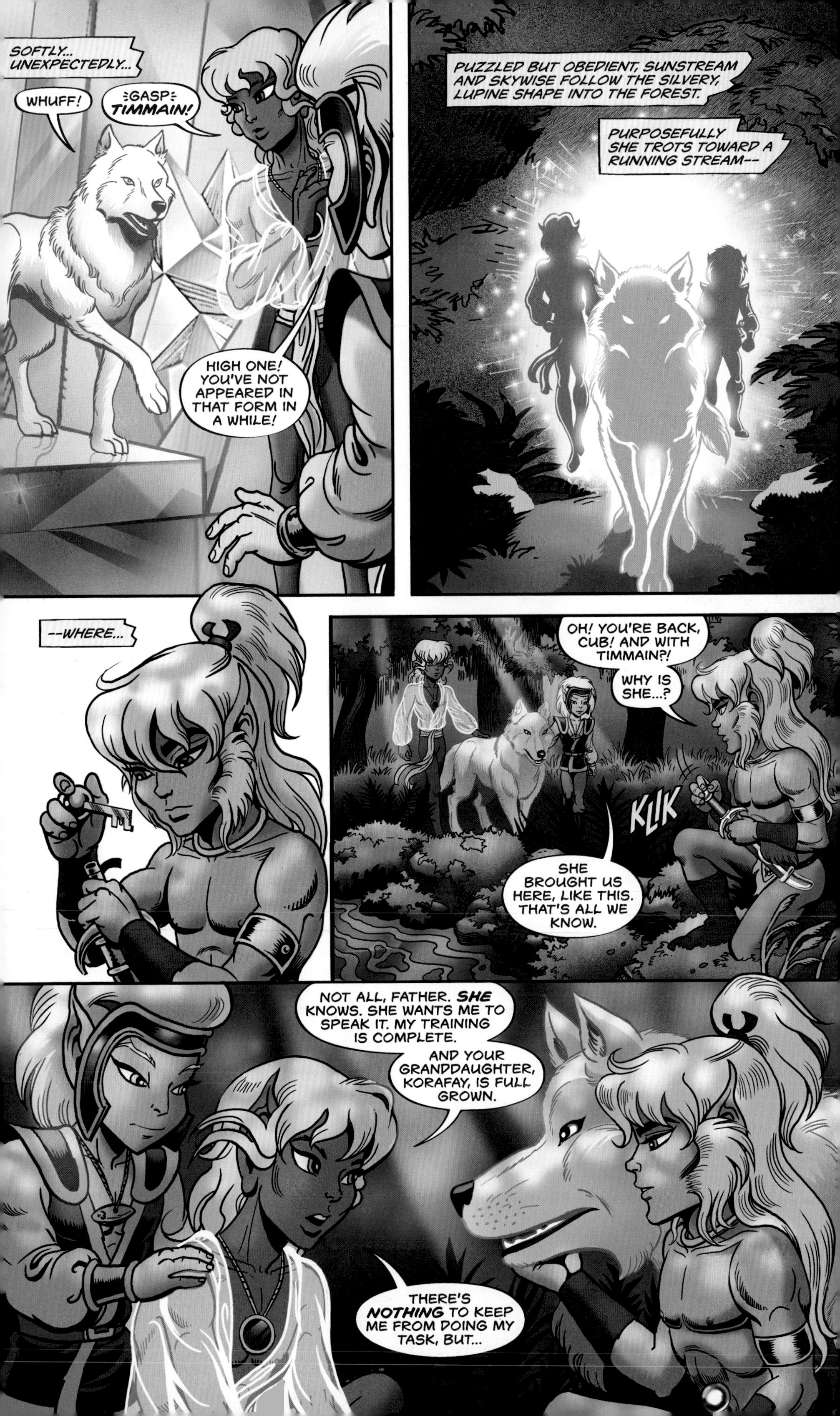
SOFTLY... UNEXPECTEDLY...
WHUFF!
:GASP: TIMMAIN!
HIGH ONE! YOU'VE NOT APPEARED IN THAT FORM IN A WHILE!
PUZZLED BUT OBEDIENT, SUNSTREAM AND SKYWISE FOLLOW THE SILVERY, LUPINE SHAPE INTO THE FOREST.
PURPOSEFULLY SHE TROTS TOWARD A RUNNING STREAM--
--WHERE...
OH! YOU'RE BACK, CUB! AND WITH TIMMAIN?!
WHY IS SHE...?
KLIK
SHE BROUGHT US HERE, LIKE THIS. THAT'S ALL WE KNOW.
NOT ALL, FATHER. SHE KNOWS. SHE WANTS ME TO SPEAK IT. MY TRAINING IS COMPLETE.
AND YOUR GRANDDAUGHTER, KORAFAY, IS FULL GROWN.
THERE'S NOTHING TO KEEP ME FROM DOING MY TASK, BUT...

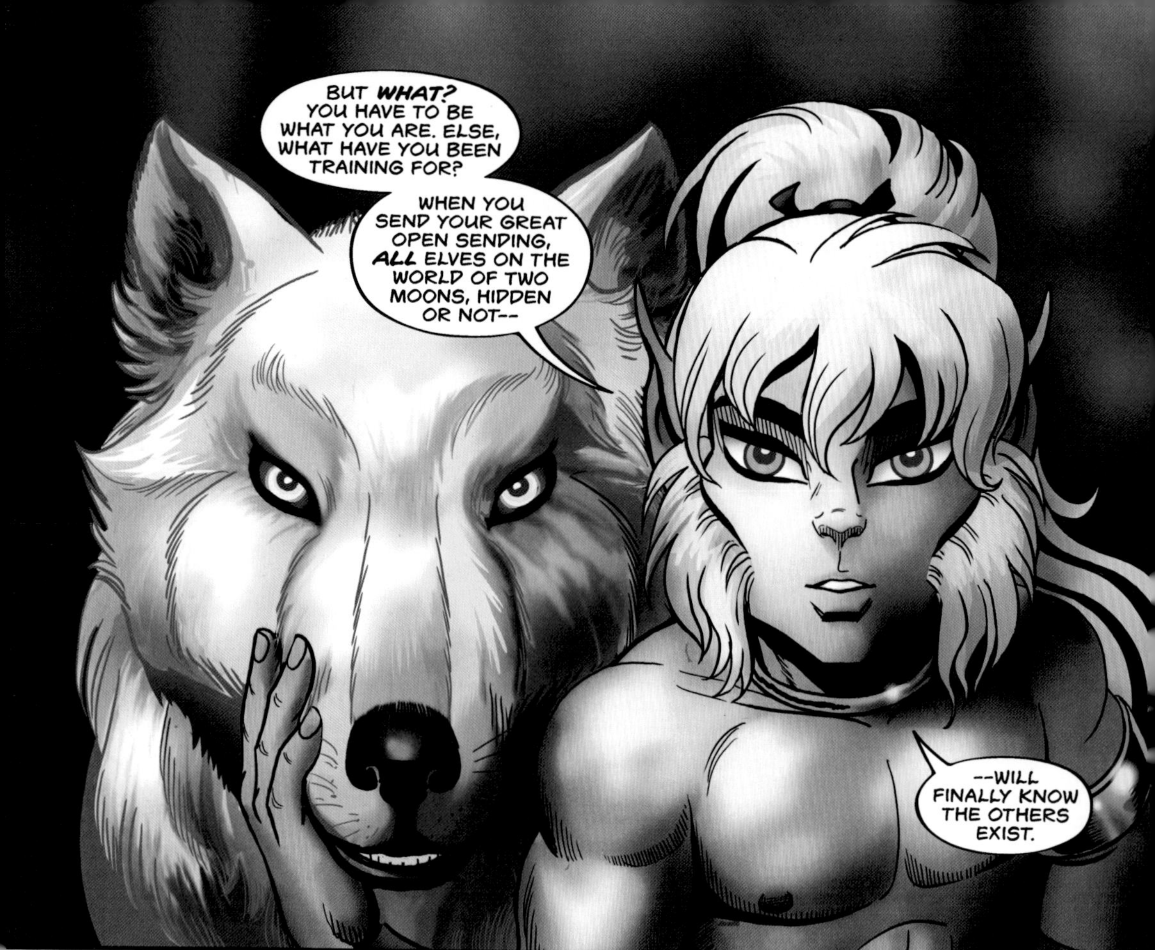
BUT *WHAT?* YOU HAVE TO BE WHAT YOU ARE. ELSE, WHAT HAVE YOU BEEN TRAINING FOR?
WHEN YOU SEND YOUR GREAT OPEN SENDING, *ALL* ELVES ON THE WORLD OF TWO MOONS, HIDDEN OR NOT--
--WILL FINALLY KNOW THE OTHERS EXIST.

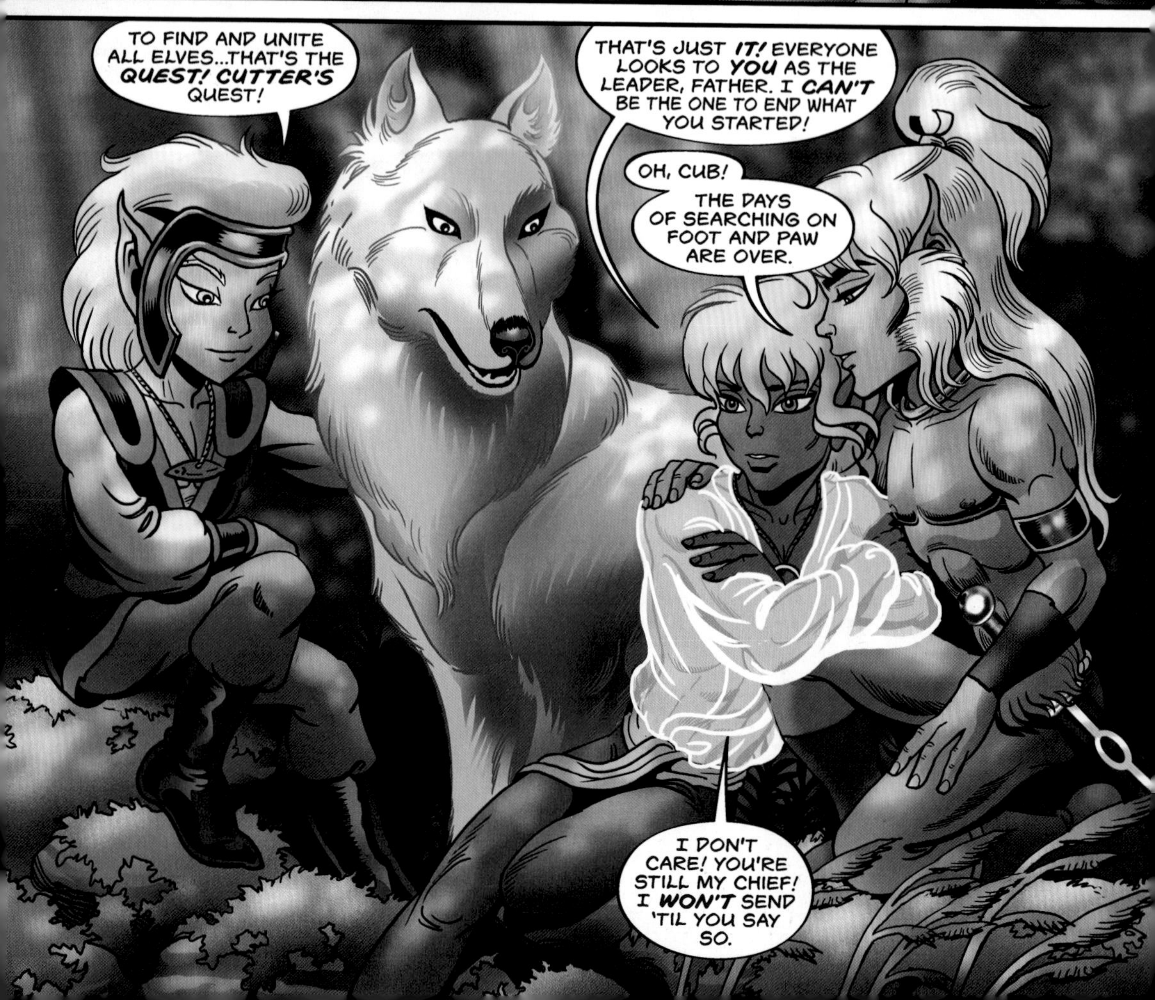
TO FIND AND UNITE ALL ELVES...THAT'S THE *QUEST! CUTTER'S* QUEST!
THAT'S JUST *IT!* EVERYONE LOOKS TO *YOU* AS THE LEADER, FATHER. I *CAN'T* BE THE ONE TO END WHAT YOU STARTED!
OH, CUB!
THE DAYS OF SEARCHING ON FOOT AND PAW ARE OVER.
I DON'T CARE! YOU'RE STILL MY CHIEF! I *WON'T* SEND 'TIL YOU SAY SO.

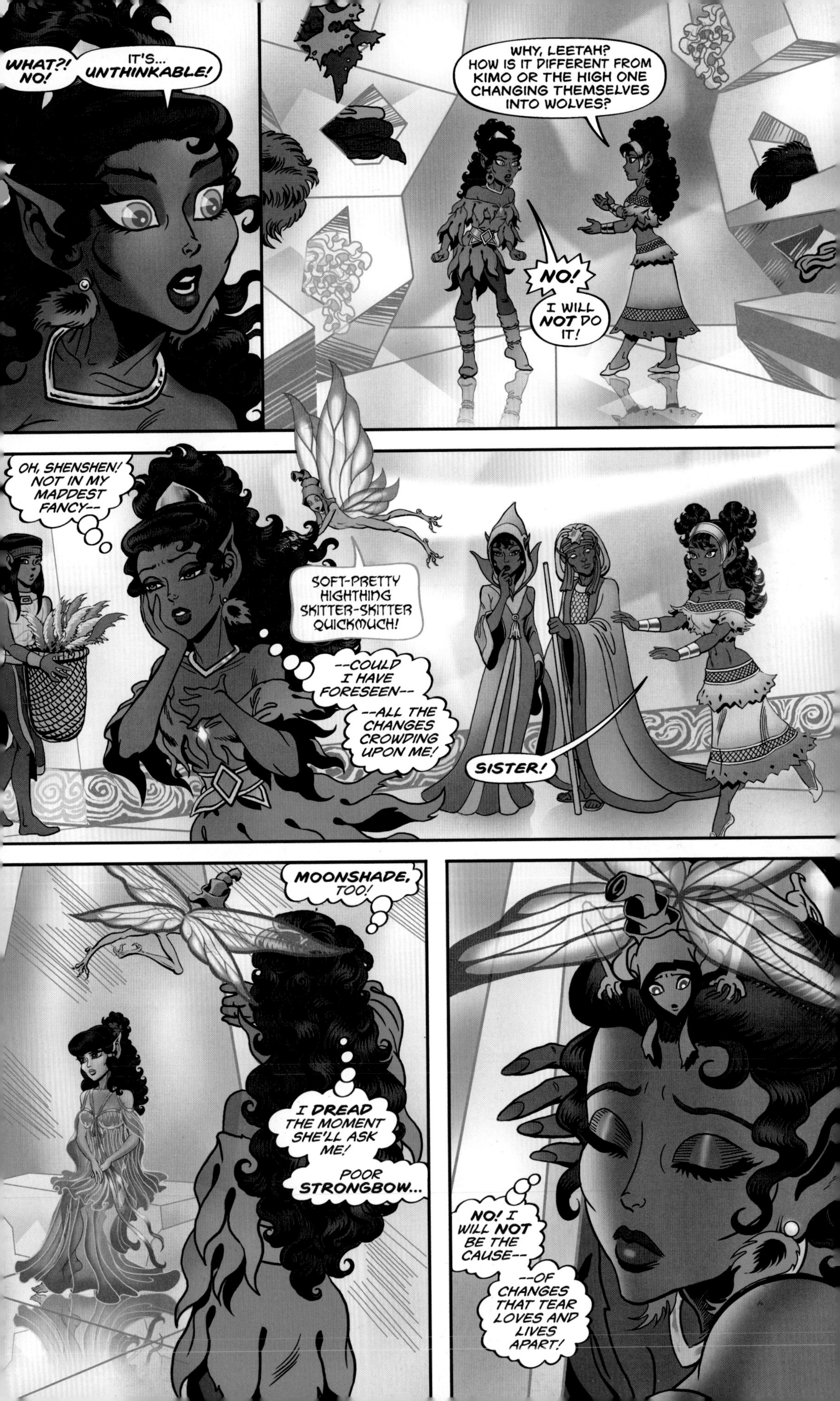
WHAT?! NO!
IT'S... UNTHINKABLE!
WHY, LEETAH? HOW IS IT DIFFERENT FROM KIMO OR THE HIGH ONE CHANGING THEMSELVES INTO WOLVES?
NO!
I WILL NOT DO IT!
OH, SHENSHEN! NOT IN MY MADDEST FANCY--
SOFT-PRETTY HIGHTHING SKITTER-SKITTER QUICKMUCH!
--COULD I HAVE FORESEEN--
--ALL THE CHANGES CROWDING UPON ME!
SISTER!
MOONSHADE, TOO!
I DREAD THE MOMENT SHE'LL ASK ME!
POOR STRONGBOW...
NO! I WILL NOT BE THE CAUSE--
--OF CHANGES THAT TEAR LOVES AND LIVES APART!

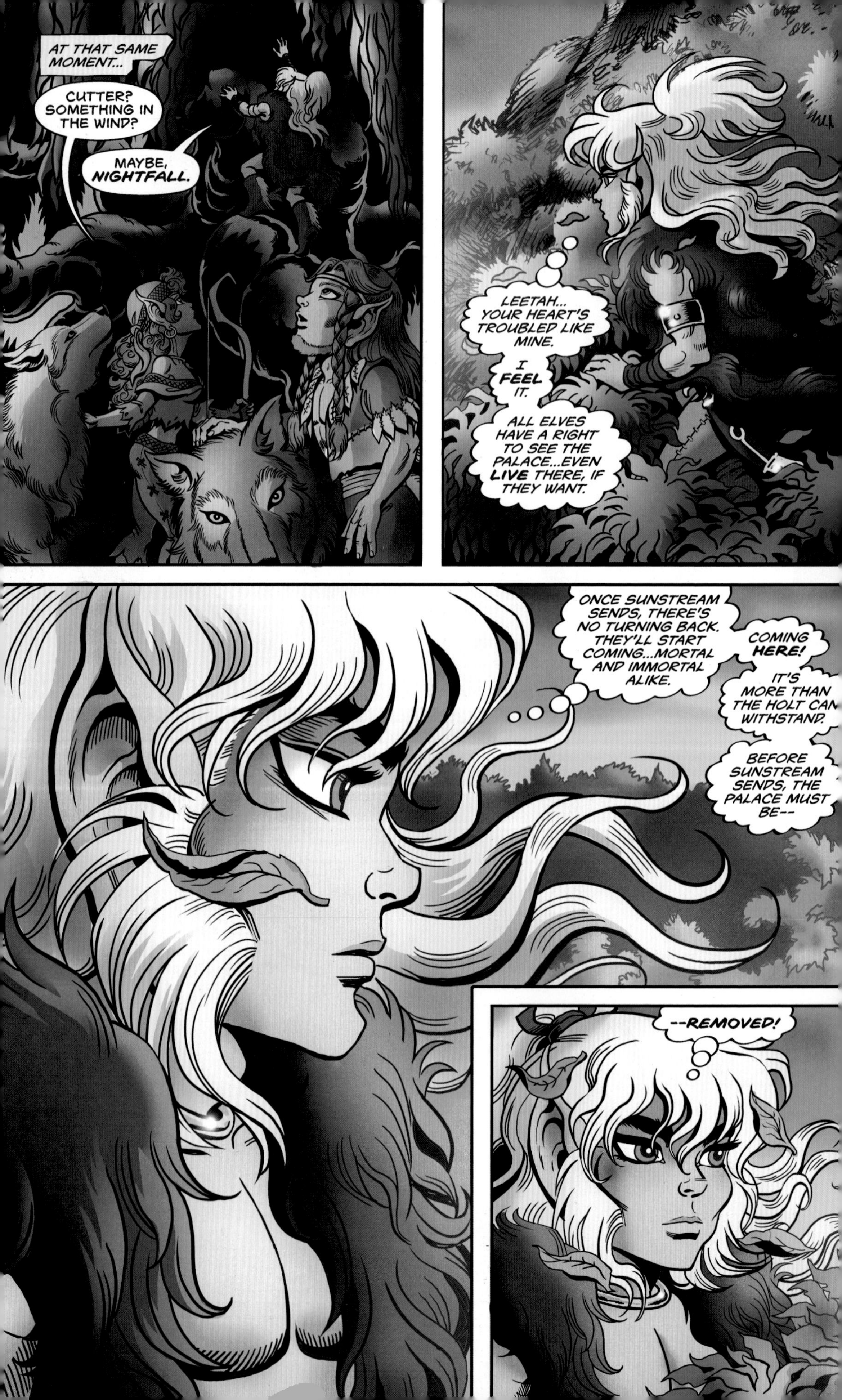

AT THAT SAME MOMENT...
CUTTER? SOMETHING IN THE WIND?
MAYBE, NIGHTFALL.
LEETAH... YOUR HEART'S TROUBLED LIKE MINE.
I FEEL IT.
ALL ELVES HAVE A RIGHT TO SEE THE PALACE...EVEN LIVE THERE, IF THEY WANT.
ONCE SUNSTREAM SENDS, THERE'S NO TURNING BACK. THEY'LL START COMING...MORTAL AND IMMORTAL ALIKE.
COMING HERE!
IT'S MORE THAN THE HOLT CAN WITHSTAND.
BEFORE SUNSTREAM SENDS, THE PALACE MUST BE--
--REMOVED!

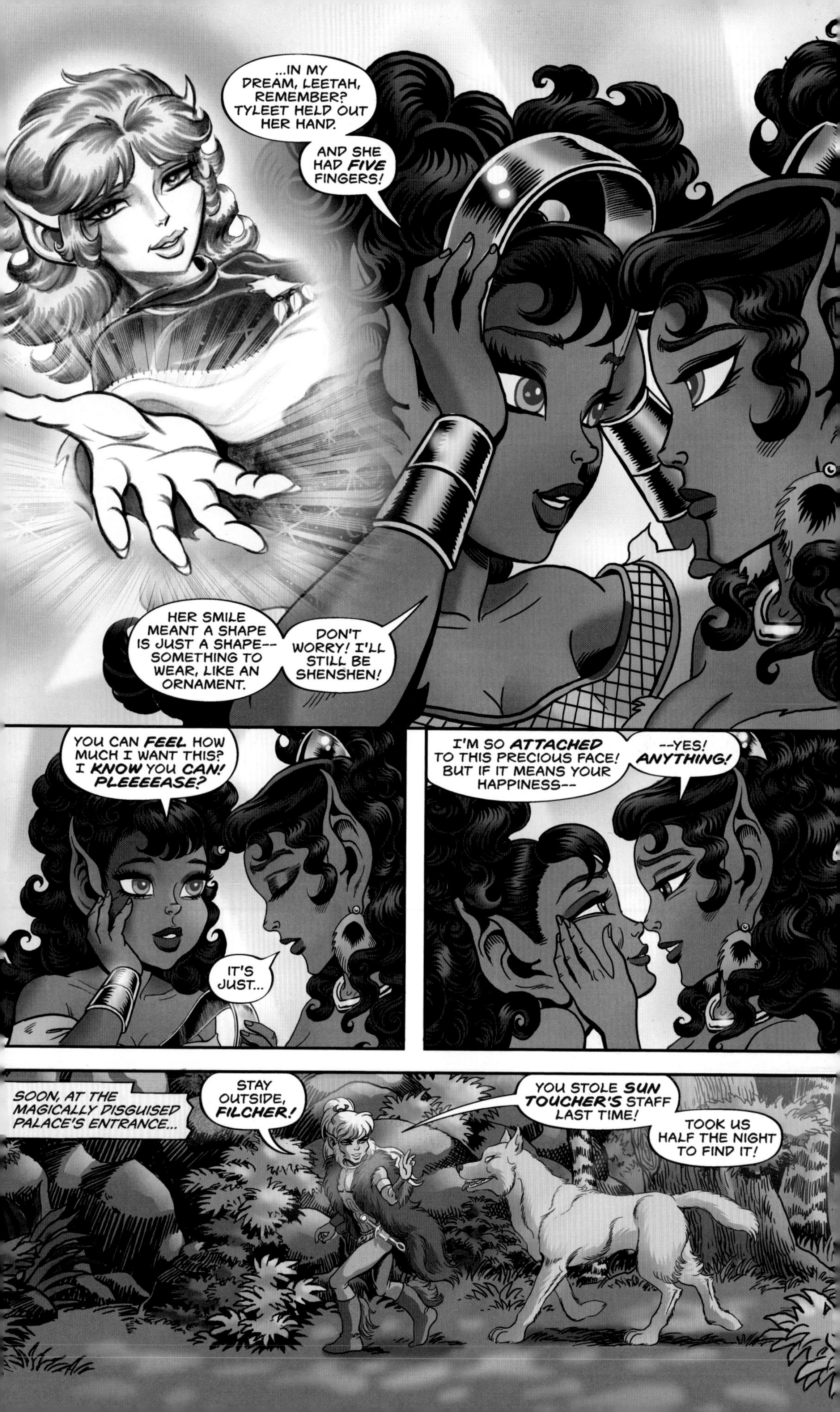
...IN MY DREAM, LEETAH, REMEMBER? TYLEET HELD OUT HER HAND.
AND SHE HAD **FIVE** FINGERS!
HER SMILE MEANT A SHAPE IS JUST A SHAPE-- SOMETHING TO WEAR, LIKE AN ORNAMENT.
DON'T WORRY! I'LL STILL BE SHENSHEN!
YOU CAN **FEEL** HOW MUCH I WANT THIS? I **KNOW** YOU **CAN! PLEEEEASE?**
IT'S JUST...
I'M SO **ATTACHED** TO THIS PRECIOUS FACE! BUT IF IT MEANS YOUR HAPPINESS--
--YES! **ANYTHING!**
SOON, AT THE MAGICALLY DISGUISED PALACE'S ENTRANCE...
STAY OUTSIDE, **FILCHER!**
YOU STOLE **SUN TOUCHER'S** STAFF LAST TIME!
TOOK US HALF THE NIGHT TO FIND IT!

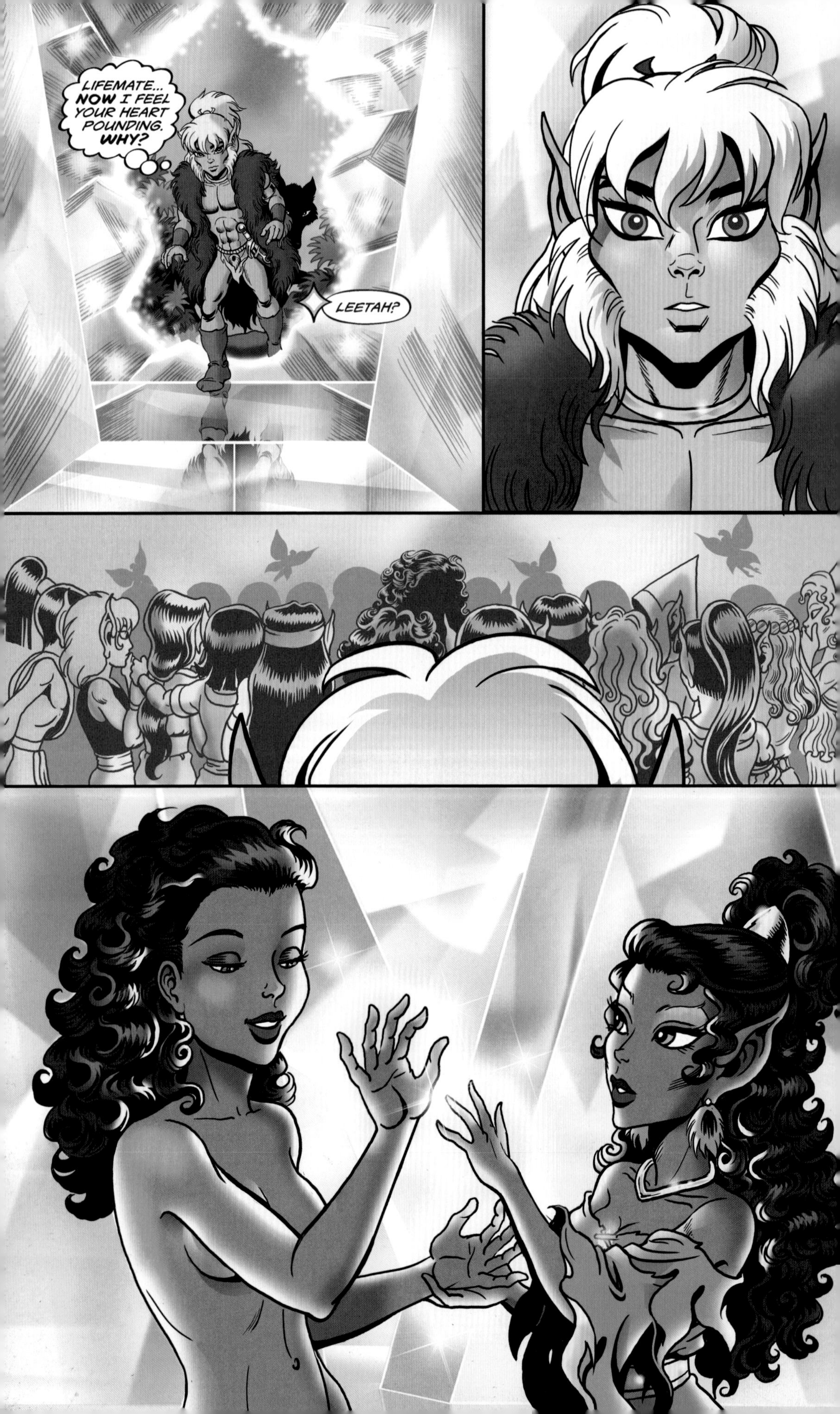
LIFEMATE... NOW I FEEL YOUR HEART POUNDING. WHY?
LEETAH?

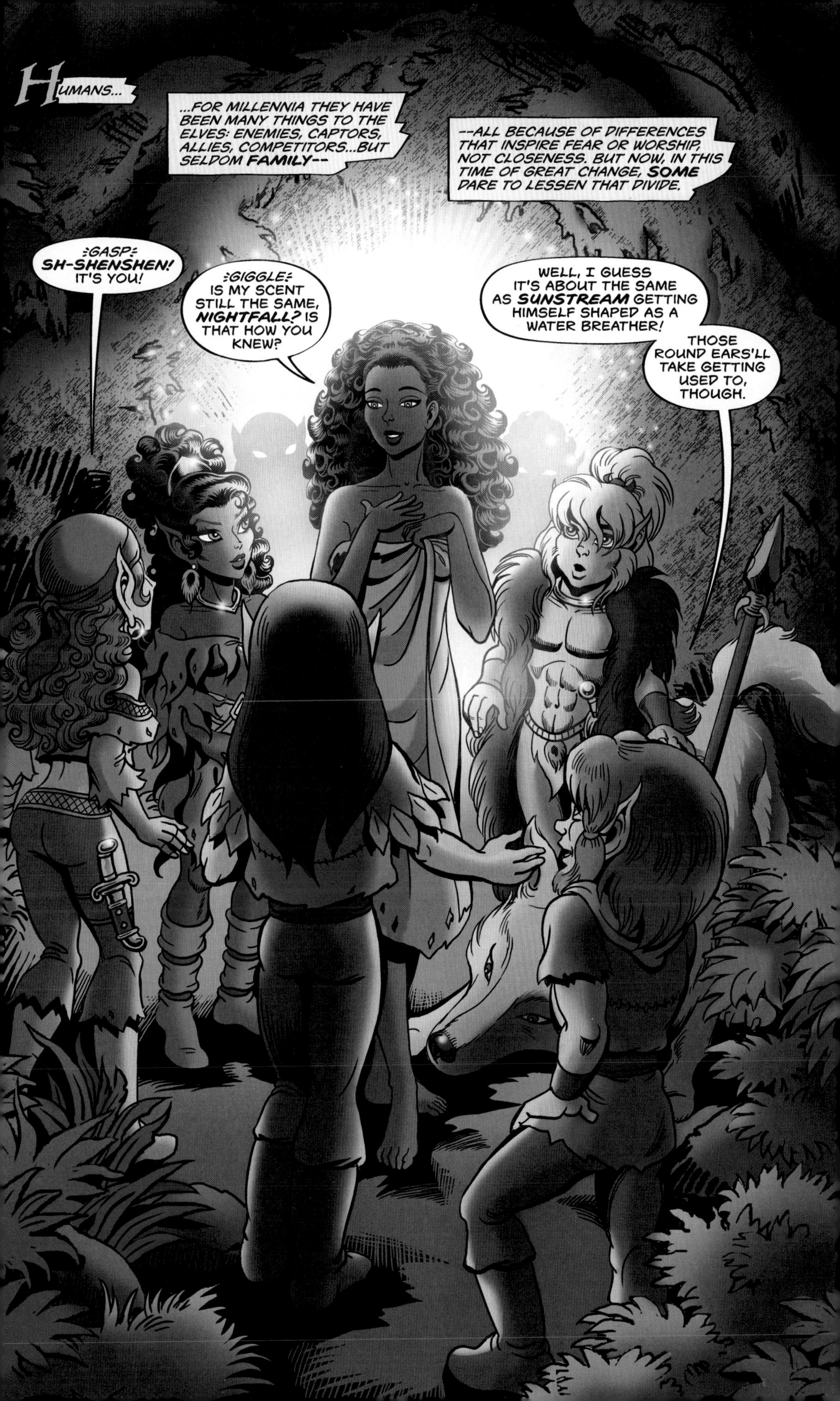
HUMANS...
...FOR MILLENNIA THEY HAVE BEEN MANY THINGS TO THE ELVES: ENEMIES, CAPTORS, ALLIES, COMPETITORS...BUT SELDOM FAMILY--
--ALL BECAUSE OF DIFFERENCES THAT INSPIRE FEAR OR WORSHIP, NOT CLOSENESS. BUT NOW, IN THIS TIME OF GREAT CHANGE, SOME DARE TO LESSEN THAT DIVIDE.
GASP SH-SHENSHEN! IT'S YOU!
GIGGLE IS MY SCENT STILL THE SAME, NIGHTFALL? IS THAT HOW YOU KNEW?
WELL, I GUESS IT'S ABOUT THE SAME AS SUNSTREAM GETTING HIMSELF SHAPED AS A WATER BREATHER!
THOSE ROUND EARS'LL TAKE GETTING USED TO, THOUGH.

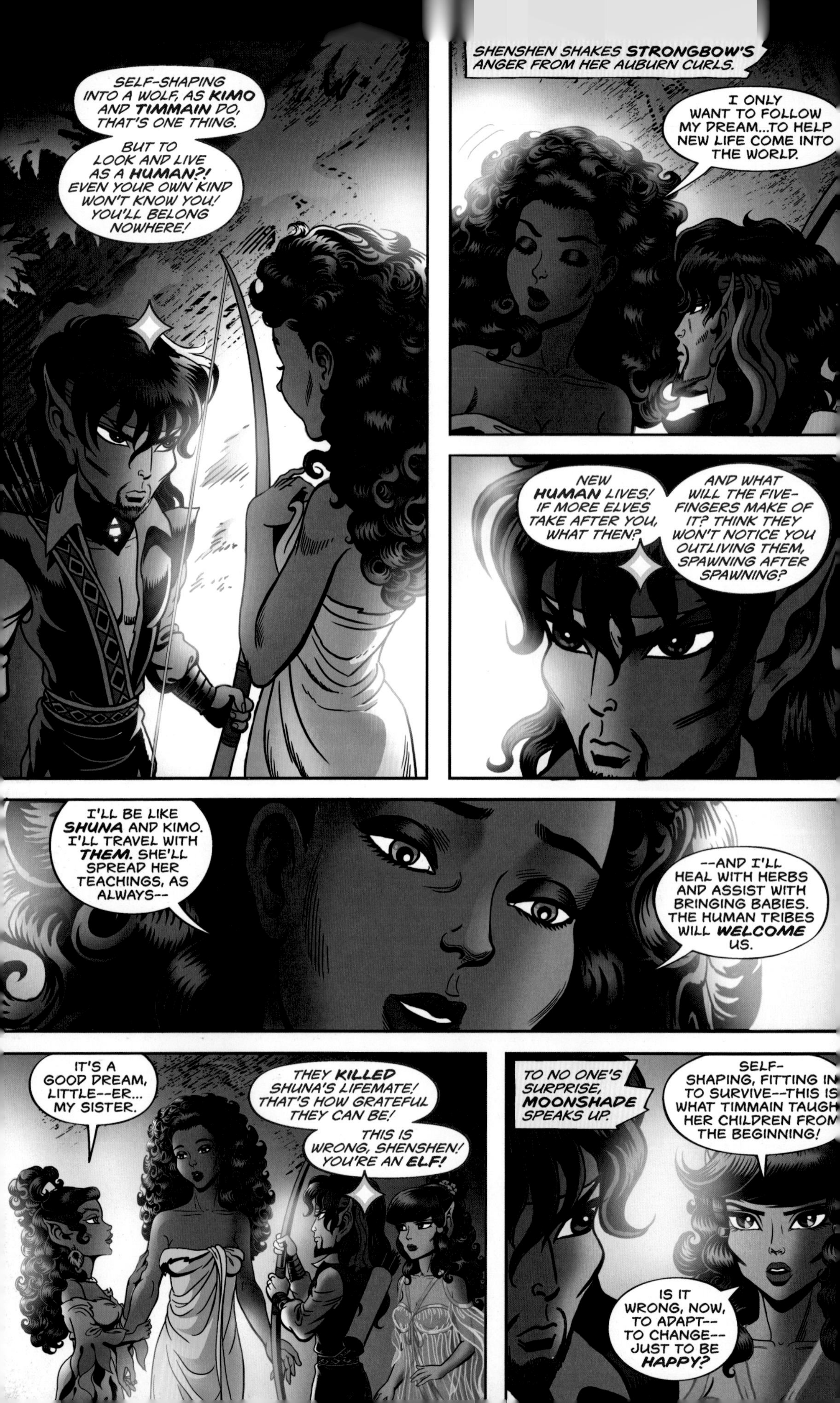

SELF-SHAPING INTO A WOLF, AS KIMO AND TIMMAIN DO, THAT'S ONE THING.
BUT TO LOOK AND LIVE AS A HUMAN?! EVEN YOUR OWN KIND WON'T KNOW YOU! YOU'LL BELONG NOWHERE!
SHENSHEN SHAKES STRONGBOW'S ANGER FROM HER AUBURN CURLS.
I ONLY WANT TO FOLLOW MY DREAM...TO HELP NEW LIFE COME INTO THE WORLD.
NEW HUMAN LIVES! IF MORE ELVES TAKE AFTER YOU, WHAT THEN?
AND WHAT WILL THE FIVE-FINGERS MAKE OF IT? THINK THEY WON'T NOTICE YOU OUTLIVING THEM, SPAWNING AFTER SPAWNING?
I'LL BE LIKE SHUNA AND KIMO. I'LL TRAVEL WITH THEM. SHE'LL SPREAD HER TEACHINGS, AS ALWAYS--
--AND I'LL HEAL WITH HERBS AND ASSIST WITH BRINGING BABIES. THE HUMAN TRIBES WILL WELCOME US.
IT'S A GOOD DREAM, LITTLE--ER... MY SISTER.
THEY KILLED SHUNA'S LIFEMATE! THAT'S HOW GRATEFUL THEY CAN BE!
THIS IS WRONG, SHENSHEN! YOU'RE AN ELF!
TO NO ONE'S SURPRISE, MOONSHADE SPEAKS UP.
SELF-SHAPING, FITTING IN TO SURVIVE--THIS IS WHAT TIMMAIN TAUGH HER CHILDREN FROM THE BEGINNING!
IS IT WRONG, NOW, TO ADAPT-- TO CHANGE-- JUST TO BE HAPPY?

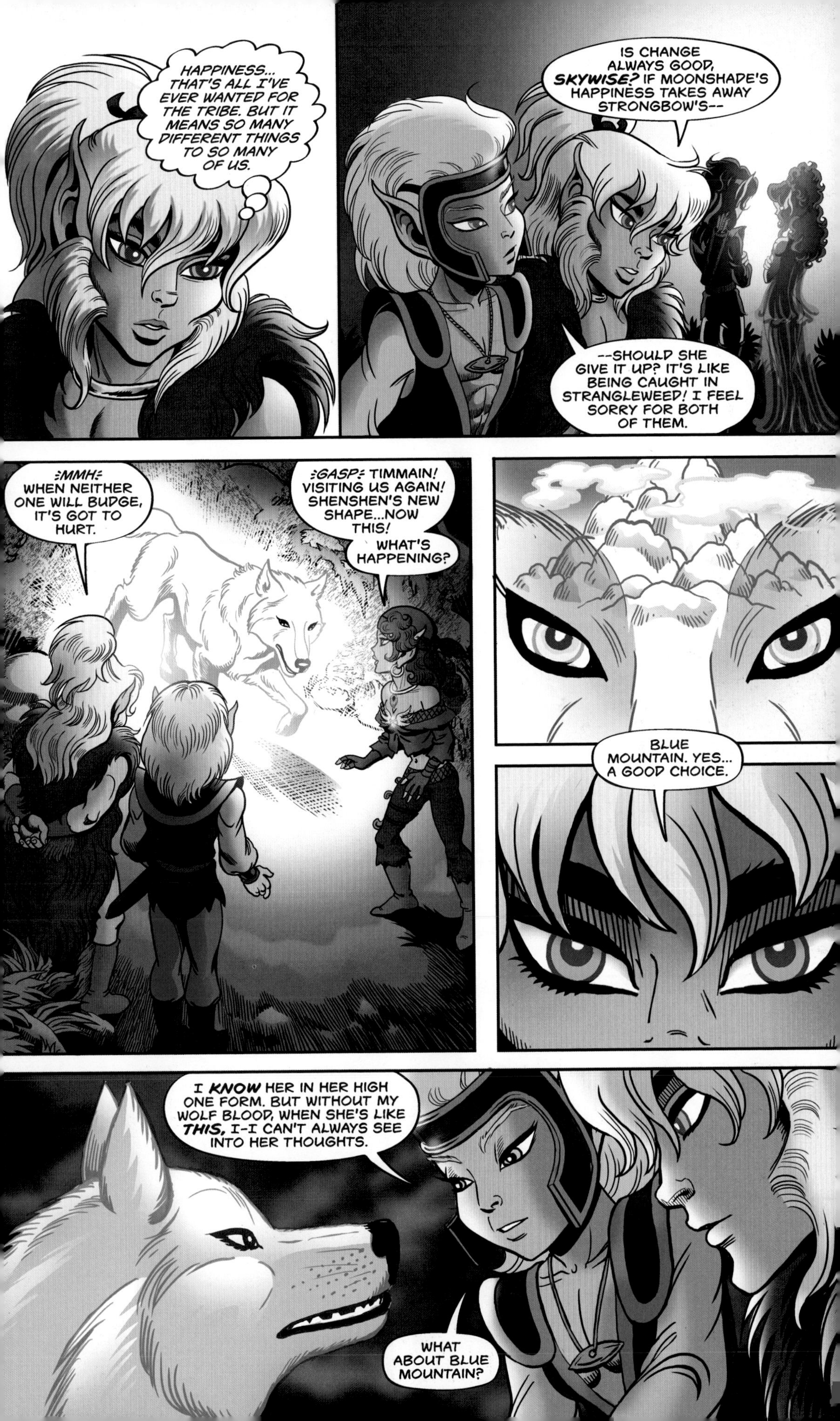
HAPPINESS... THAT'S ALL I'VE EVER WANTED FOR THE TRIBE. BUT IT MEANS SO MANY DIFFERENT THINGS TO SO MANY OF US.
IS CHANGE ALWAYS GOOD, SKYWISE? IF MOONSHADE'S HAPPINESS TAKES AWAY STRONGBOW'S--
--SHOULD SHE GIVE IT UP? IT'S LIKE BEING CAUGHT IN STRANGLEWEED! I FEEL SORRY FOR BOTH OF THEM.
MMH WHEN NEITHER ONE WILL BUDGE, IT'S GOT TO HURT.
GASP TIMMAIN! VISITING US AGAIN! SHENSHEN'S NEW SHAPE...NOW THIS!
WHAT'S HAPPENING?
BLUE MOUNTAIN. YES... A GOOD CHOICE.
I KNOW HER IN HER HIGH ONE FORM. BUT WITHOUT MY WOLF BLOOD, WHEN SHE'S LIKE THIS, I-I CAN'T ALWAYS SEE INTO HER THOUGHTS.
WHAT ABOUT BLUE MOUNTAIN?

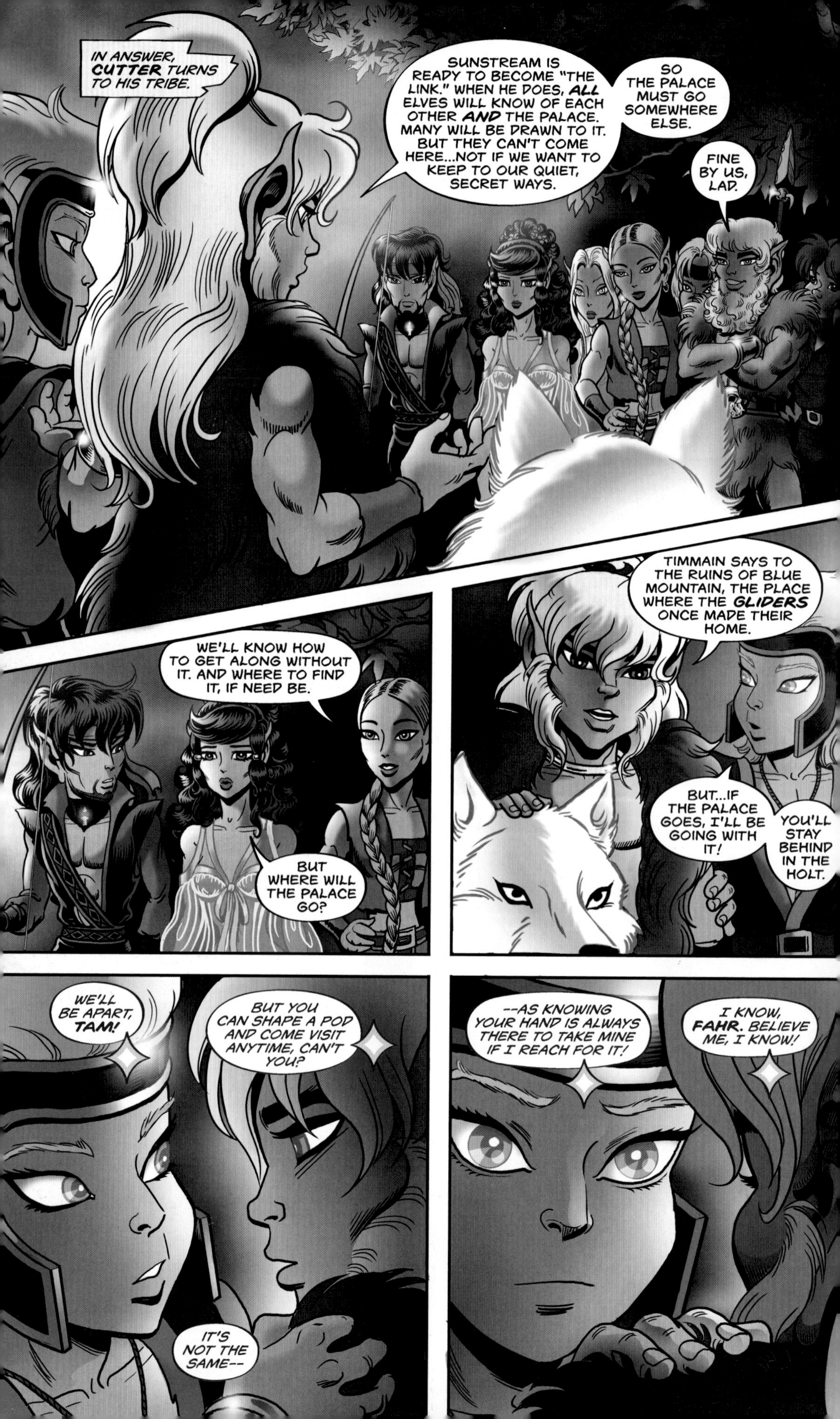
IN ANSWER, **CUTTER** TURNS TO HIS TRIBE.
SUNSTREAM IS READY TO BECOME "THE LINK." WHEN HE DOES, **ALL** ELVES WILL KNOW OF EACH OTHER **AND** THE PALACE. MANY WILL BE DRAWN TO IT. BUT THEY CAN'T COME HERE...NOT IF WE WANT TO KEEP TO OUR QUIET, SECRET WAYS.
SO THE PALACE MUST GO SOMEWHERE ELSE.
FINE BY US, LAD.
WE'LL KNOW HOW TO GET ALONG WITHOUT IT. AND WHERE TO FIND IT, IF NEED BE.
BUT WHERE WILL THE PALACE GO?
TIMMAIN SAYS TO THE RUINS OF BLUE MOUNTAIN, THE PLACE WHERE THE **GLIDERS** ONCE MADE THEIR HOME.
BUT...IF THE PALACE GOES, I'LL BE GOING WITH IT!
YOU'LL STAY BEHIND IN THE HOLT.
WE'LL BE APART, **TAM!**
BUT YOU CAN SHAPE A POD AND COME VISIT ANYTIME, CAN'T YOU?
IT'S NOT THE SAME--
--AS KNOWING YOUR HAND IS ALWAYS THERE TO TAKE MINE IF I REACH FOR IT!
I KNOW, **FAHR.** BELIEVE ME, I KNOW!

FEAR. AND YET...

...ELSEWHERE IN THE WORLD...

:ULP:

...FEARLESSNESS BURSTS INTO THE LIGHT IN A SHOWER OF SUN-DRENCHED FOAM.

SHOOOSH

GIVE ME LEAVE, FRIENDS, TO GO RAISE THE SEA LEVEL A BIT.

HAR HAR! TOO MUCH WATERY SOUP FOR BREAKFAST, EH?

...?!

DO THE SPARKLING SUNBEAMS TRICK MY EYES?

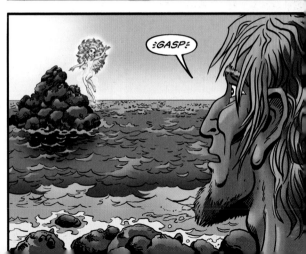

:GASP:

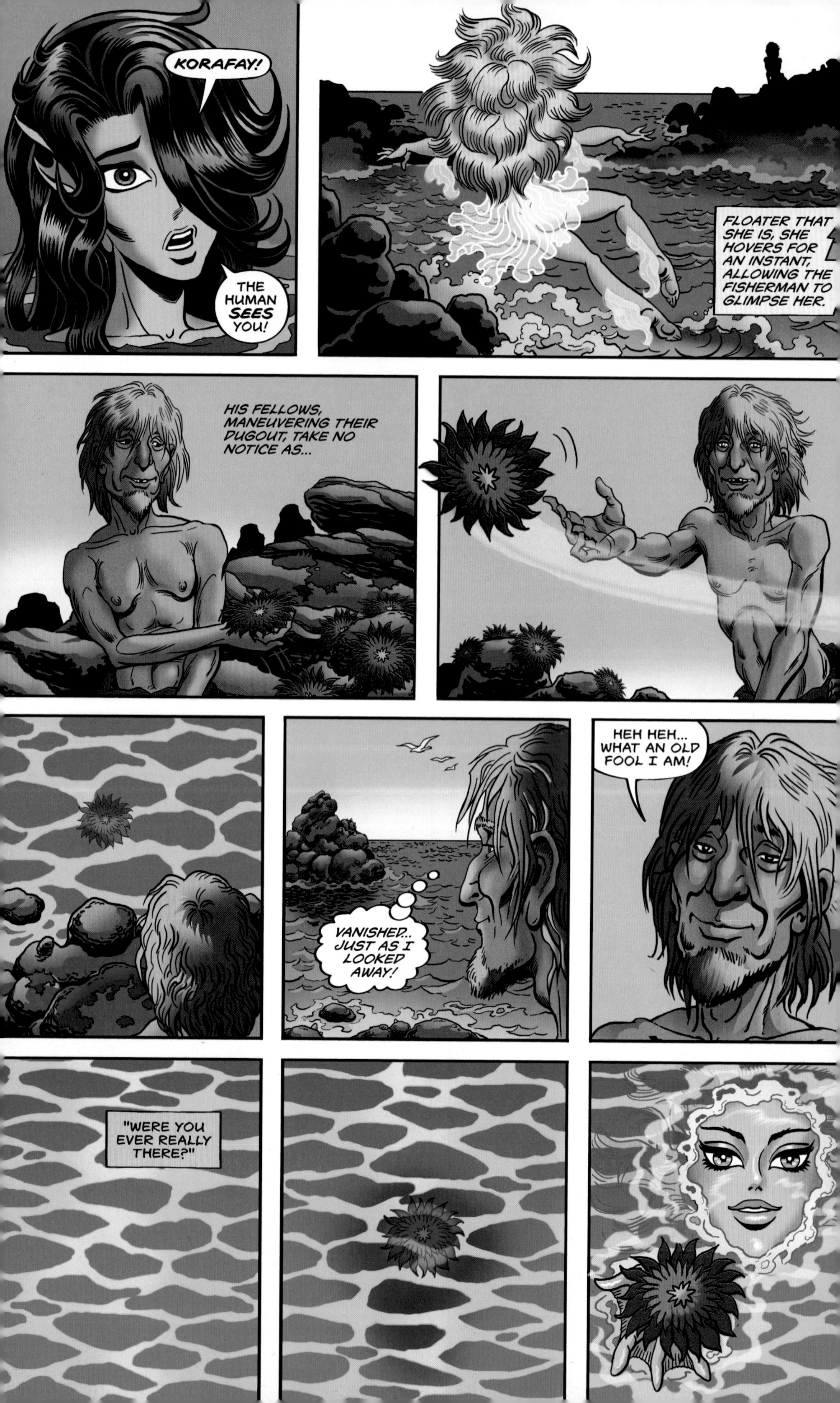
KORAFAY!
THE HUMAN SEES YOU!
FLOATER THAT SHE IS, SHE HOVERS FOR AN INSTANT, ALLOWING THE FISHERMAN TO GLIMPSE HER.
HIS FELLOWS, MANEUVERING THEIR DUGOUT, TAKE NO NOTICE AS...
VANISHED... JUST AS I LOOKED AWAY!
HEH HEH... WHAT AN OLD FOOL I AM!
"WERE YOU EVER REALLY THERE?"

HEH HEH HEH

SPLASH

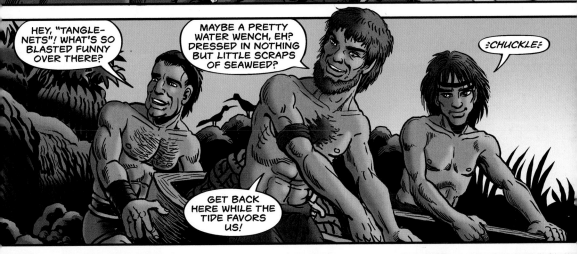

HEY, "TANGLE-NETS"! WHAT'S SO BLASTED FUNNY OVER THERE?

MAYBE A PRETTY WATER WENCH, EH? DRESSED IN NOTHING BUT LITTLE SCRAPS OF SEAWEED?

::CHUCKLE::

GET BACK HERE WHILE THE TIDE FAVORS US!

YOU LET HIM SEE YOU!

HUMANS CAN FEEL LOVE FOR US, REEF. THERE ARE GOOD ONES AS WELL AS BAD.

BUT WHAT IF HE'S BAD? WHAT IF HE TELLS AND THEY COME LOOKING FOR US?

HE WON'T.

SOMEHOW... I KNOW IT.

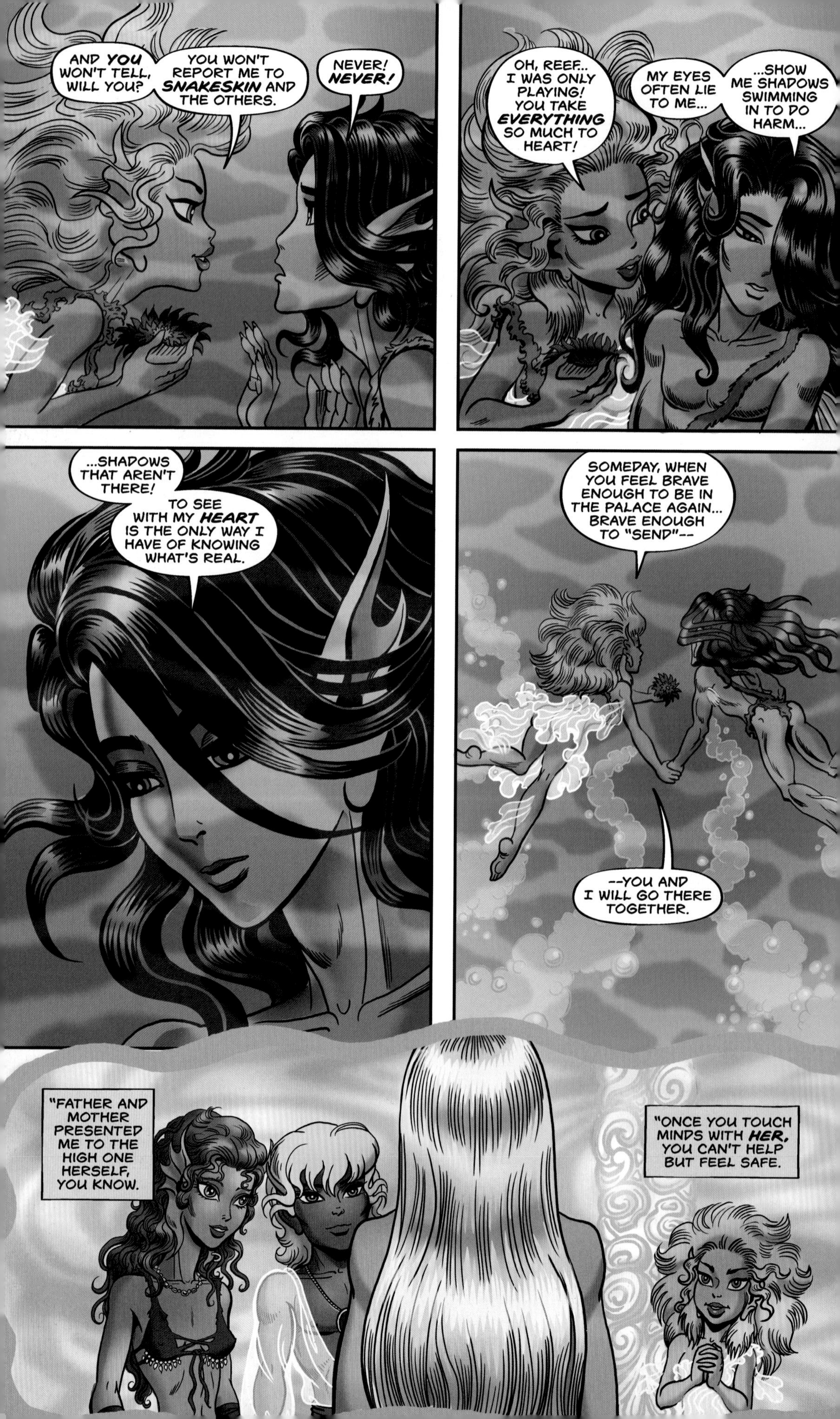
AND YOU WON'T TELL, WILL YOU?
YOU WON'T REPORT ME TO SNAKESKIN AND THE OTHERS.
NEVER! NEVER!
OH, REEF... I WAS ONLY PLAYING! YOU TAKE EVERYTHING SO MUCH TO HEART!
MY EYES OFTEN LIE TO ME...
...SHOW ME SHADOWS SWIMMING IN TO DO HARM...
...SHADOWS THAT AREN'T THERE!
TO SEE WITH MY HEART IS THE ONLY WAY I HAVE OF KNOWING WHAT'S REAL.
SOMEDAY, WHEN YOU FEEL BRAVE ENOUGH TO BE IN THE PALACE AGAIN... BRAVE ENOUGH TO "SEND"--
--YOU AND I WILL GO THERE TOGETHER.
"FATHER AND MOTHER PRESENTED ME TO THE HIGH ONE HERSELF, YOU KNOW.
"ONCE YOU TOUCH MINDS WITH HER, YOU CAN'T HELP BUT FEEL SAFE.

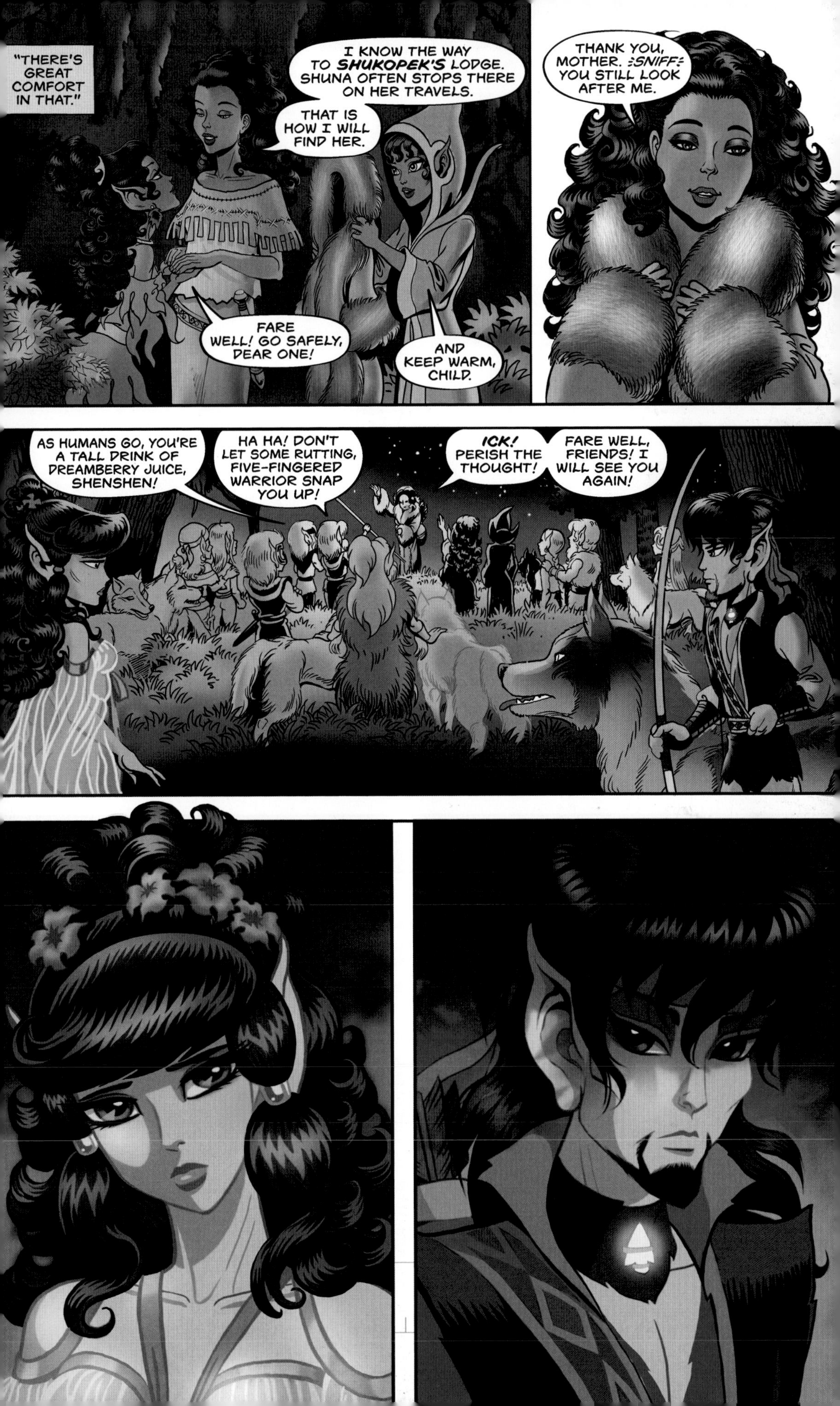

"THERE'S GREAT COMFORT IN THAT."
I KNOW THE WAY TO SHUKOPEK'S LODGE. SHUNA OFTEN STOPS THERE ON HER TRAVELS.
THAT IS HOW I WILL FIND HER.
FARE WELL! GO SAFELY, DEAR ONE!
AND KEEP WARM, CHILD.
THANK YOU, MOTHER. :SNIFF: YOU STILL LOOK AFTER ME.
AS HUMANS GO, YOU'RE A TALL DRINK OF DREAMBERRY JUICE, SHENSHEN!
HA HA! DON'T LET SOME RUTTING, FIVE-FINGERED WARRIOR SNAP YOU UP!
ICK! PERISH THE THOUGHT!
FARE WELL, FRIENDS! I WILL SEE YOU AGAIN!

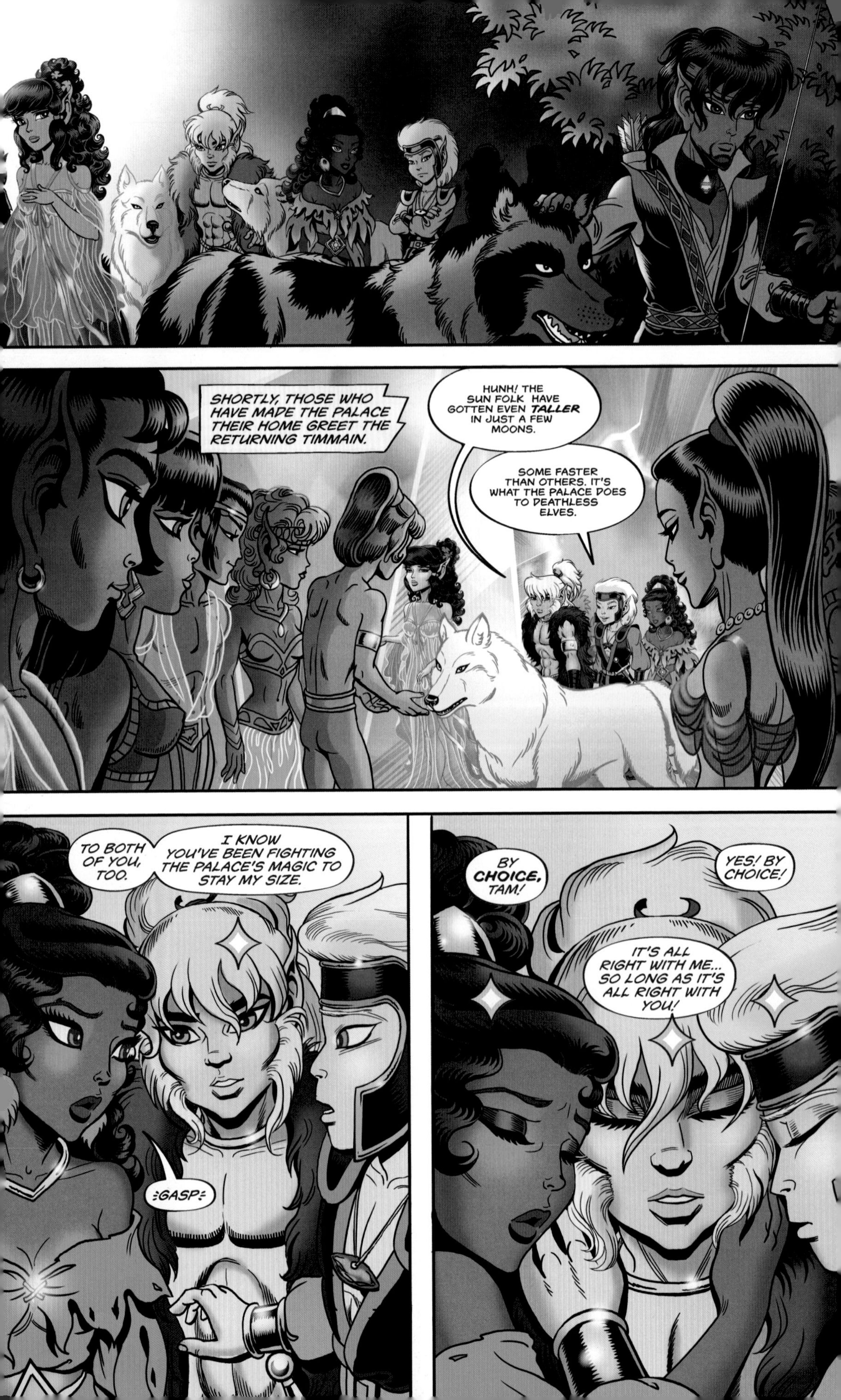
SHORTLY, THOSE WHO HAVE MADE THE PALACE THEIR HOME GREET THE RETURNING TIMMAIN.
HUNH! THE SUN FOLK HAVE GOTTEN EVEN TALLER IN JUST A FEW MOONS.
SOME FASTER THAN OTHERS. IT'S WHAT THE PALACE DOES TO DEATHLESS ELVES.
TO BOTH OF YOU, TOO.
I KNOW YOU'VE BEEN FIGHTING THE PALACE'S MAGIC TO STAY MY SIZE.
GASP
BY CHOICE, TAM!
YES! BY CHOICE!
IT'S ALL RIGHT WITH ME... SO LONG AS IT'S ALL RIGHT WITH YOU!

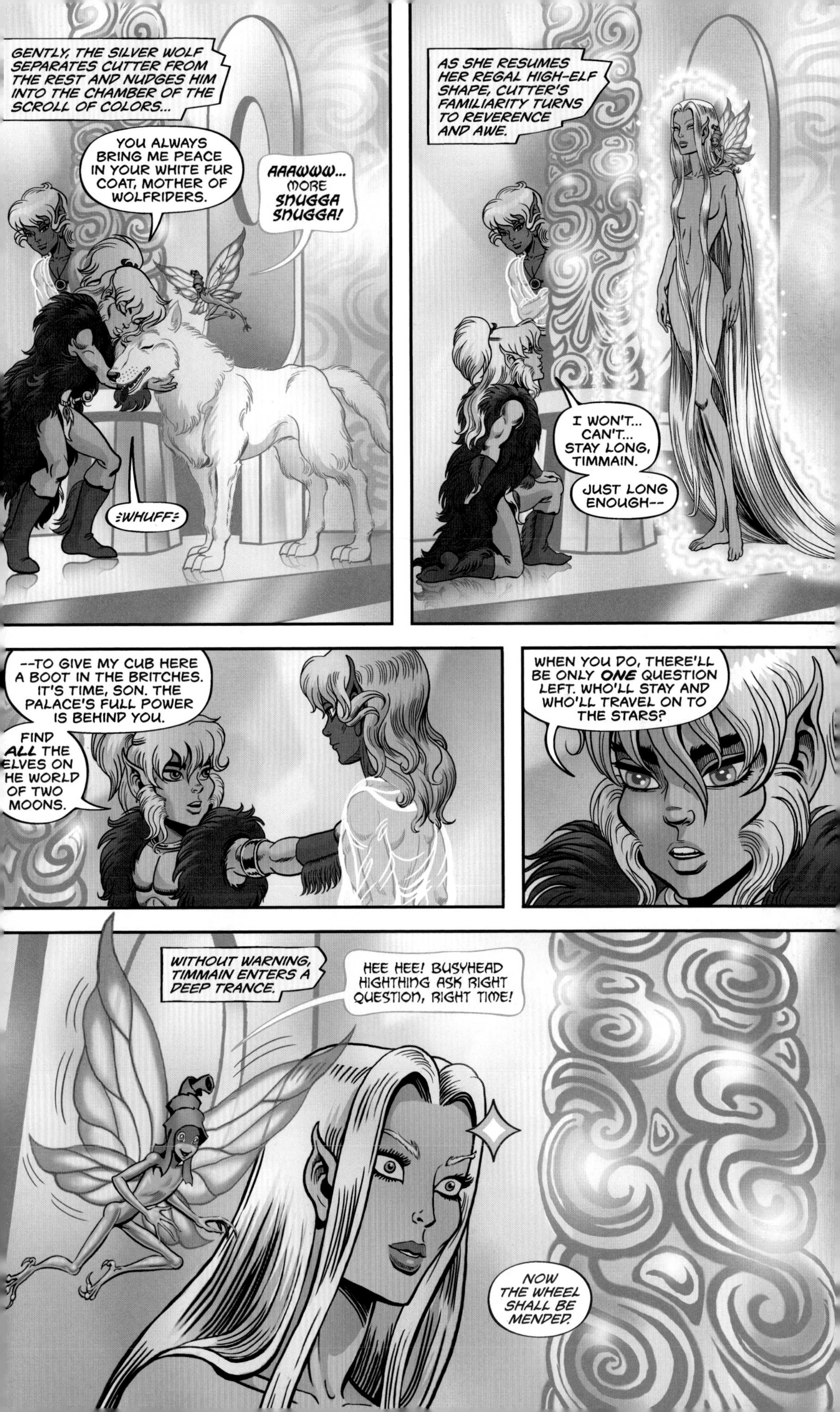
GENTLY, THE SILVER WOLF SEPARATES CUTTER FROM THE REST AND NUDGES HIM INTO THE CHAMBER OF THE SCROLL OF COLORS...
YOU ALWAYS BRING ME PEACE IN YOUR WHITE FUR COAT, MOTHER OF WOLFRIDERS.
AAAWWW... MORE SNUGGA SNUGGA!
WHUFF
AS SHE RESUMES HER REGAL HIGH-ELF SHAPE, CUTTER'S FAMILIARITY TURNS TO REVERENCE AND AWE.
I WON'T... CAN'T... STAY LONG, TIMMAIN.
JUST LONG ENOUGH--
--TO GIVE MY CUB HERE A BOOT IN THE BRITCHES. IT'S TIME, SON. THE PALACE'S FULL POWER IS BEHIND YOU.
FIND ALL THE ELVES ON HE WORLD OF TWO MOONS.
WHEN YOU DO, THERE'LL BE ONLY ONE QUESTION LEFT. WHO'LL STAY AND WHO'LL TRAVEL ON TO THE STARS?
WITHOUT WARNING, TIMMAIN ENTERS A DEEP TRANCE.
HEE HEE! BUSYHEAD HIGHTHING ASK RIGHT QUESTION, RIGHT TIME!
NOW THE WHEEL SHALL BE MENDED.

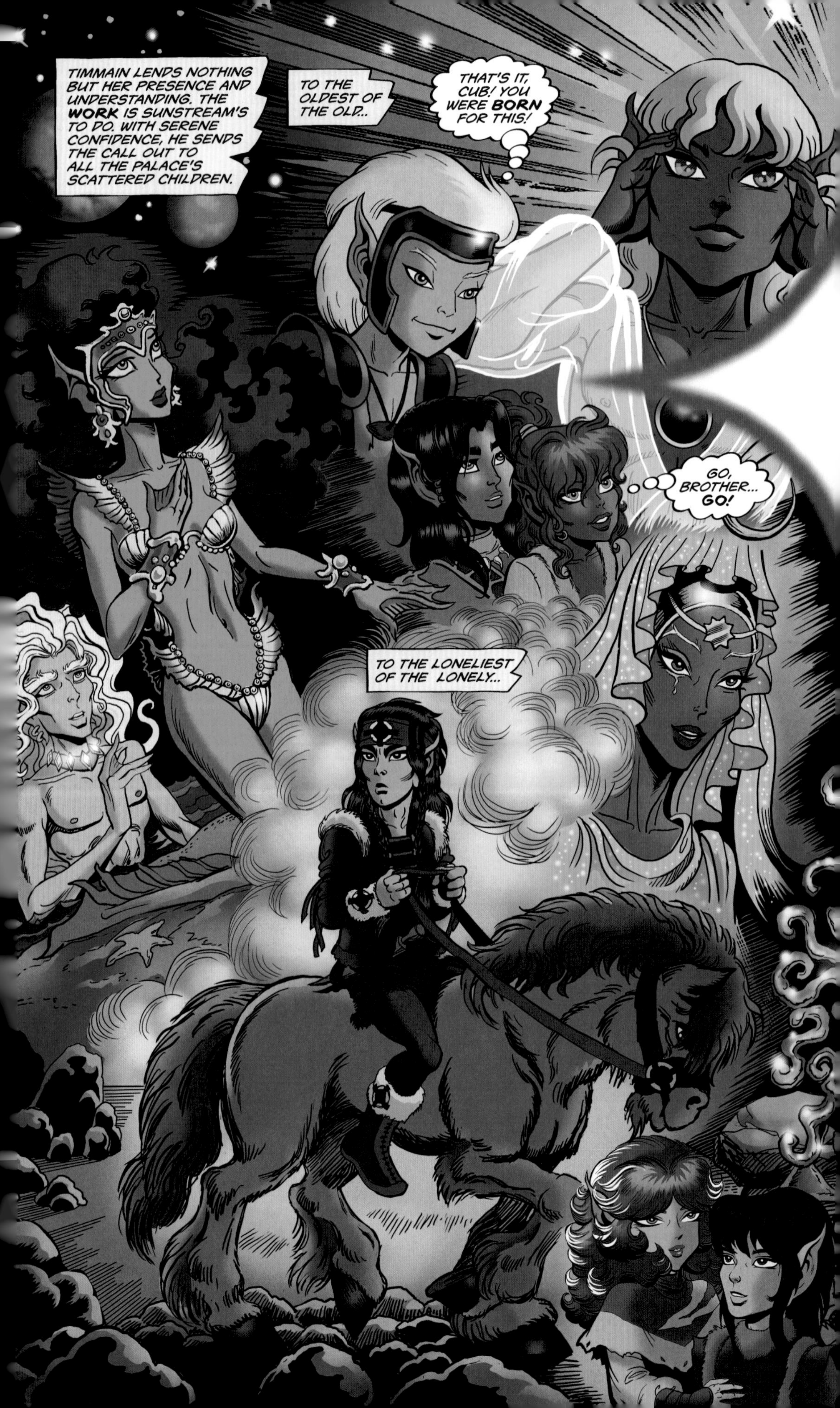

TIMMAIN LENDS NOTHING BUT HER PRESENCE AND UNDERSTANDING. THE **WORK** IS SUNSTREAM'S TO DO. WITH SERENE CONFIDENCE, HE SENDS THE CALL OUT TO ALL THE PALACE'S SCATTERED CHILDREN.
TO THE OLDEST OF THE OLD..
THAT'S IT, CUB! YOU WERE **BORN** FOR THIS!
GO, BROTHER... **GO!**
TO THE LONELIEST OF THE LONELY...

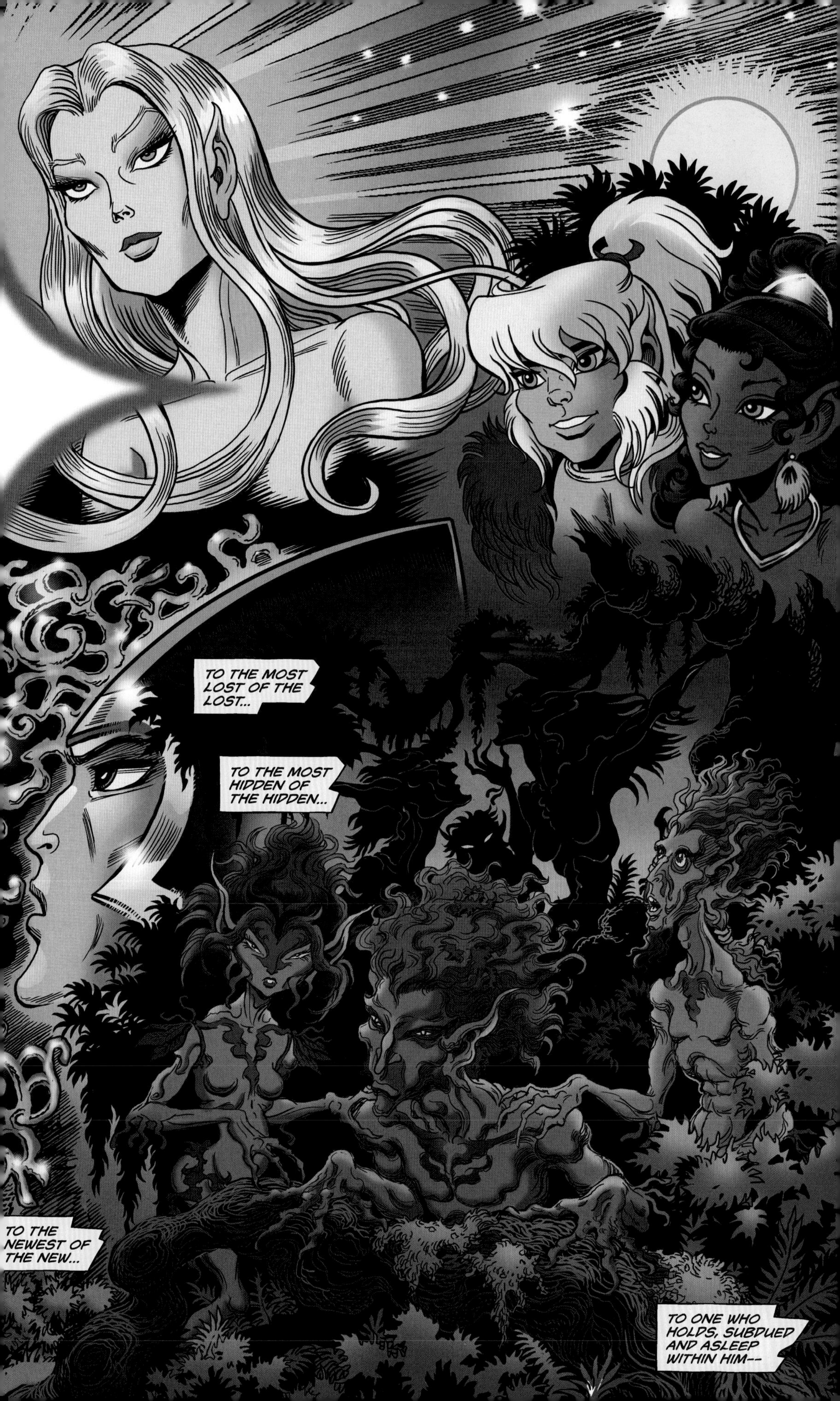
TO THE MOST LOST OF THE LOST...
TO THE MOST HIDDEN OF THE HIDDEN...
TO THE NEWEST OF THE NEW...
TO ONE WHO HOLDS, SUBDUED AND ASLEEP WITHIN HIM--

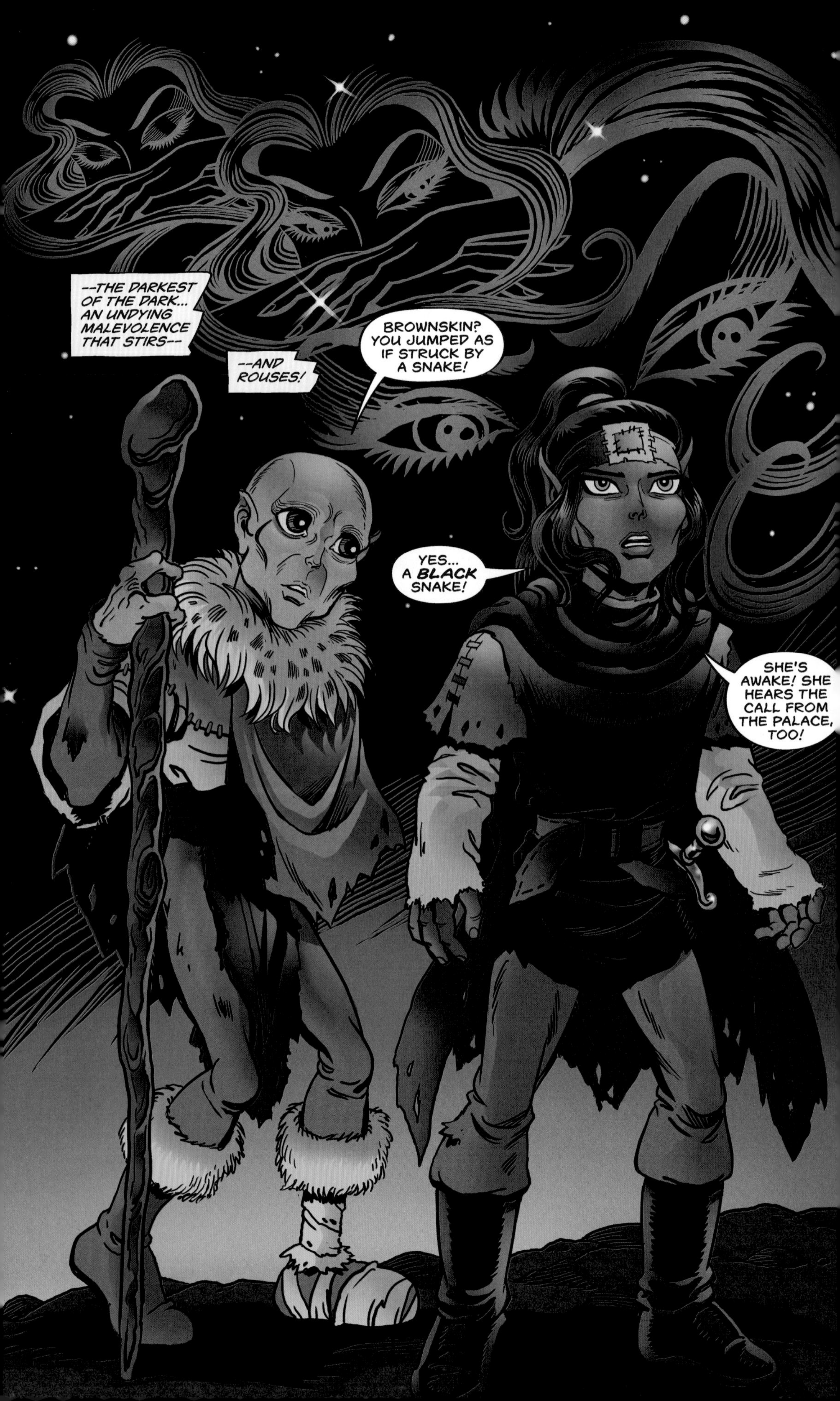
--THE DARKEST OF THE DARK... AN UNDYING MALEVOLENCE THAT STIRS--
--AND ROUSES!
BROWNSKIN? YOU JUMPED AS IF STRUCK BY A SNAKE!
YES... A BLACK SNAKE!
SHE'S AWAKE! SHE HEARS THE CALL FROM THE PALACE, TOO!

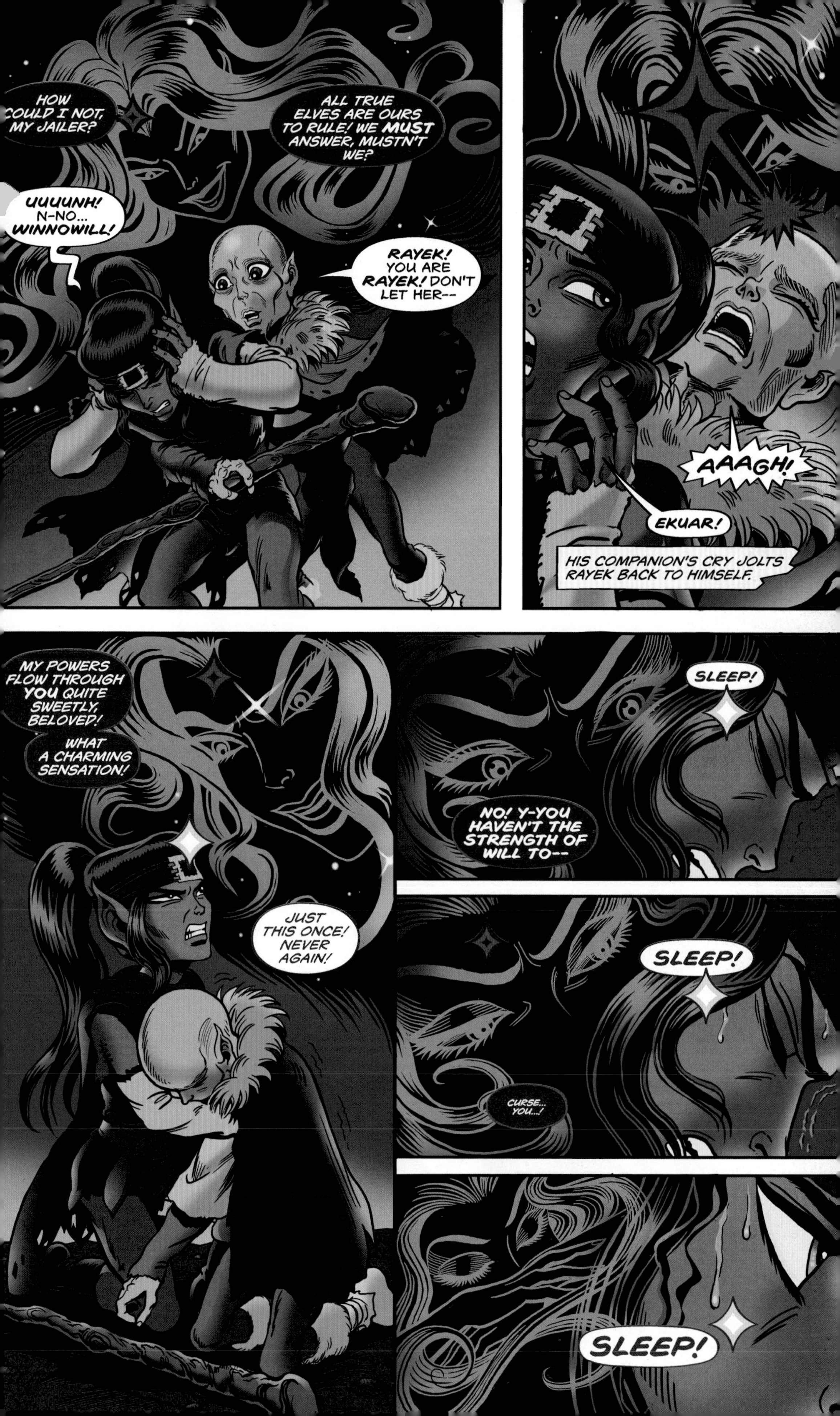
HOW COULD I NOT, MY JAILER?
ALL TRUE ELVES ARE OURS TO RULE! WE MUST ANSWER, MUSTN'T WE?
UUUUNH! N-NO... WINNOWILL!
RAYEK! YOU ARE RAYEK! DON'T LET HER--
AAAGH!
EKUAR!
HIS COMPANION'S CRY JOLTS RAYEK BACK TO HIMSELF.
MY POWERS FLOW THROUGH YOU QUITE SWEETLY, BELOVED!
WHAT A CHARMING SENSATION!
JUST THIS ONCE! NEVER AGAIN!
SLEEP!
NO! Y-YOU HAVEN'T THE STRENGTH OF WILL TO--
SLEEP!
CURSE... YOU...!
SLEEP!

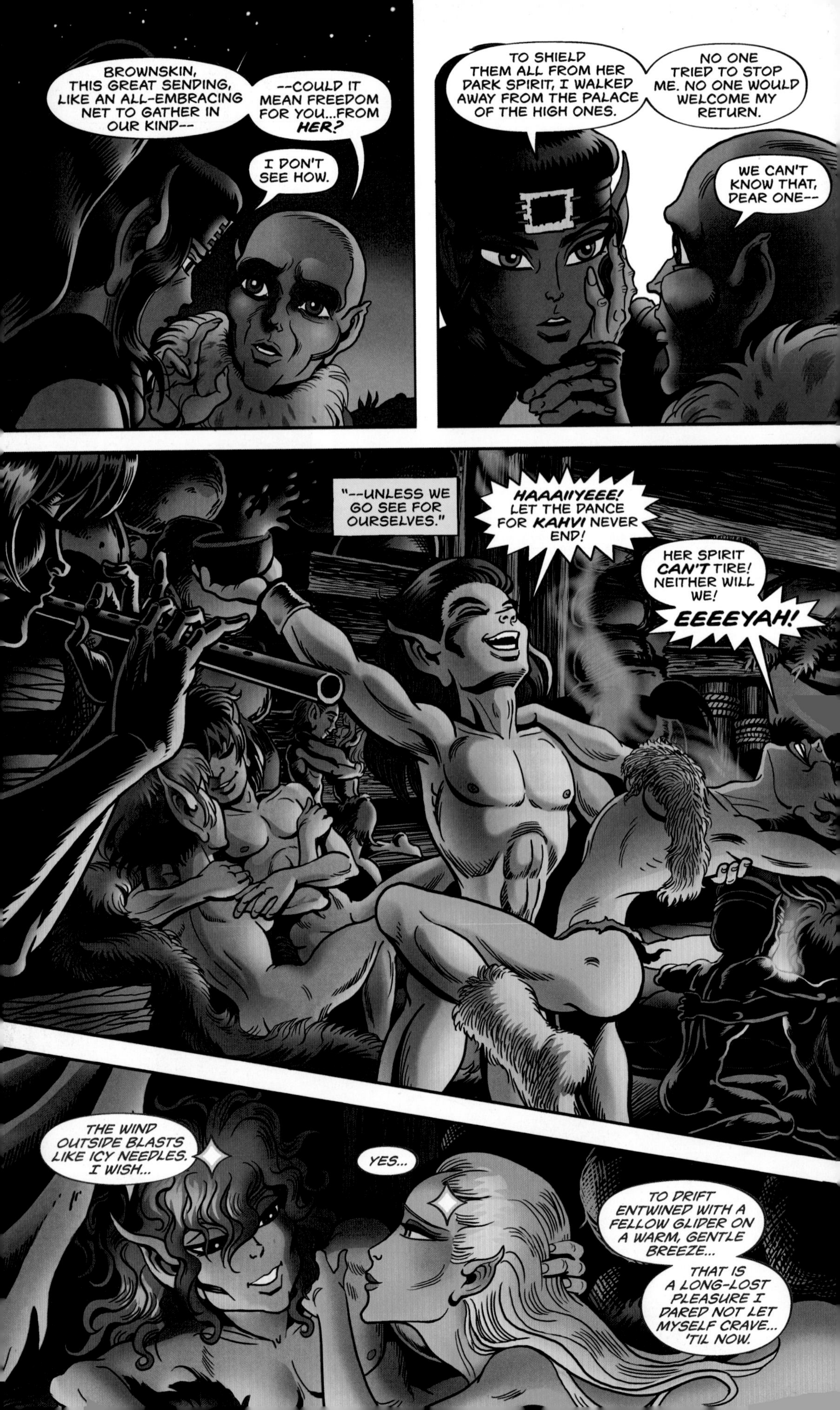
BROWNSKIN, THIS GREAT SENDING, LIKE AN ALL-EMBRACING NET TO GATHER IN OUR KIND--
--COULD IT MEAN FREEDOM FOR YOU...FROM HER?
I DON'T SEE HOW.
TO SHIELD THEM ALL FROM HER DARK SPIRIT, I WALKED AWAY FROM THE PALACE OF THE HIGH ONES.
NO ONE TRIED TO STOP ME. NO ONE WOULD WELCOME MY RETURN.
WE CAN'T KNOW THAT, DEAR ONE--
"--UNLESS WE GO SEE FOR OURSELVES."
HAAAIIYEEE! LET THE DANCE FOR KAHVI NEVER END!
HER SPIRIT CAN'T TIRE! NEITHER WILL WE!
EEEEYAH!
THE WIND OUTSIDE BLASTS LIKE ICY NEEDLES. I WISH...
YES...
TO DRIFT ENTWINED WITH A FELLOW GLIDER ON A WARM, GENTLE BREEZE...
THAT IS A LONG-LOST PLEASURE I DARED NOT LET MYSELF CRAVE... 'TIL NOW.

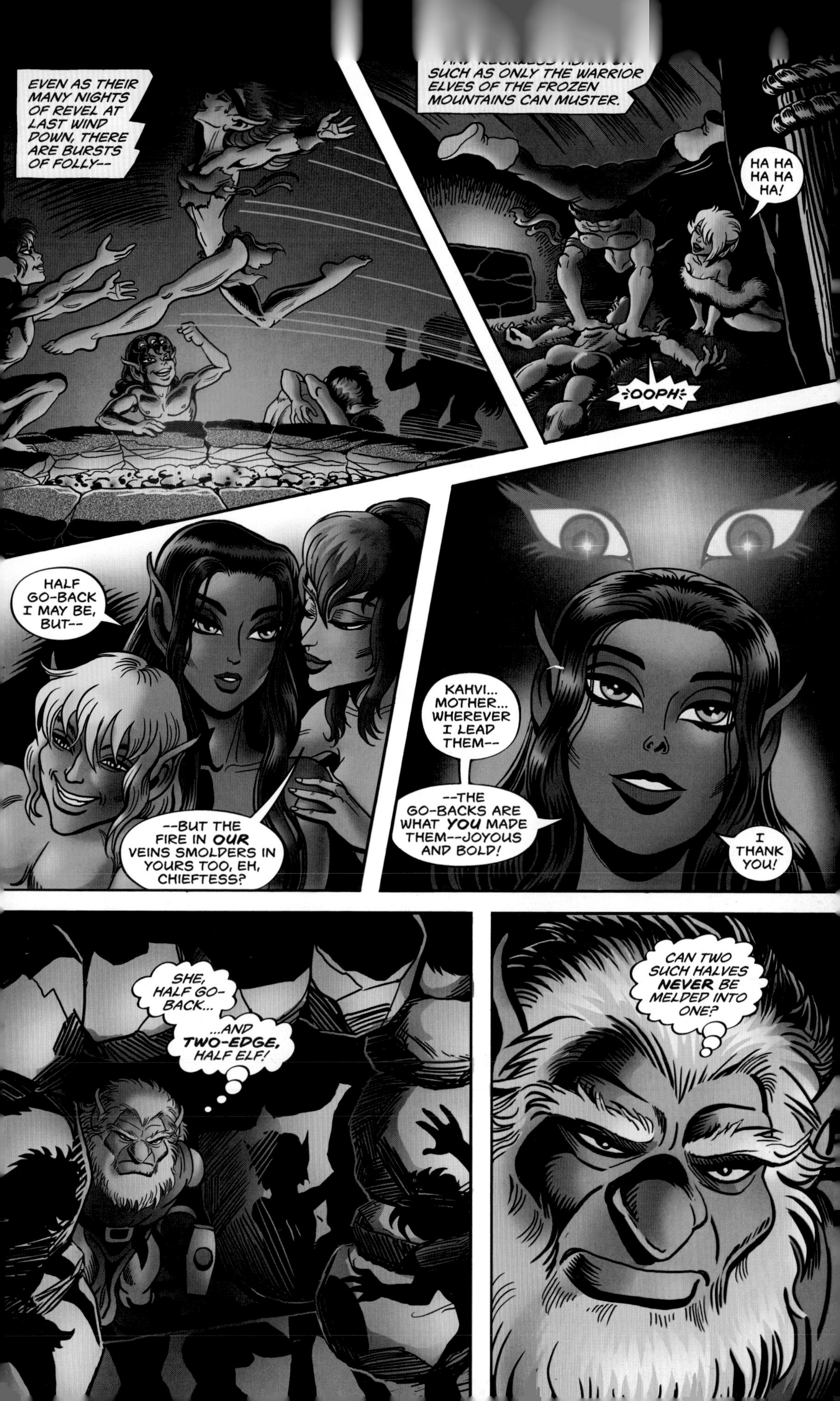
EVEN AS THEIR MANY NIGHTS OF REVEL AT LAST WIND DOWN, THERE ARE BURSTS OF FOLLY--
SUCH AS ONLY THE WARRIOR ELVES OF THE FROZEN MOUNTAINS CAN MUSTER.
HA HA HA HA HA!
OOPH
HALF GO-BACK I MAY BE, BUT--
--BUT THE FIRE IN OUR VEINS SMOLDERS IN YOURS TOO, EH, CHIEFTESS?
KAHVI... MOTHER... WHEREVER I LEAD THEM--
--THE GO-BACKS ARE WHAT YOU MADE THEM--JOYOUS AND BOLD!
I THANK YOU!
SHE, HALF GO-BACK...
...AND TWO-EDGE, HALF ELF!
CAN TWO SUCH HALVES NEVER BE MELDED INTO ONE?

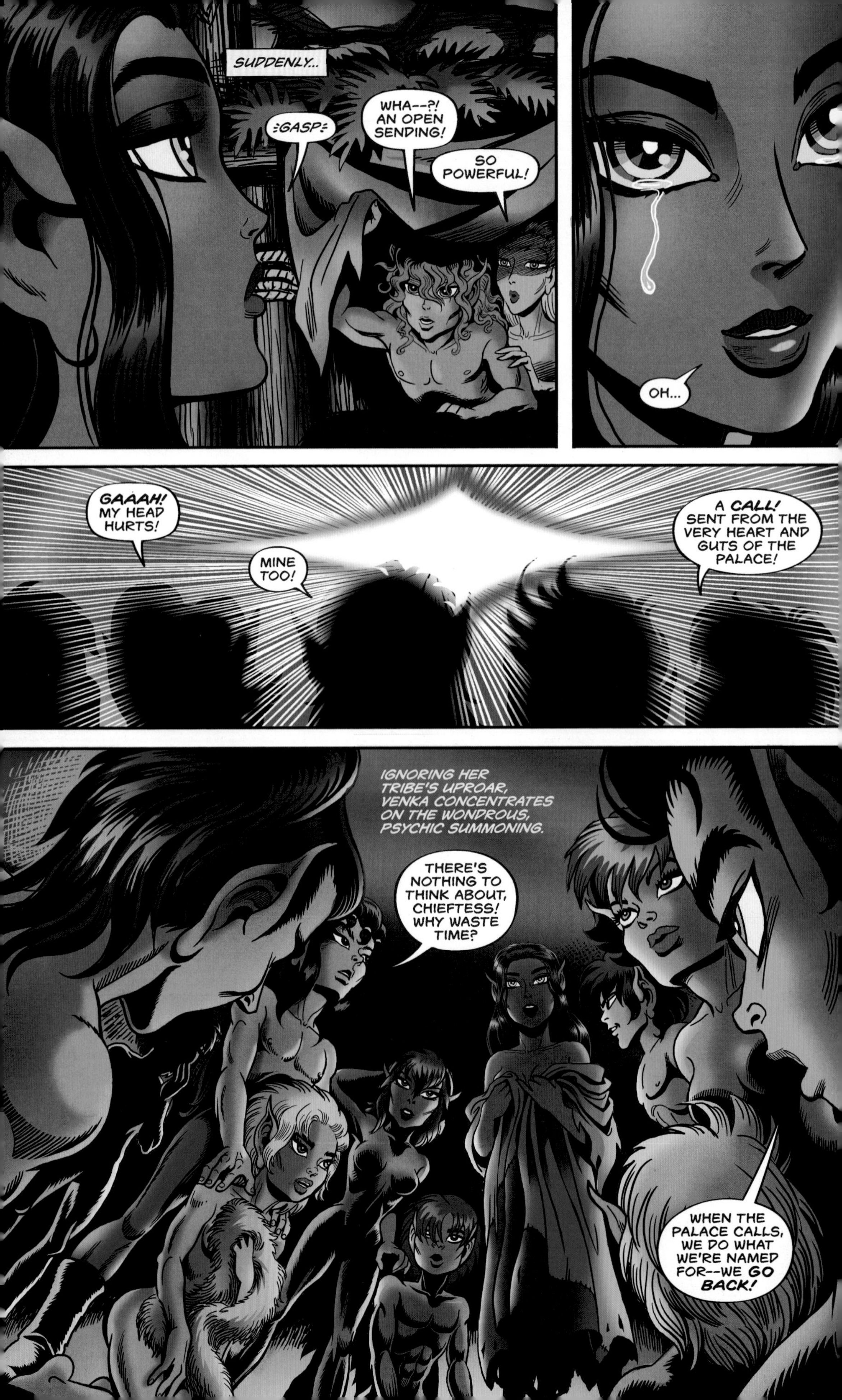
SUDDENLY...
:GASP:
WHA--?! AN OPEN SENDING!
SO POWERFUL!
OH...
GAAAH! MY HEAD HURTS!
MINE TOO!
A CALL! SENT FROM THE VERY HEART AND GUTS OF THE PALACE!
IGNORING HER TRIBE'S UPROAR, VENKA CONCENTRATES ON THE WONDROUS, PSYCHIC SUMMONING.
THERE'S NOTHING TO THINK ABOUT, CHIEFTESS! WHY WASTE TIME?
WHEN THE PALACE CALLS, WE DO WHAT WE'RE NAMED FOR--WE GO BACK!

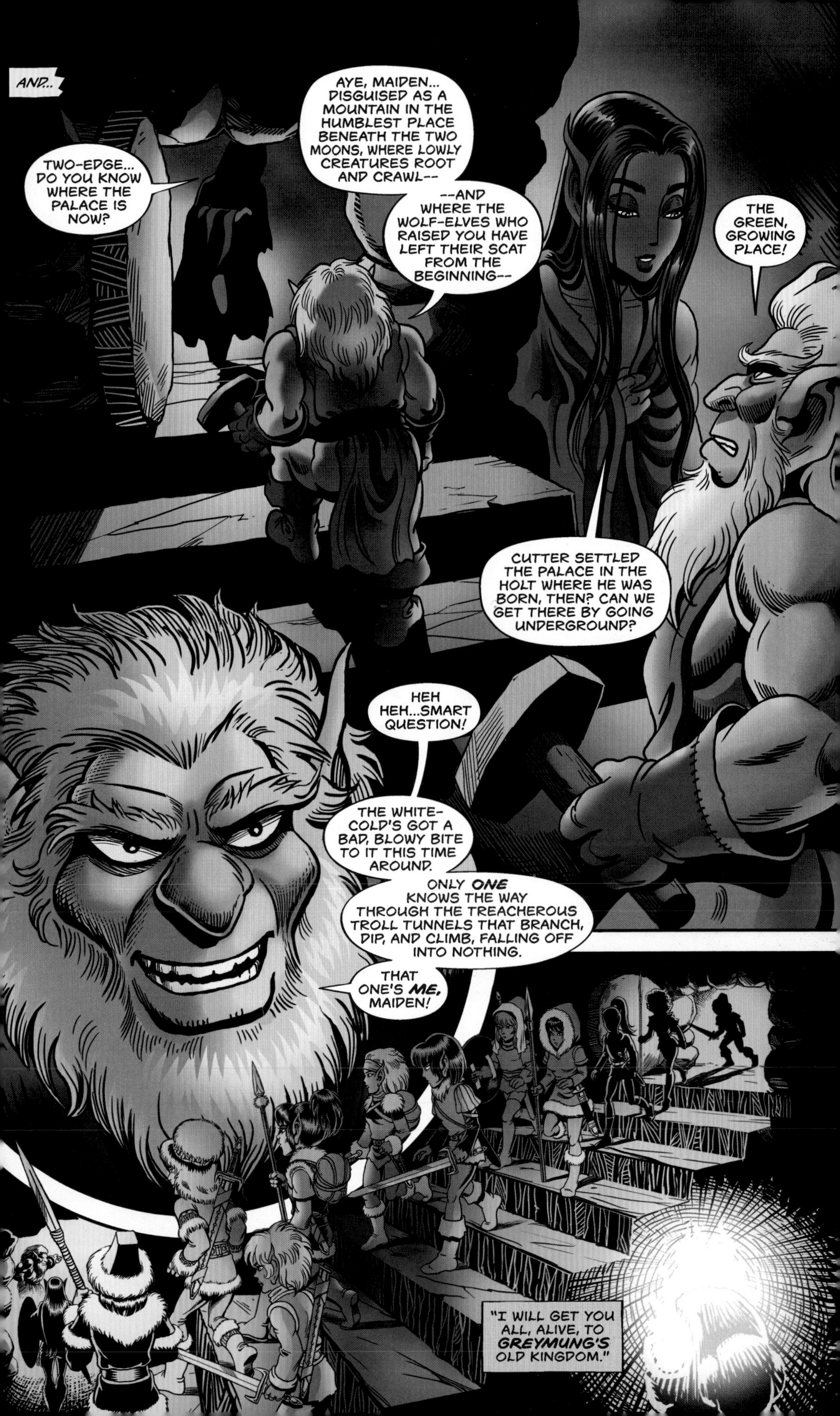
AND...
TWO-EDGE... DO YOU KNOW WHERE THE PALACE IS NOW?
AYE, MAIDEN... DISGUISED AS A MOUNTAIN IN THE HUMBLEST PLACE BENEATH THE TWO MOONS, WHERE LOWLY CREATURES ROOT AND CRAWL--
--AND WHERE THE WOLF-ELVES WHO RAISED YOU HAVE LEFT THEIR SCAT FROM THE BEGINNING--
THE GREEN, GROWING PLACE!
CUTTER SETTLED THE PALACE IN THE HOLT WHERE HE WAS BORN, THEN? CAN WE GET THERE BY GOING UNDERGROUND?
HEH HEH...SMART QUESTION!
THE WHITE-COLD'S GOT A BAD, BLOWY BITE TO IT THIS TIME AROUND.
ONLY ONE KNOWS THE WAY THROUGH THE TREACHEROUS TROLL TUNNELS THAT BRANCH, DIP, AND CLIMB, FALLING OFF INTO NOTHING.
THAT ONE'S ME, MAIDEN!
"I WILL GET YOU ALL, ALIVE, TO GREYMUNG'S OLD KINGDOM."

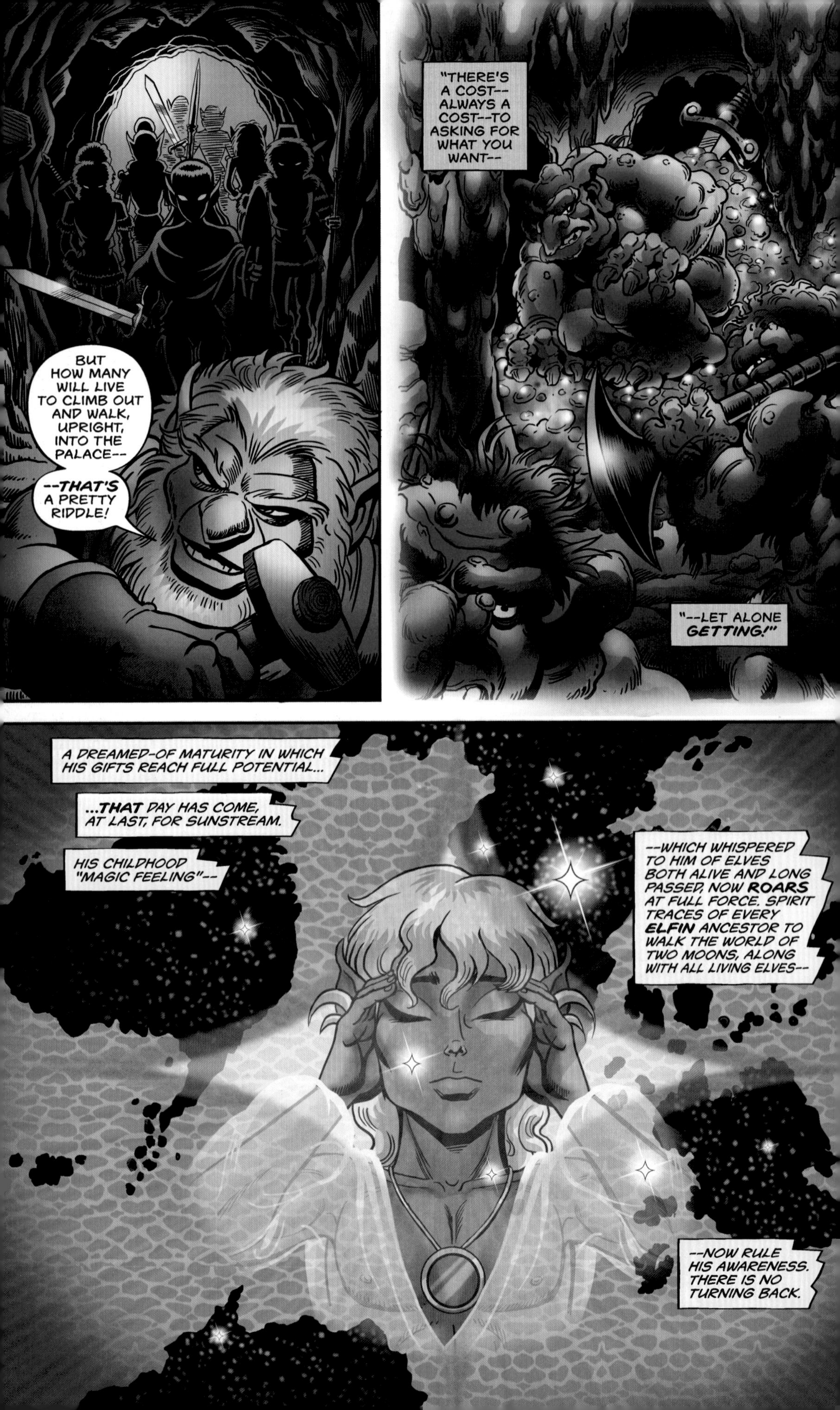

BUT HOW MANY WILL LIVE TO CLIMB OUT AND WALK, UPRIGHT, INTO THE PALACE--
--THAT'S A PRETTY RIDDLE!
"THERE'S A COST-- ALWAYS A COST--TO ASKING FOR WHAT YOU WANT--
"--LET ALONE GETTING!"
A DREAMED-OF MATURITY IN WHICH HIS GIFTS REACH FULL POTENTIAL...
...THAT DAY HAS COME, AT LAST, FOR SUNSTREAM.
HIS CHILDHOOD "MAGIC FEELING"--
--WHICH WHISPERED TO HIM OF ELVES BOTH ALIVE AND LONG PASSED, NOW ROARS AT FULL FORCE. SPIRIT TRACES OF EVERY ELFIN ANCESTOR TO WALK THE WORLD OF TWO MOONS, ALONG WITH ALL LIVING ELVES--
--NOW RULE HIS AWARENESS. THERE IS NO TURNING BACK.

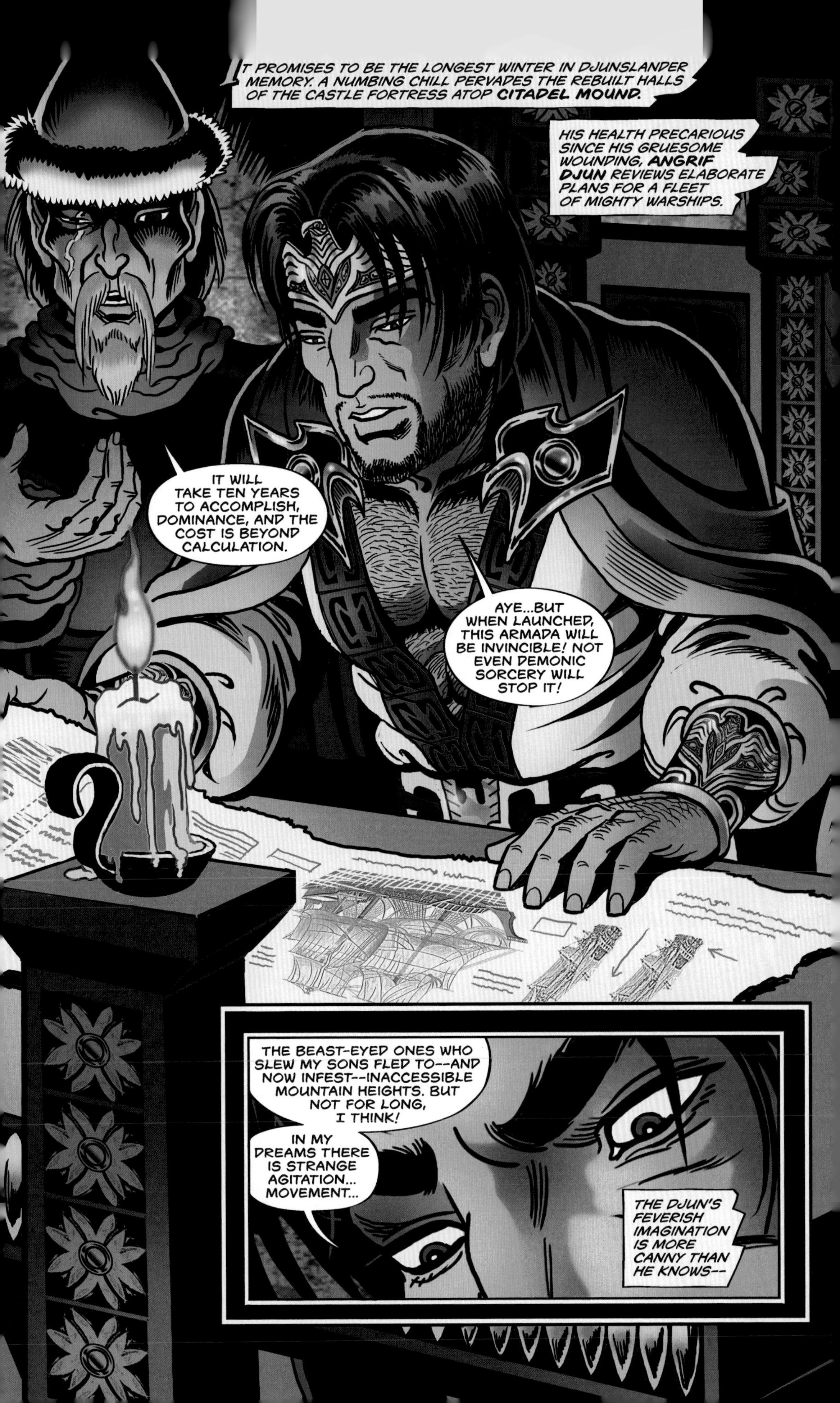
IT PROMISES TO BE THE LONGEST WINTER IN DJUNSLANDER MEMORY. A NUMBING CHILL PERVADES THE REBUILT HALLS OF THE CASTLE FORTRESS ATOP CITADEL MOUND.
HIS HEALTH PRECARIOUS SINCE HIS GRUESOME WOUNDING, ANGRIF DJUN REVIEWS ELABORATE PLANS FOR A FLEET OF MIGHTY WARSHIPS.
IT WILL TAKE TEN YEARS TO ACCOMPLISH, DOMINANCE, AND THE COST IS BEYOND CALCULATION.
AYE...BUT WHEN LAUNCHED, THIS ARMADA WILL BE INVINCIBLE! NOT EVEN DEMONIC SORCERY WILL STOP IT!
THE BEAST-EYED ONES WHO SLEW MY SONS FLED TO--AND NOW INFEST--INACCESSIBLE MOUNTAIN HEIGHTS. BUT NOT FOR LONG, I THINK!
IN MY DREAMS THERE IS STRANGE AGITATION... MOVEMENT...
THE DJUN'S FEVERISH IMAGINATION IS MORE CANNY THAN HE KNOWS--

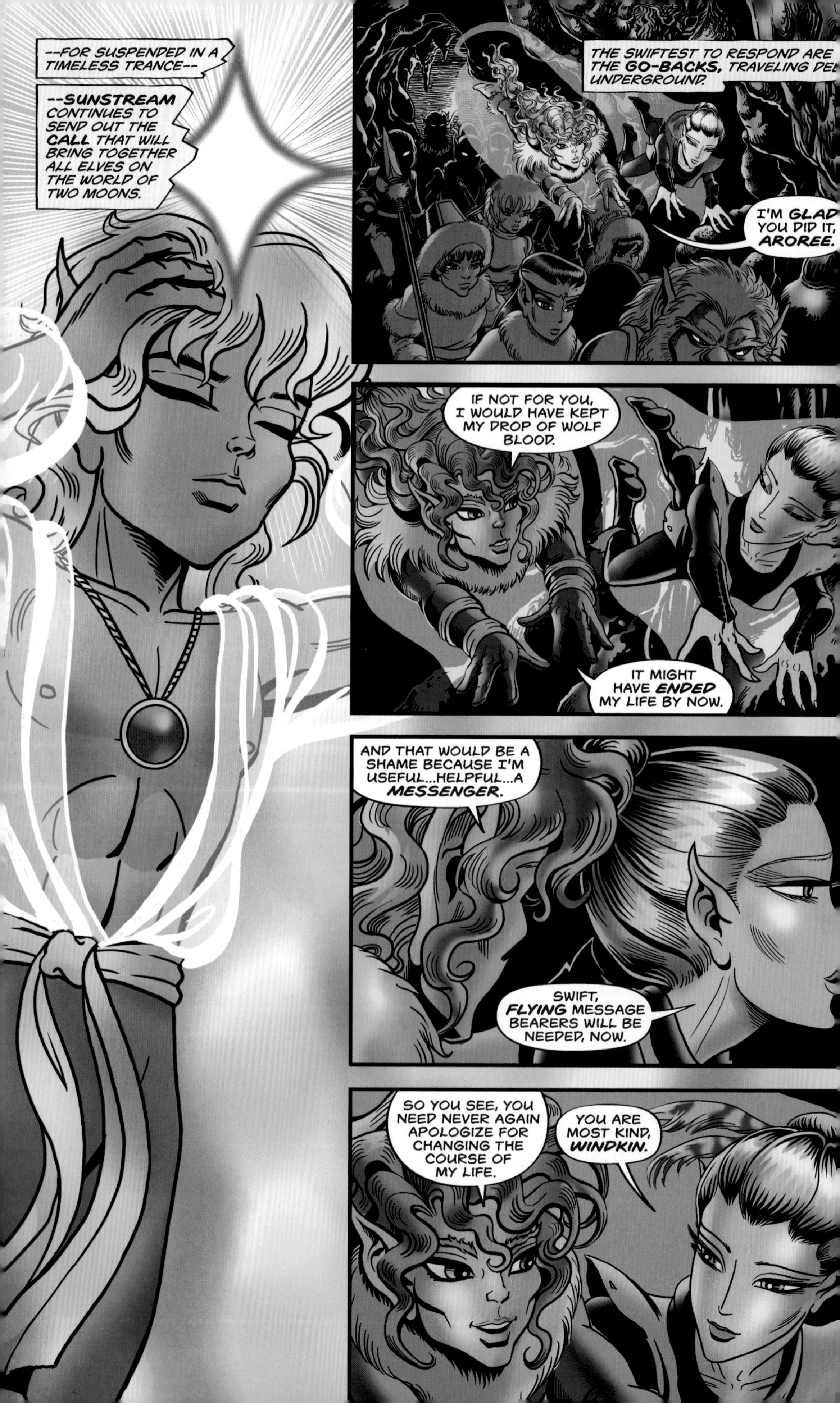
--FOR SUSPENDED IN A TIMELESS TRANCE--
--SUNSTREAM CONTINUES TO SEND OUT THE CALL THAT WILL BRING TOGETHER ALL ELVES ON THE WORLD OF TWO MOONS.
THE SWIFTEST TO RESPOND ARE THE GO-BACKS, TRAVELING DE UNDERGROUND.
I'M GLAD YOU DID IT, AROREE.
IF NOT FOR YOU, I WOULD HAVE KEPT MY DROP OF WOLF BLOOD.
IT MIGHT HAVE ENDED MY LIFE BY NOW.
AND THAT WOULD BE A SHAME BECAUSE I'M USEFUL...HELPFUL...A MESSENGER.
SWIFT, FLYING MESSAGE BEARERS WILL BE NEEDED, NOW.
SO YOU SEE, YOU NEED NEVER AGAIN APOLOGIZE FOR CHANGING THE COURSE OF MY LIFE.
YOU ARE MOST KIND, WINDKIN.

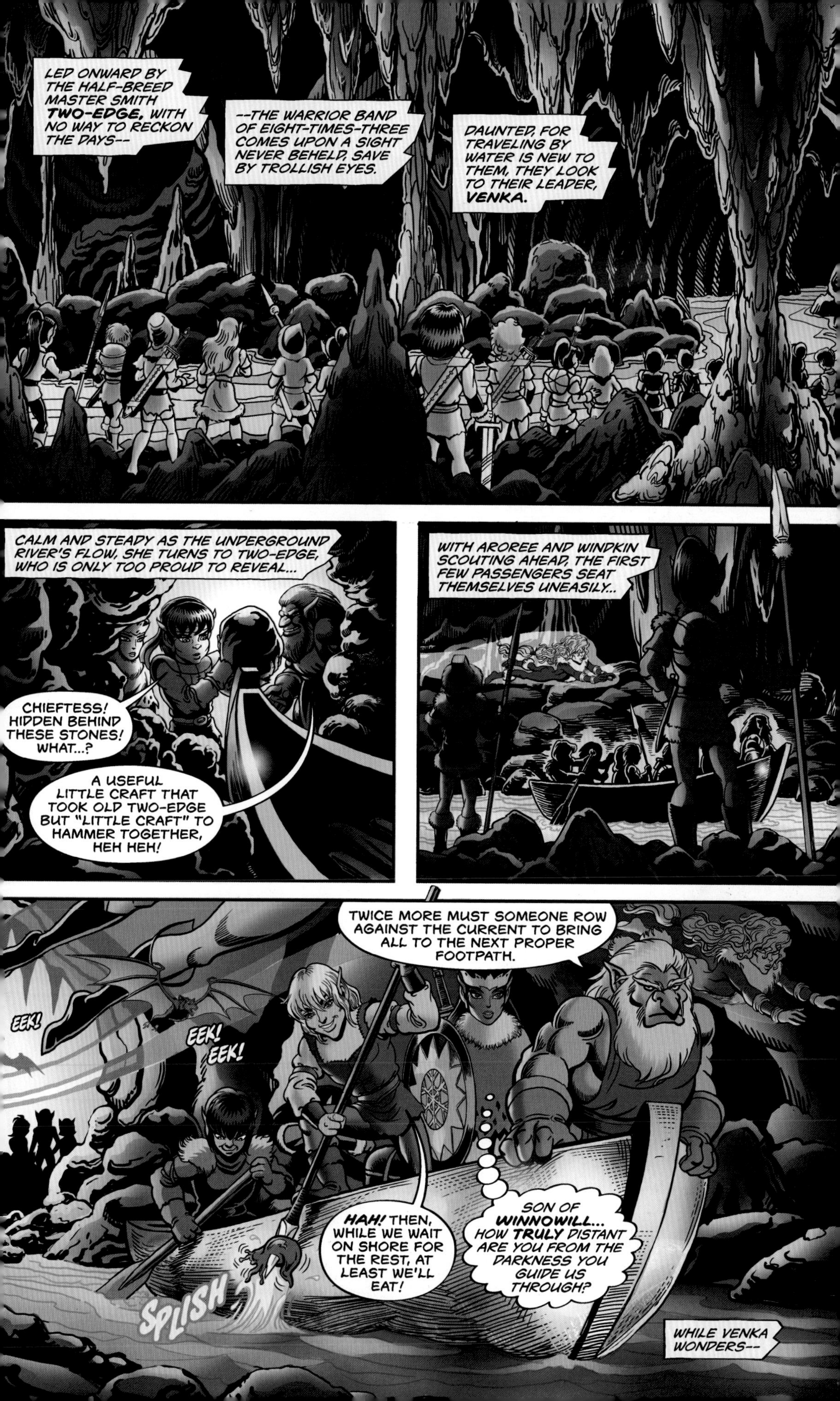
LED ONWARD BY THE HALF-BREED MASTER SMITH **TWO-EDGE,** WITH NO WAY TO RECKON THE DAYS--
--THE WARRIOR BAND OF EIGHT-TIMES-THREE COMES UPON A SIGHT NEVER BEHELD, SAVE BY TROLLISH EYES.
DAUNTED, FOR TRAVELING BY WATER IS NEW TO THEM, THEY LOOK TO THEIR LEADER, **VENKA.**
CALM AND STEADY AS THE UNDERGROUND RIVER'S FLOW, SHE TURNS TO TWO-EDGE, WHO IS ONLY TOO PROUD TO REVEAL...
CHIEFTESS! HIDDEN BEHIND THESE STONES! WHAT...?
A USEFUL LITTLE CRAFT THAT TOOK OLD TWO-EDGE BUT "LITTLE CRAFT" TO HAMMER TOGETHER, HEH HEH!
WITH AROREE AND WINDKIN SCOUTING AHEAD, THE FIRST FEW PASSENGERS SEAT THEMSELVES UNEASILY...
TWICE MORE MUST SOMEONE ROW AGAINST THE CURRENT TO BRING ALL TO THE NEXT PROPER FOOTPATH.
EEK!
EEK! EEK!
HAH! THEN, WHILE WE WAIT ON SHORE FOR THE REST, AT LEAST WE'LL EAT!
SPLISH
SON OF **WINNOWILL...** HOW **TRULY** DISTANT ARE YOU FROM THE DARKNESS YOU GUIDE US THROUGH?
WHILE VENKA WONDERS--

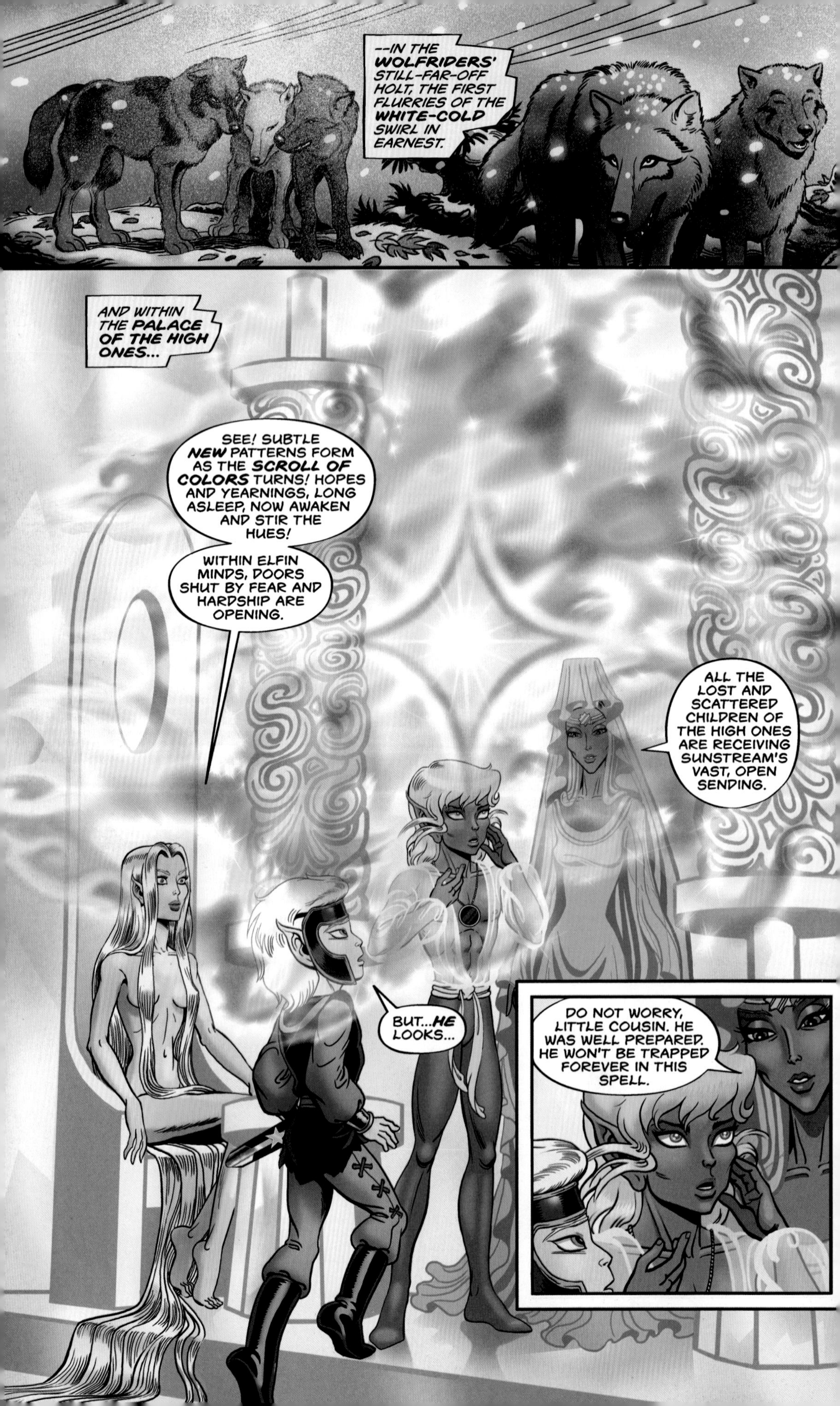
--IN THE WOLFRIDERS' STILL-FAR-OFF HOLT, THE FIRST FLURRIES OF THE WHITE-COLD SWIRL IN EARNEST.
AND WITHIN THE PALACE OF THE HIGH ONES...
SEE! SUBTLE NEW PATTERNS FORM AS THE SCROLL OF COLORS TURNS! HOPES AND YEARNINGS, LONG ASLEEP, NOW AWAKEN AND STIR THE HUES!
WITHIN ELFIN MINDS, DOORS SHUT BY FEAR AND HARDSHIP ARE OPENING.
ALL THE LOST AND SCATTERED CHILDREN OF THE HIGH ONES ARE RECEIVING SUNSTREAM'S VAST, OPEN SENDING.
BUT...HE LOOKS...
DO NOT WORRY, LITTLE COUSIN. HE WAS WELL PREPARED. HE WON'T BE TRAPPED FOREVER IN THIS SPELL.

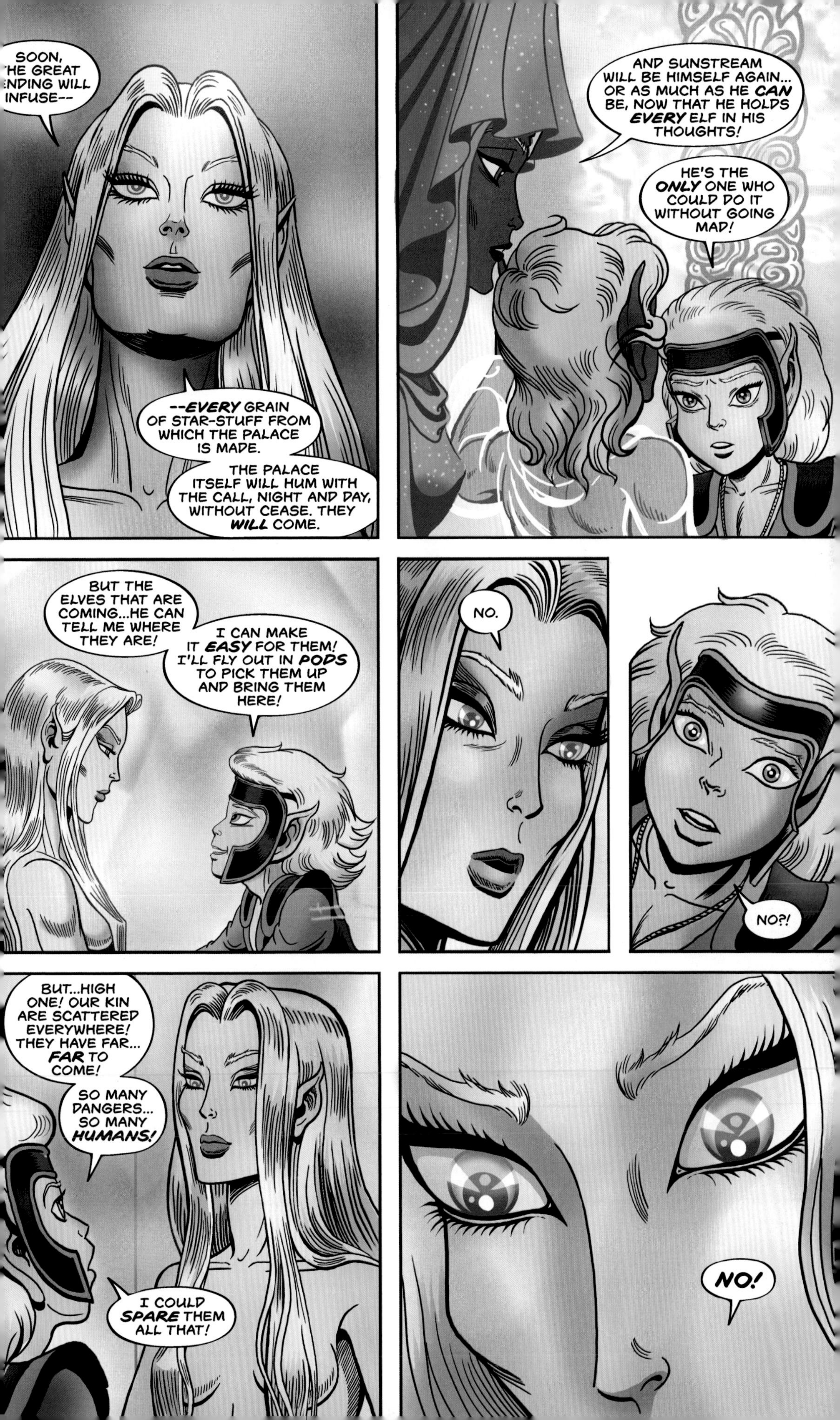
SOON, THE GREAT ENDING WILL INFUSE--
--EVERY GRAIN OF STAR-STUFF FROM WHICH THE PALACE IS MADE.
THE PALACE ITSELF WILL HUM WITH THE CALL, NIGHT AND DAY, WITHOUT CEASE. THEY WILL COME.
AND SUNSTREAM WILL BE HIMSELF AGAIN... OR AS MUCH AS HE CAN BE, NOW THAT HE HOLDS EVERY ELF IN HIS THOUGHTS!
HE'S THE ONLY ONE WHO COULD DO IT WITHOUT GOING MAD!
BUT THE ELVES THAT ARE COMING...HE CAN TELL ME WHERE THEY ARE!
I CAN MAKE IT EASY FOR THEM! I'LL FLY OUT IN PODS TO PICK THEM UP AND BRING THEM HERE!
NO.
NO?!
BUT...HIGH ONE! OUR KIN ARE SCATTERED EVERYWHERE! THEY HAVE FAR... FAR TO COME!
SO MANY DANGERS... SO MANY HUMANS!
I COULD SPARE THEM ALL THAT!
NO!

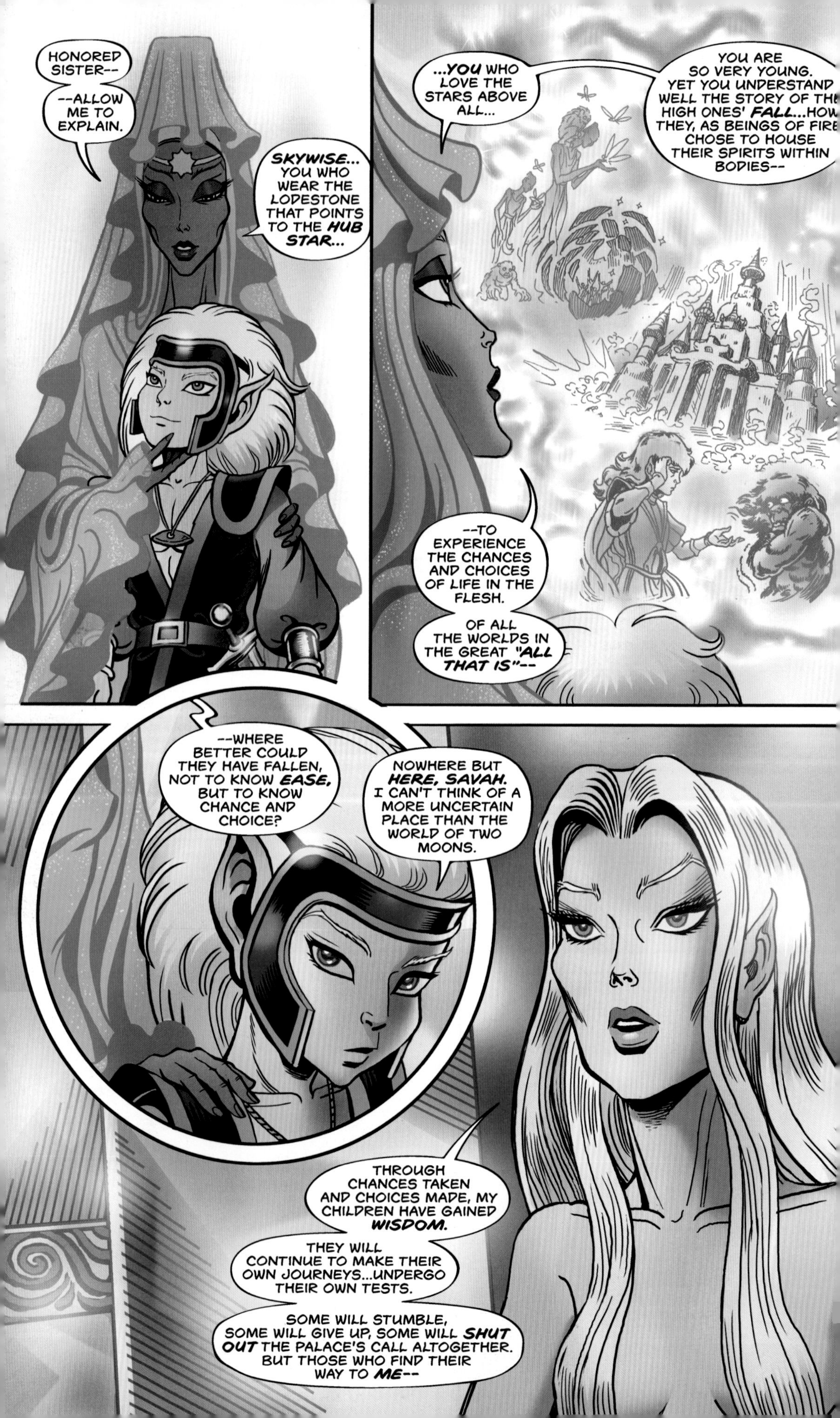
HONORED SISTER--
--ALLOW ME TO EXPLAIN.
SKYWISE... YOU WHO WEAR THE LODESTONE THAT POINTS TO THE HUB STAR...
...YOU WHO LOVE THE STARS ABOVE ALL...
YOU ARE SO VERY YOUNG. YET YOU UNDERSTAND WELL THE STORY OF THE HIGH ONES' FALL...HOW THEY, AS BEINGS OF FIRE CHOSE TO HOUSE THEIR SPIRITS WITHIN BODIES--
--TO EXPERIENCE THE CHANCES AND CHOICES OF LIFE IN THE FLESH.
OF ALL THE WORLDS IN THE GREAT "ALL THAT IS"--
--WHERE BETTER COULD THEY HAVE FALLEN, NOT TO KNOW EASE, BUT TO KNOW CHANCE AND CHOICE?
NOWHERE BUT HERE, SAVAH. I CAN'T THINK OF A MORE UNCERTAIN PLACE THAN THE WORLD OF TWO MOONS.
THROUGH CHANCES TAKEN AND CHOICES MADE, MY CHILDREN HAVE GAINED WISDOM.
THEY WILL CONTINUE TO MAKE THEIR OWN JOURNEYS...UNDERGO THEIR OWN TESTS.
SOME WILL STUMBLE, SOME WILL GIVE UP, SOME WILL SHUT OUT THE PALACE'S CALL ALTOGETHER. BUT THOSE WHO FIND THEIR WAY TO ME--

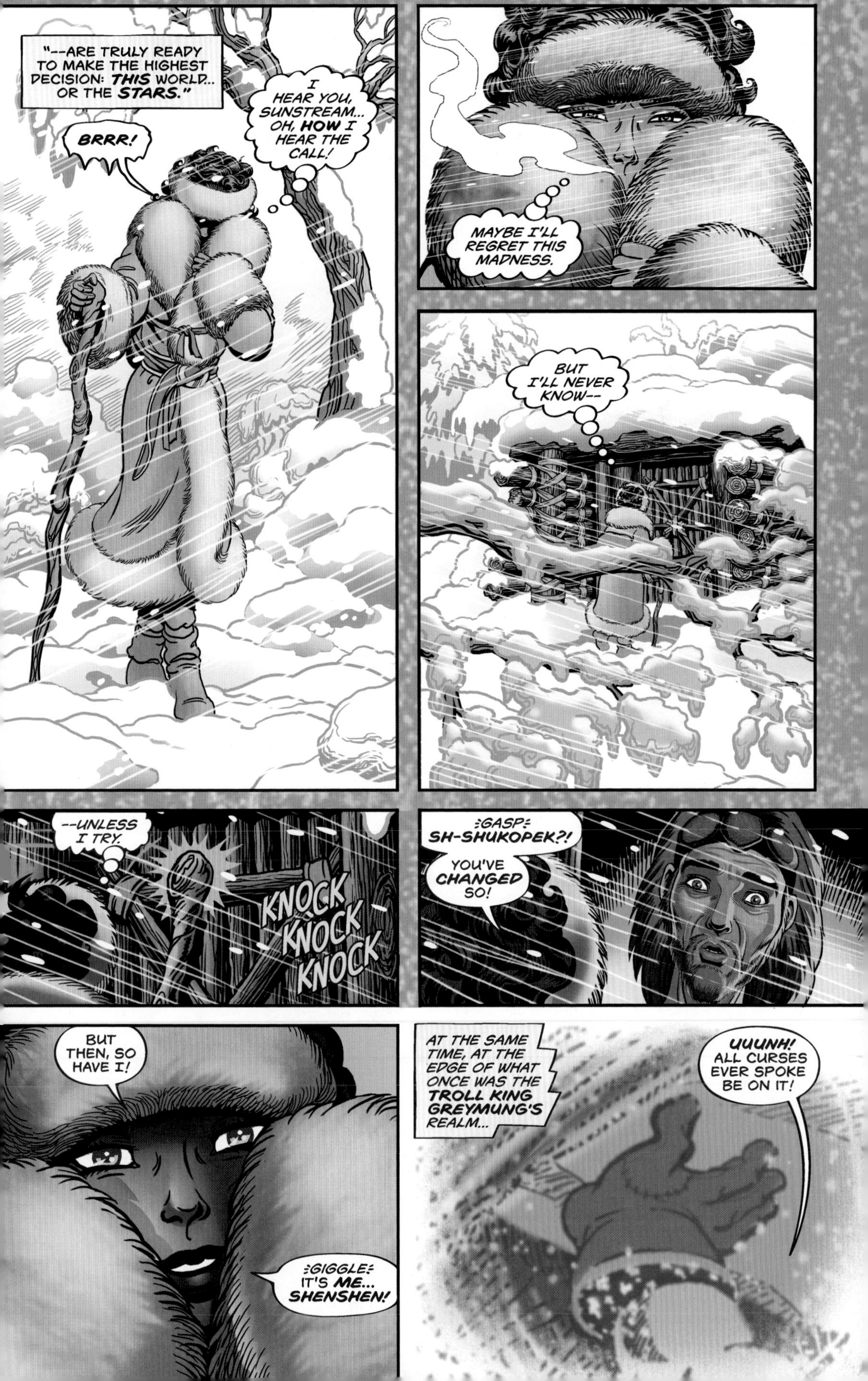
"--ARE TRULY READY TO MAKE THE HIGHEST DECISION: THIS WORLD... OR THE STARS."
BRRR!
I HEAR YOU, SUNSTREAM... OH, HOW I HEAR THE CALL!
MAYBE I'LL REGRET THIS MADNESS.
BUT I'LL NEVER KNOW--
--UNLESS I TRY.
KNOCK KNOCK KNOCK
GASP SH-SHUKOPEK?!
YOU'VE CHANGED SO!
BUT THEN, SO HAVE I!
GIGGLE IT'S ME... SHENSHEN!
AT THE SAME TIME, AT THE EDGE OF WHAT ONCE WAS THE TROLL KING GREYMUNG'S REALM...
UUUNH! ALL CURSES EVER SPOKE BE ON IT!

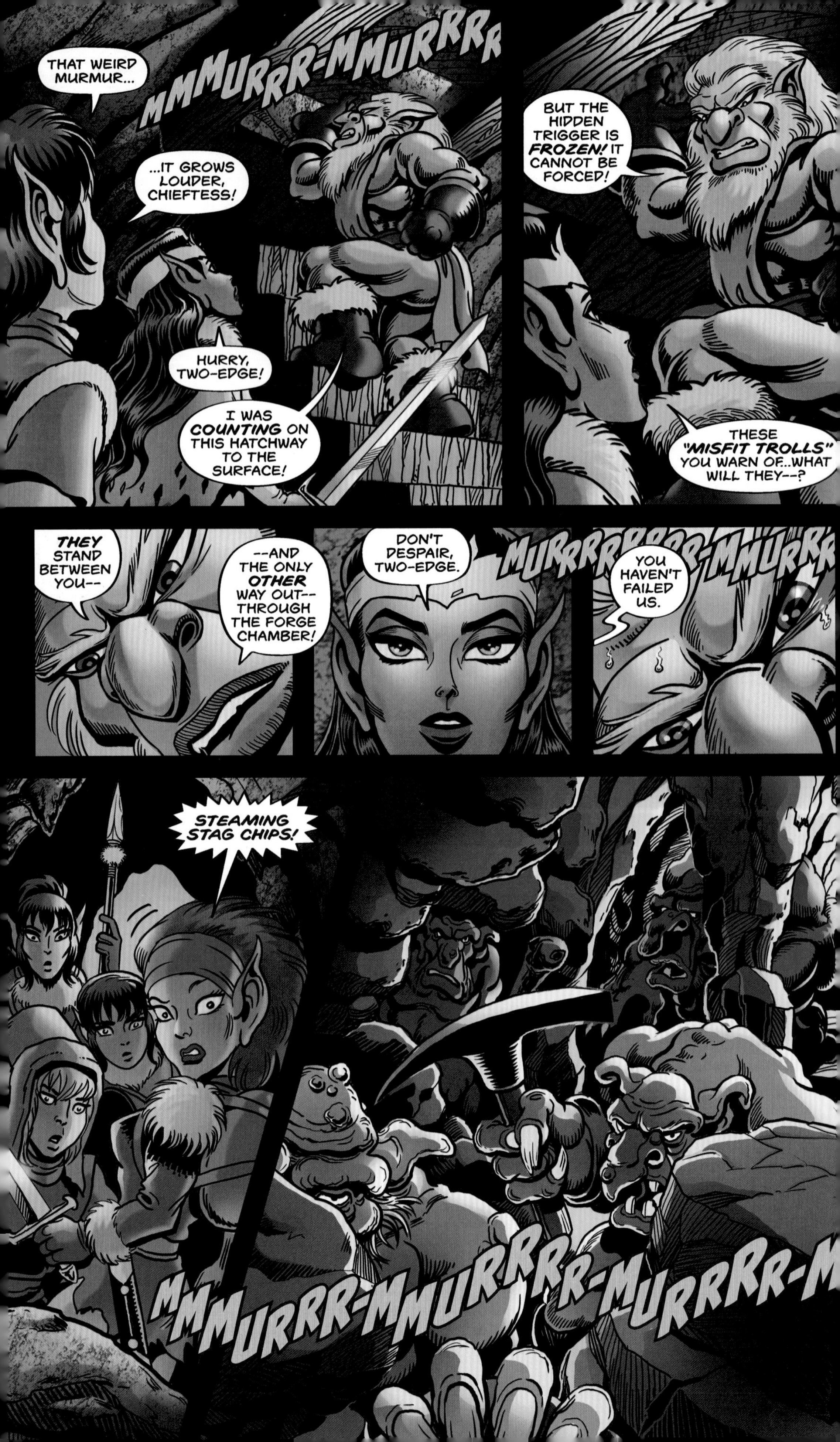
THAT WEIRD MURMUR...
MMMURRR-MMURRRR
...IT GROWS LOUDER, CHIEFTESS!
HURRY, TWO-EDGE!
I WAS COUNTING ON THIS HATCHWAY TO THE SURFACE!
BUT THE HIDDEN TRIGGER IS FROZEN! IT CANNOT BE FORCED!
THESE "MISFIT TROLLS" YOU WARN OF...WHAT WILL THEY--?
THEY STAND BETWEEN YOU--
--AND THE ONLY OTHER WAY OUT--THROUGH THE FORGE CHAMBER!
DON'T DESPAIR, TWO-EDGE.
MURRRRRRR-MMURR
YOU HAVEN'T FAILED US.
STEAMING STAG CHIPS!
MMMURRR-MMURRRR-MURRRR-M

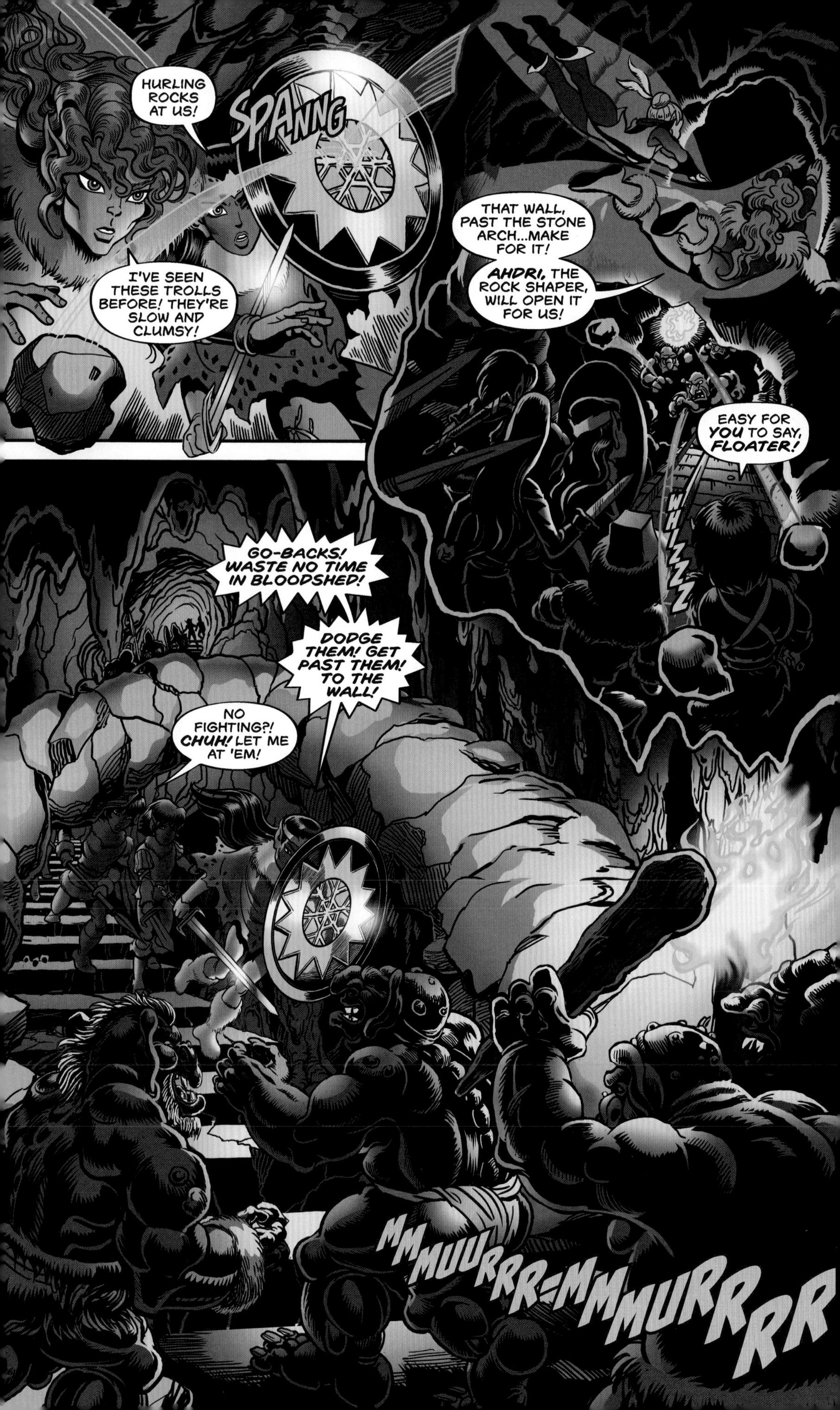
HURLING ROCKS AT US!
SPANNG
I'VE SEEN THESE TROLLS BEFORE! THEY'RE SLOW AND CLUMSY!
THAT WALL, PAST THE STONE ARCH...MAKE FOR IT!
AHDRI, THE ROCK SHAPER, WILL OPEN IT FOR US!
EASY FOR YOU TO SAY, FLOATER!
WHIZZZ
GO-BACKS! WASTE NO TIME IN BLOODSHED!
DODGE THEM! GET PAST THEM! TO THE WALL!
NO FIGHTING?! CHUH! LET ME AT 'EM!
MMMUURRRR=MMMURRRR

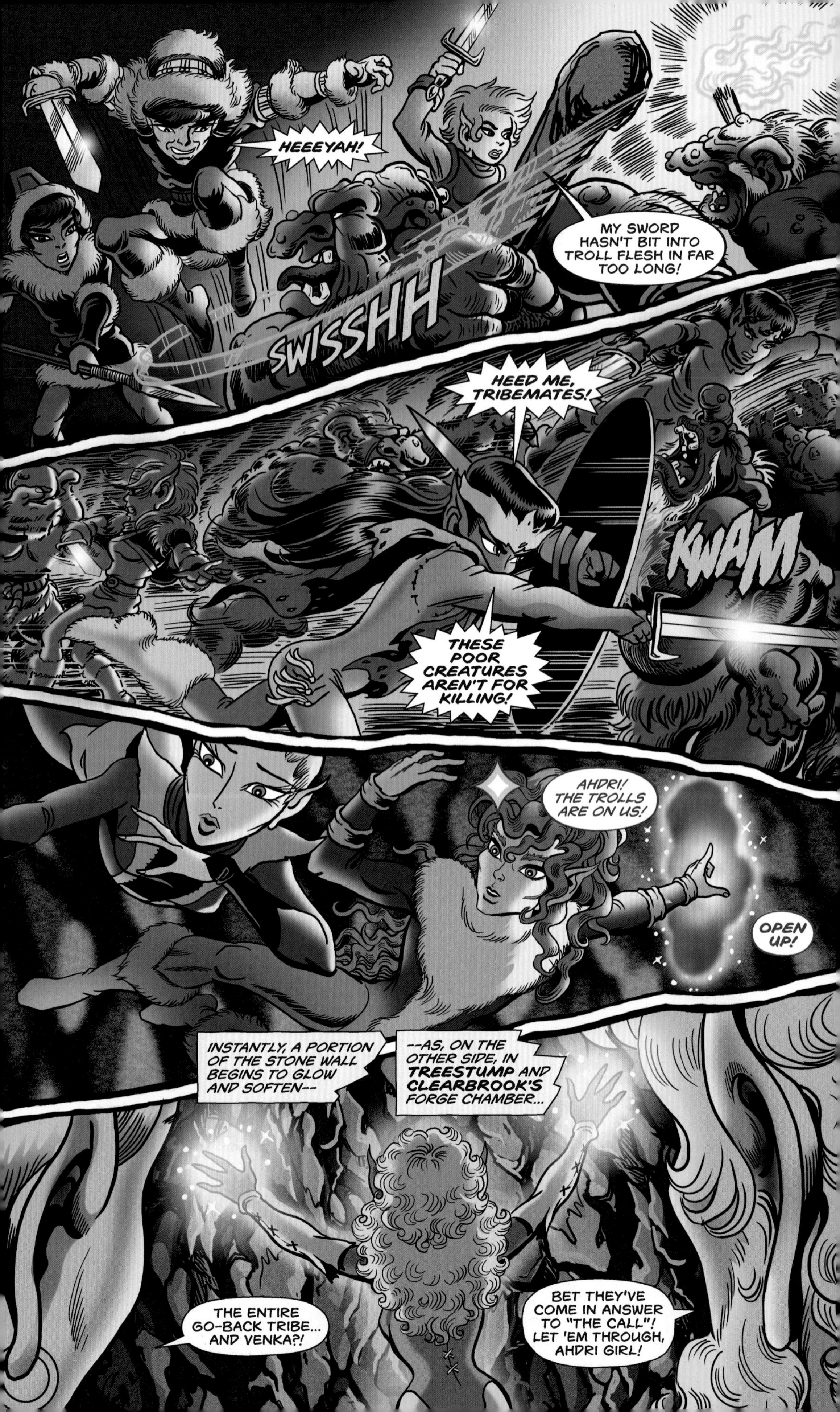
HEEEYAH!
MY SWORD HASN'T BIT INTO TROLL FLESH IN FAR TOO LONG!
SWISSHH
HEED ME, TRIBEMATES!
THESE POOR CREATURES AREN'T FOR KILLING!
KWAM
AHDRI! THE TROLLS ARE ON US!
OPEN UP!
INSTANTLY, A PORTION OF THE STONE WALL BEGINS TO GLOW AND SOFTEN--
--AS, ON THE OTHER SIDE, IN TREESTUMP AND CLEARBROOK'S FORGE CHAMBER...
THE ENTIRE GO-BACK TRIBE... AND VENKA?!
BET THEY'VE COME IN ANSWER TO "THE CALL"! LET 'EM THROUGH, AHDRI GIRL!

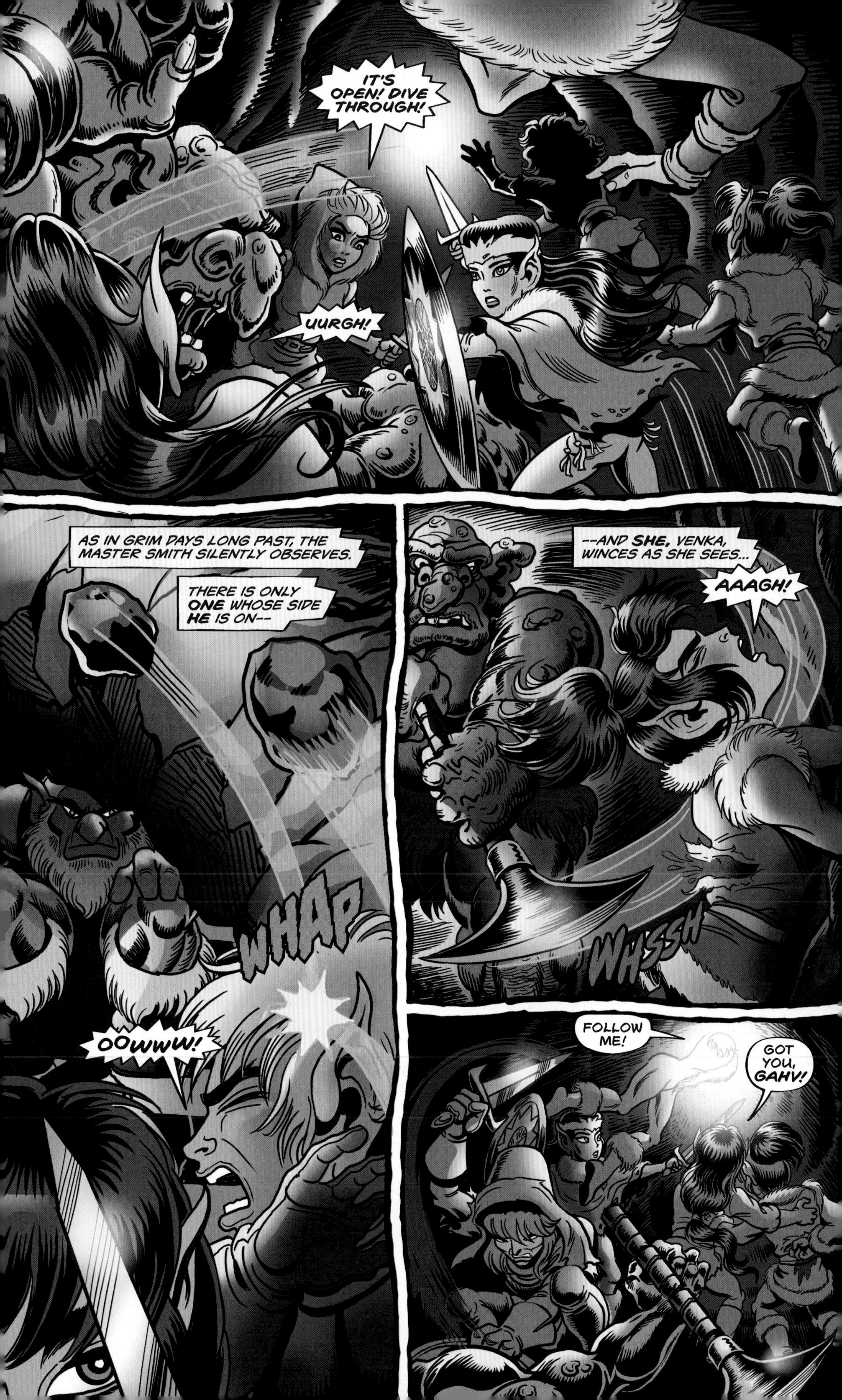
IT'S OPEN! DIVE THROUGH!
UURGH!
AS IN GRIM DAYS LONG PAST, THE MASTER SMITH SILENTLY OBSERVES.
THERE IS ONLY ONE WHOSE SIDE HE IS ON--
WHAP
OOWWW!
--AND SHE, VENKA, WINCES AS SHE SEES...
AAAGH!
WHSSH
FOLLOW ME!
GOT YOU, GAHV!

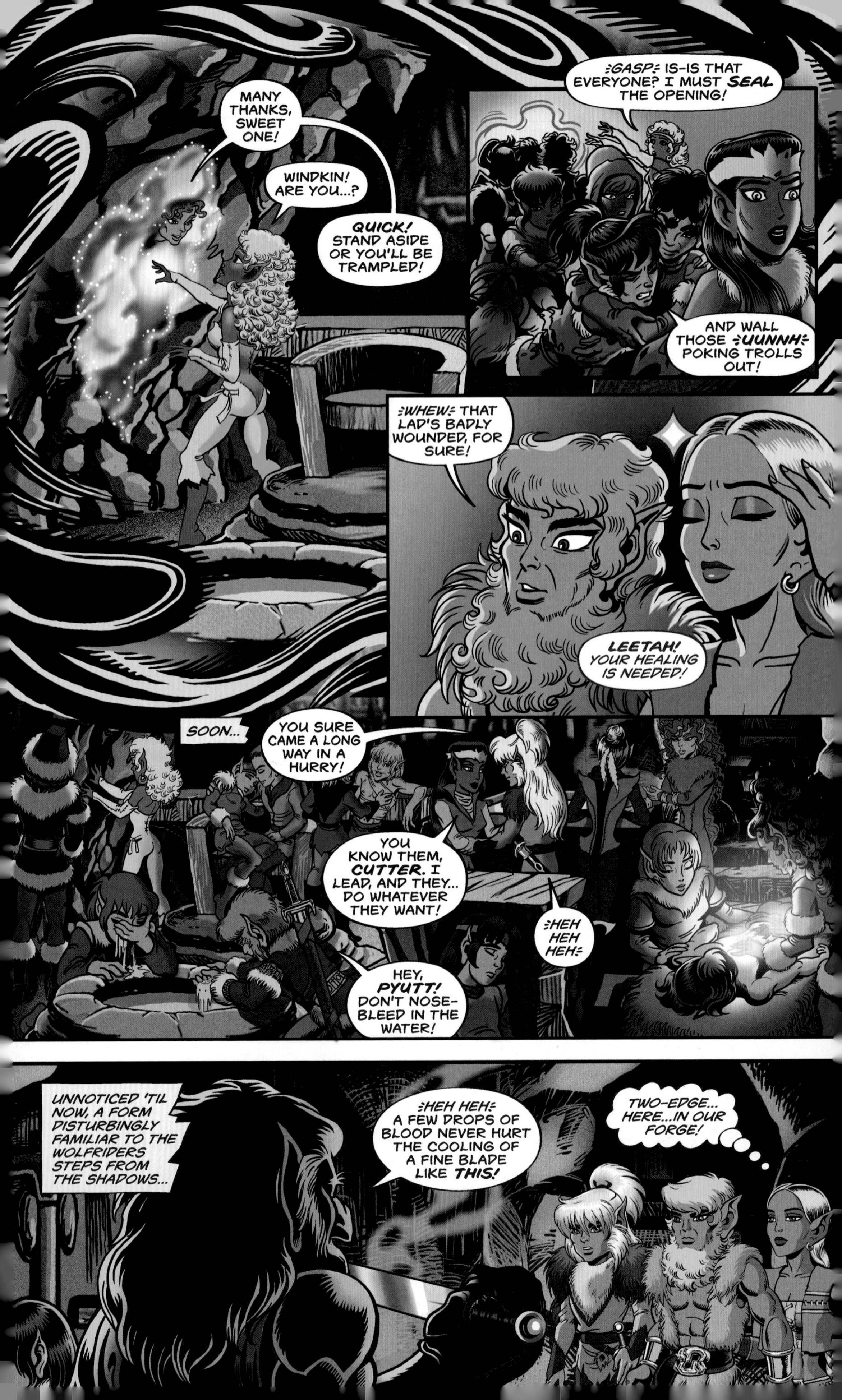

MANY THANKS, SWEET ONE!
WINDKIN! ARE YOU...?
QUICK! STAND ASIDE OR YOU'LL BE TRAMPLED!
:GASP: IS-IS THAT EVERYONE? I MUST SEAL THE OPENING!
AND WALL THOSE :UUNNH: POKING TROLLS OUT!
:WHEW: THAT LAD'S BADLY WOUNDED, FOR SURE!
LEETAH! YOUR HEALING IS NEEDED!
SOON...
YOU SURE CAME A LONG WAY IN A HURRY!
YOU KNOW THEM, CUTTER. I LEAD, AND THEY... DO WHATEVER THEY WANT!
:HEH HEH HEH:
HEY, PYUTT! DON'T NOSE-BLEED IN THE WATER!
UNNOTICED 'TIL NOW, A FORM DISTURBINGLY FAMILIAR TO THE WOLFRIDERS STEPS FROM THE SHADOWS...
:HEH HEH: A FEW DROPS OF BLOOD NEVER HURT THE COOLING OF A FINE BLADE LIKE THIS!
TWO-EDGE... HERE...IN OUR FORGE!

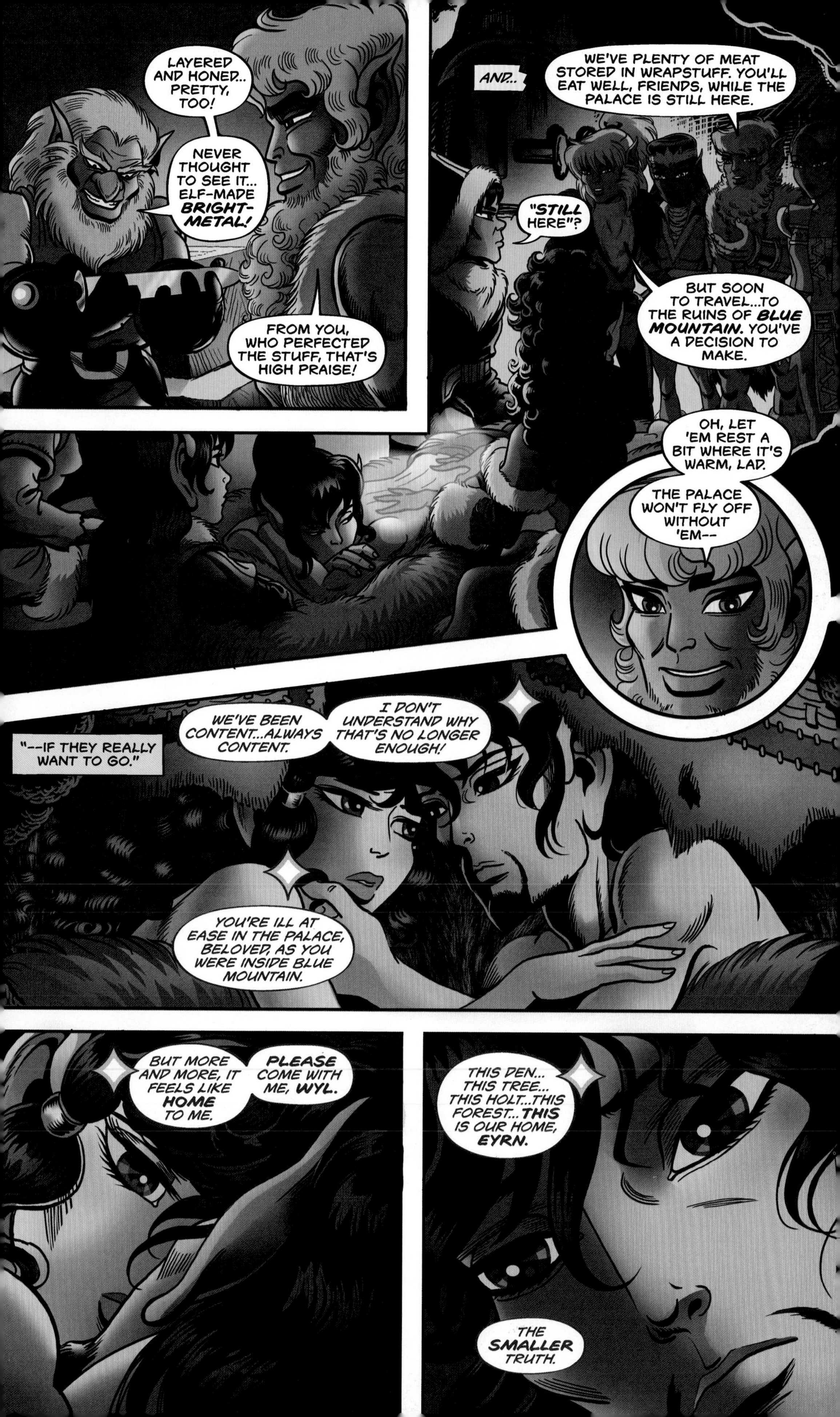
LAYERED AND HONED... PRETTY, TOO!
NEVER THOUGHT TO SEE IT... ELF-MADE BRIGHT-METAL!
FROM YOU, WHO PERFECTED THE STUFF, THAT'S HIGH PRAISE!
AND...
WE'VE PLENTY OF MEAT STORED IN WRAPSTUFF. YOU'LL EAT WELL, FRIENDS, WHILE THE PALACE IS STILL HERE.
"STILL HERE"?
BUT SOON TO TRAVEL...TO THE RUINS OF BLUE MOUNTAIN. YOU'VE A DECISION TO MAKE.
OH, LET 'EM REST A BIT WHERE IT'S WARM, LAD.
THE PALACE WON'T FLY OFF WITHOUT 'EM--
"--IF THEY REALLY WANT TO GO."
WE'VE BEEN CONTENT...ALWAYS CONTENT.
I DON'T UNDERSTAND WHY THAT'S NO LONGER ENOUGH!
YOU'RE ILL AT EASE IN THE PALACE, BELOVED, AS YOU WERE INSIDE BLUE MOUNTAIN.
BUT MORE AND MORE, IT FEELS LIKE HOME TO ME.
PLEASE COME WITH ME, WYL.
THIS DEN... THIS TREE... THIS HOLT...THIS FOREST...THIS IS OUR HOME, EYRN.
THE SMALLER TRUTH.

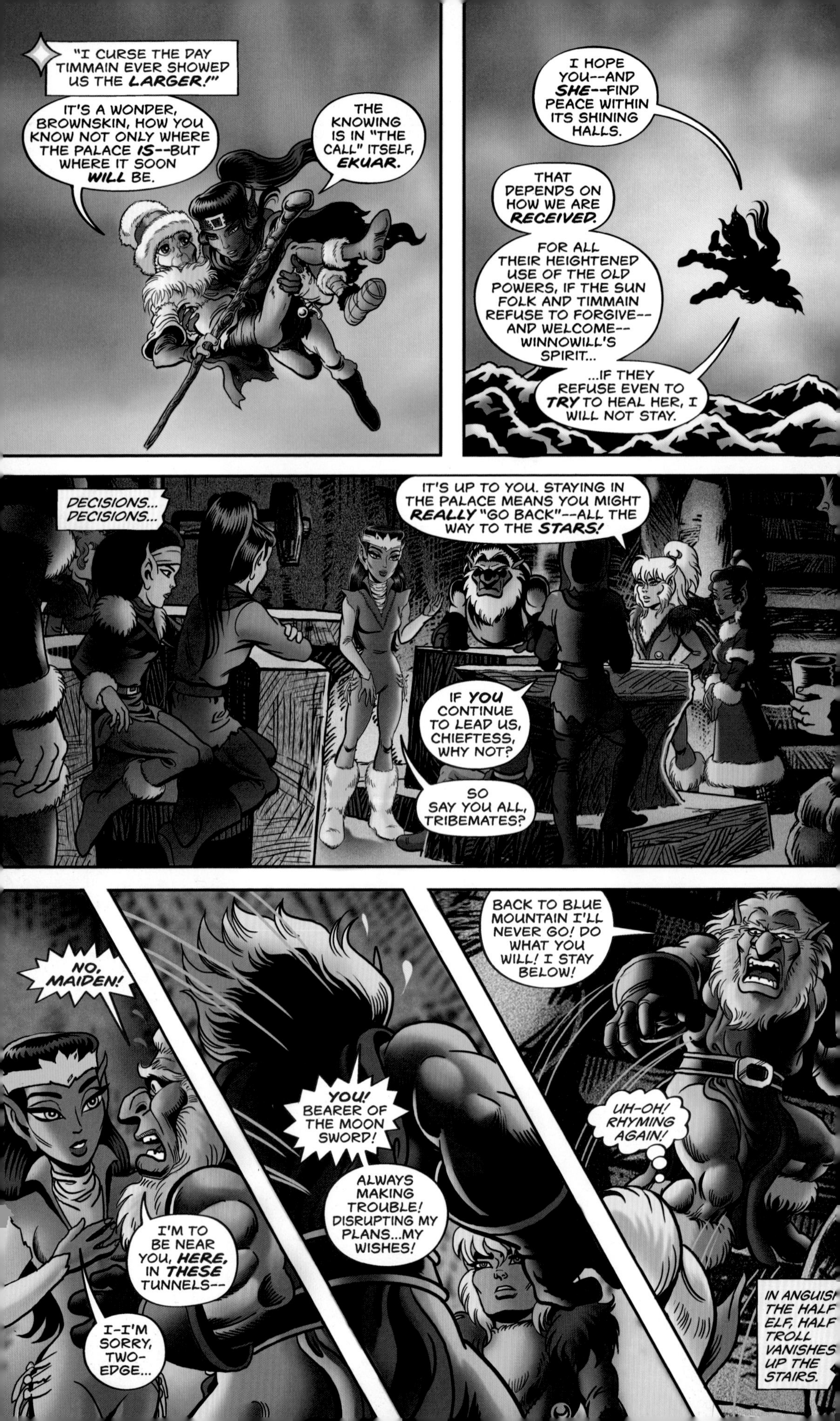
"I CURSE THE DAY TIMMAIN EVER SHOWED US THE LARGER!"
IT'S A WONDER, BROWNSKIN, HOW YOU KNOW NOT ONLY WHERE THE PALACE IS--BUT WHERE IT SOON WILL BE.
THE KNOWING IS IN "THE CALL" ITSELF, EKUAR.
I HOPE YOU--AND SHE--FIND PEACE WITHIN ITS SHINING HALLS.
THAT DEPENDS ON HOW WE ARE RECEIVED.
FOR ALL THEIR HEIGHTENED USE OF THE OLD POWERS, IF THE SUN FOLK AND TIMMAIN REFUSE TO FORGIVE-- AND WELCOME-- WINNOWILL'S SPIRIT...
...IF THEY REFUSE EVEN TO TRY TO HEAL HER, I WILL NOT STAY.
DECISIONS... DECISIONS...
IT'S UP TO YOU. STAYING IN THE PALACE MEANS YOU MIGHT REALLY "GO BACK"--ALL THE WAY TO THE STARS!
IF YOU CONTINUE TO LEAD US, CHIEFTESS, WHY NOT?
SO SAY YOU ALL, TRIBEMATES?
NO, MAIDEN!
I'M TO BE NEAR YOU, HERE, IN THESE TUNNELS--
I-I'M SORRY, TWO-EDGE...
YOU! BEARER OF THE MOON SWORD!
ALWAYS MAKING TROUBLE! DISRUPTING MY PLANS...MY WISHES!
BACK TO BLUE MOUNTAIN I'LL NEVER GO! DO WHAT YOU WILL! I STAY BELOW!
UH-OH! RHYMING AGAIN!
IN ANGUISH THE HALF ELF, HALF TROLL VANISHES UP THE STAIRS.

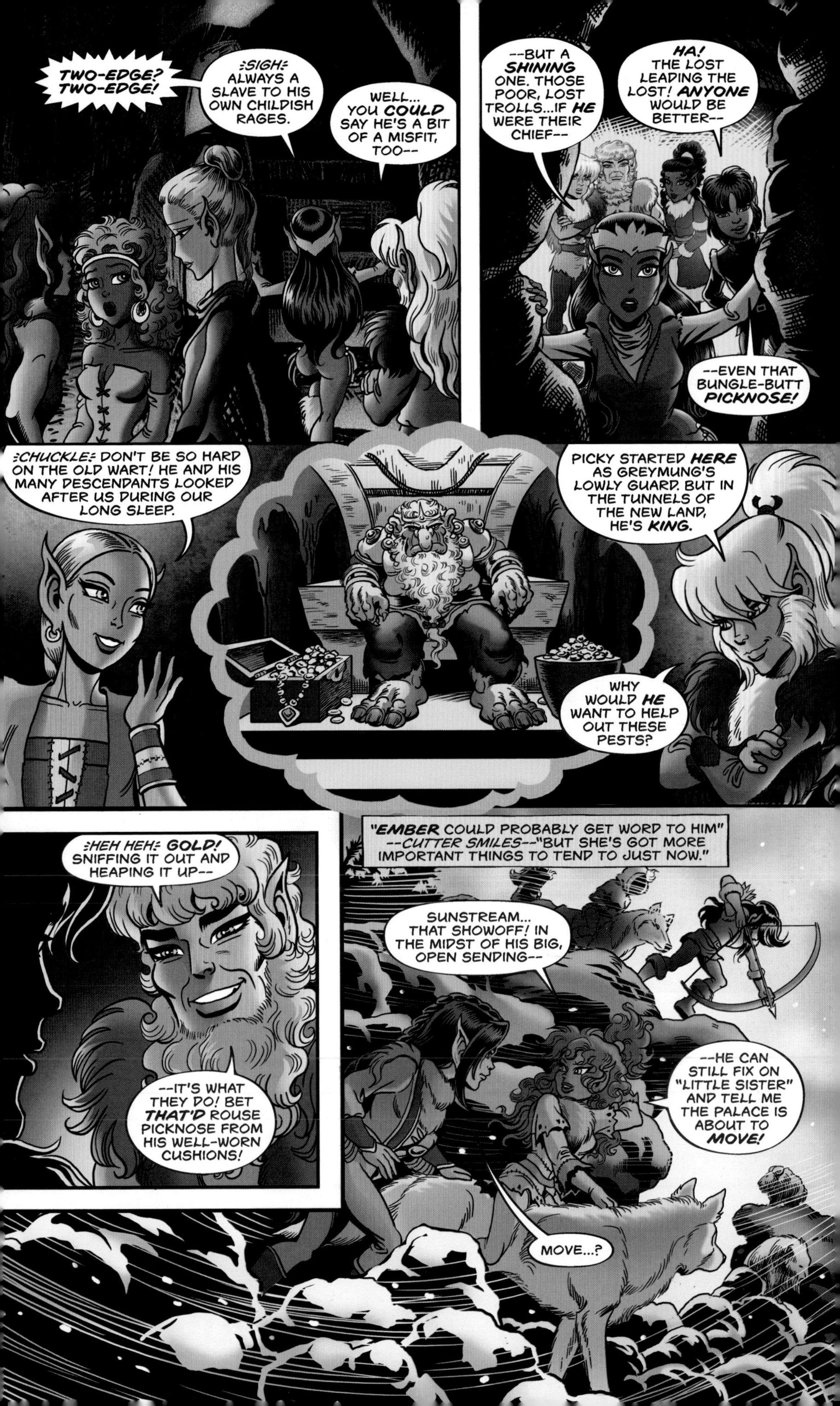

TWO-EDGE? TWO-EDGE!
:SIGH: ALWAYS A SLAVE TO HIS OWN CHILDISH RAGES.
WELL... YOU COULD SAY HE'S A BIT OF A MISFIT, TOO--
--BUT A SHINING ONE. THOSE POOR, LOST TROLLS...IF HE WERE THEIR CHIEF--
HA! THE LOST LEADING THE LOST! ANYONE WOULD BE BETTER--
--EVEN THAT BUNGLE-BUTT PICKNOSE!
:CHUCKLE: DON'T BE SO HARD ON THE OLD WART! HE AND HIS MANY DESCENDANTS LOOKED AFTER US DURING OUR LONG SLEEP.
PICKY STARTED HERE AS GREYMUNG'S LOWLY GUARD. BUT IN THE TUNNELS OF THE NEW LAND, HE'S KING.
WHY WOULD HE WANT TO HELP OUT THESE PESTS?
:HEH HEH: GOLD! SNIFFING IT OUT AND HEAPING IT UP--
--IT'S WHAT THEY DO! BET THAT'D ROUSE PICKNOSE FROM HIS WELL-WORN CUSHIONS!
"EMBER COULD PROBABLY GET WORD TO HIM" --CUTTER SMILES--"BUT SHE'S GOT MORE IMPORTANT THINGS TO TEND TO JUST NOW."
SUNSTREAM... THAT SHOWOFF! IN THE MIDST OF HIS BIG, OPEN SENDING--
--HE CAN STILL FIX ON "LITTLE SISTER" AND TELL ME THE PALACE IS ABOUT TO MOVE!
MOVE...?

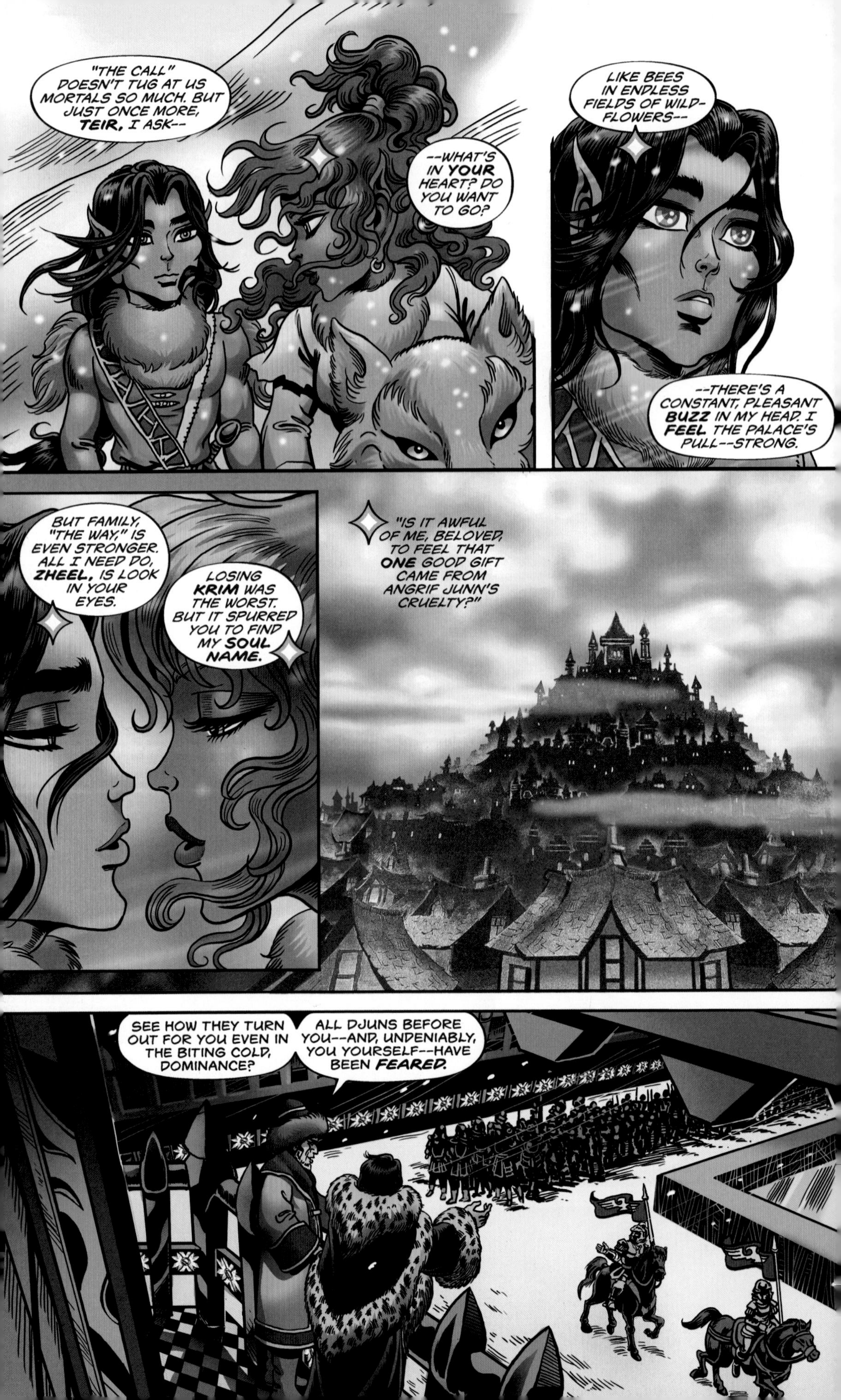
"THE CALL" DOESN'T TUG AT US MORTALS SO MUCH. BUT JUST ONCE MORE, TEIR, I ASK--
--WHAT'S IN YOUR HEART? DO YOU WANT TO GO?
LIKE BEES IN ENDLESS FIELDS OF WILD-FLOWERS--
--THERE'S A CONSTANT, PLEASANT BUZZ IN MY HEAD. I FEEL THE PALACE'S PULL--STRONG.
BUT FAMILY, "THE WAY," IS EVEN STRONGER. ALL I NEED DO, ZHEEL, IS LOOK IN YOUR EYES.
LOSING KRIM WAS THE WORST. BUT IT SPURRED YOU TO FIND MY SOUL NAME.
"IS IT AWFUL OF ME, BELOVED, TO FEEL THAT ONE GOOD GIFT CAME FROM ANGRIF JUNN'S CRUELTY?"
SEE HOW THEY TURN OUT FOR YOU EVEN IN THE BITING COLD, DOMINANCE?
ALL DJUNS BEFORE YOU--AND, UNDENIABLY, YOU YOURSELF--HAVE BEEN FEARED.

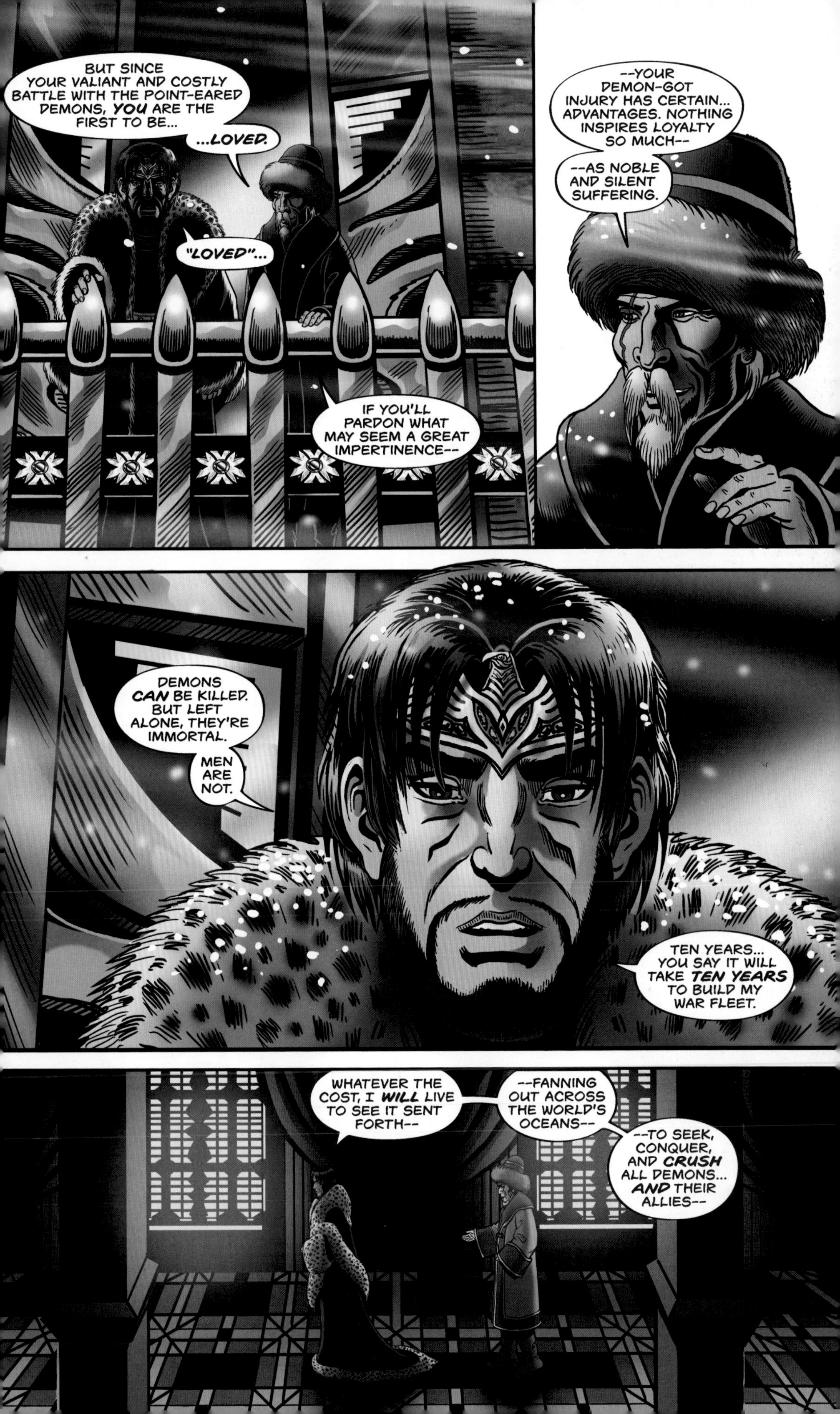
BUT SINCE YOUR VALIANT AND COSTLY BATTLE WITH THE POINT-EARED DEMONS, YOU ARE THE FIRST TO BE...
...LOVED.
"LOVED"...
IF YOU'LL PARDON WHAT MAY SEEM A GREAT IMPERTINENCE--
--YOUR DEMON-GOT INJURY HAS CERTAIN... ADVANTAGES. NOTHING INSPIRES LOYALTY SO MUCH--
--AS NOBLE AND SILENT SUFFERING.
DEMONS CAN BE KILLED. BUT LEFT ALONE, THEY'RE IMMORTAL.
MEN ARE NOT.
TEN YEARS... YOU SAY IT WILL TAKE TEN YEARS TO BUILD MY WAR FLEET.
WHATEVER THE COST, I WILL LIVE TO SEE IT SENT FORTH--
--FANNING OUT ACROSS THE WORLD'S OCEANS--
--TO SEEK, CONQUER, AND CRUSH ALL DEMONS... AND THEIR ALLIES--

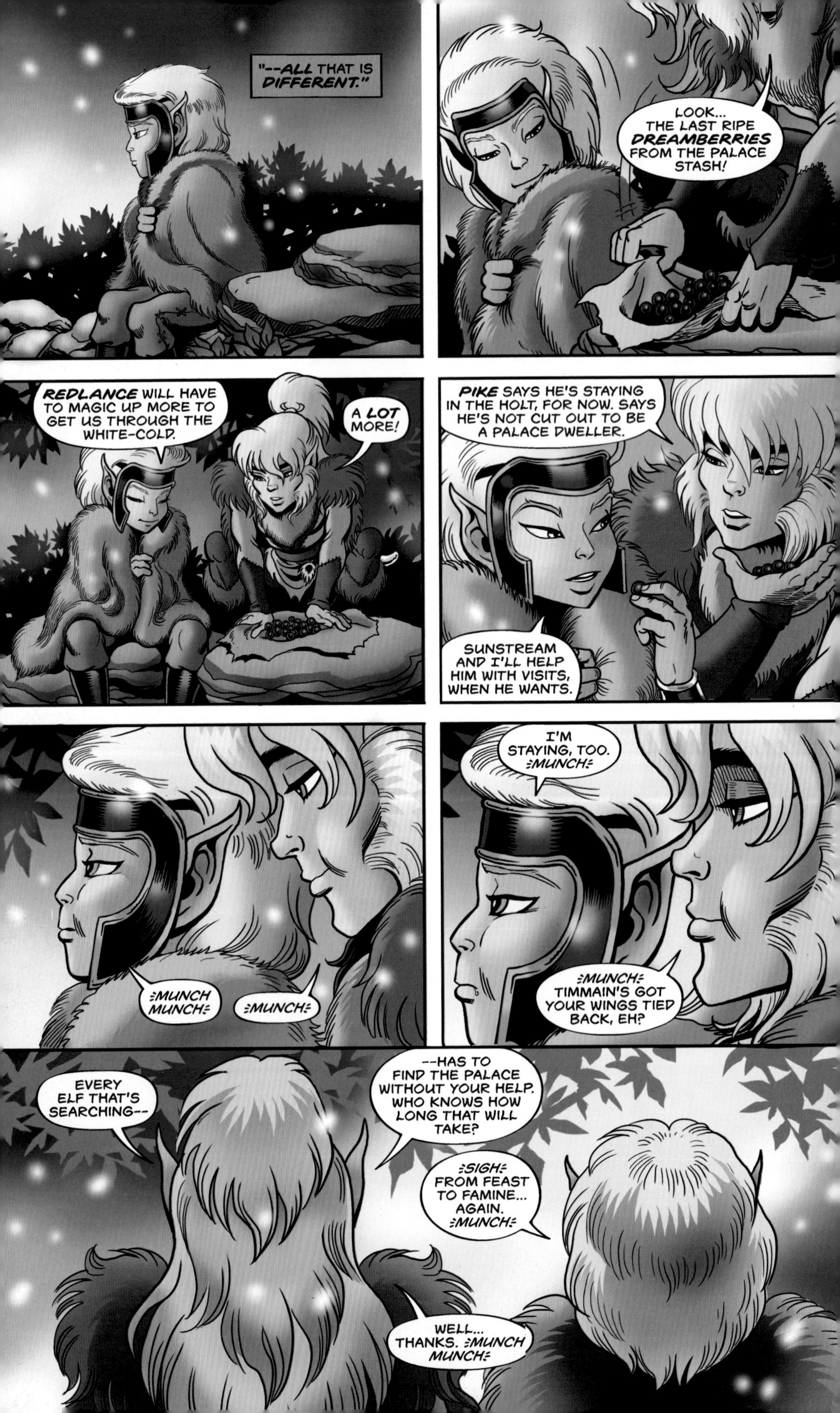
"--ALL THAT IS DIFFERENT."
LOOK... THE LAST RIPE DREAMBERRIES FROM THE PALACE STASH!
REDLANCE WILL HAVE TO MAGIC UP MORE TO GET US THROUGH THE WHITE-COLD.
A LOT MORE!
PIKE SAYS HE'S STAYING IN THE HOLT, FOR NOW. SAYS HE'S NOT CUT OUT TO BE A PALACE DWELLER.
SUNSTREAM AND I'LL HELP HIM WITH VISITS, WHEN HE WANTS.
:MUNCH MUNCH:
:MUNCH:
I'M STAYING, TOO. :MUNCH:
:MUNCH: TIMMAIN'S GOT YOUR WINGS TIED BACK, EH?
EVERY ELF THAT'S SEARCHING--
--HAS TO FIND THE PALACE WITHOUT YOUR HELP. WHO KNOWS HOW LONG THAT WILL TAKE?
:SIGH: FROM FEAST TO FAMINE... AGAIN. :MUNCH:
WELL... THANKS. :MUNCH MUNCH:

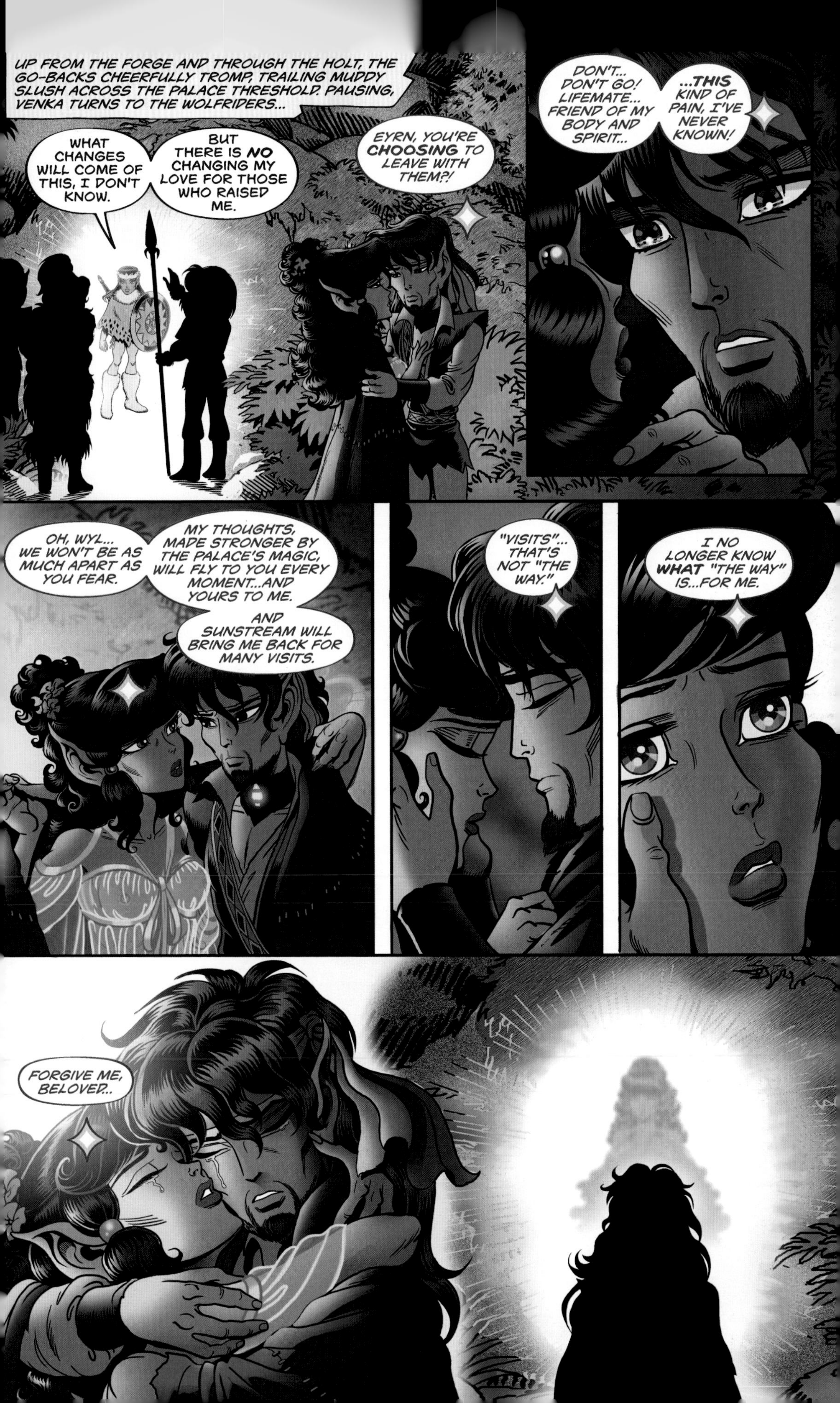
UP FROM THE FORGE AND THROUGH THE HOLT, THE GO-BACKS CHEERFULLY TROMP, TRAILING MUDDY SLUSH ACROSS THE PALACE THRESHOLD. PAUSING, VENKA TURNS TO THE WOLFRIDERS...
WHAT CHANGES WILL COME OF THIS, I DON'T KNOW.
BUT THERE IS NO CHANGING MY LOVE FOR THOSE WHO RAISED ME.
EYRN, YOU'RE CHOOSING TO LEAVE WITH THEM?!
DON'T... DON'T GO! LIFEMATE... FRIEND OF MY BODY AND SPIRIT...
...THIS KIND OF PAIN, I'VE NEVER KNOWN!
OH, WYL... WE WON'T BE AS MUCH APART AS YOU FEAR.
MY THOUGHTS, MADE STRONGER BY THE PALACE'S MAGIC, WILL FLY TO YOU EVERY MOMENT...AND YOURS TO ME.
AND SUNSTREAM WILL BRING ME BACK FOR MANY VISITS.
"VISITS"... THAT'S NOT "THE WAY."
I NO LONGER KNOW WHAT "THE WAY" IS...FOR ME.
FORGIVE ME, BELOVED...

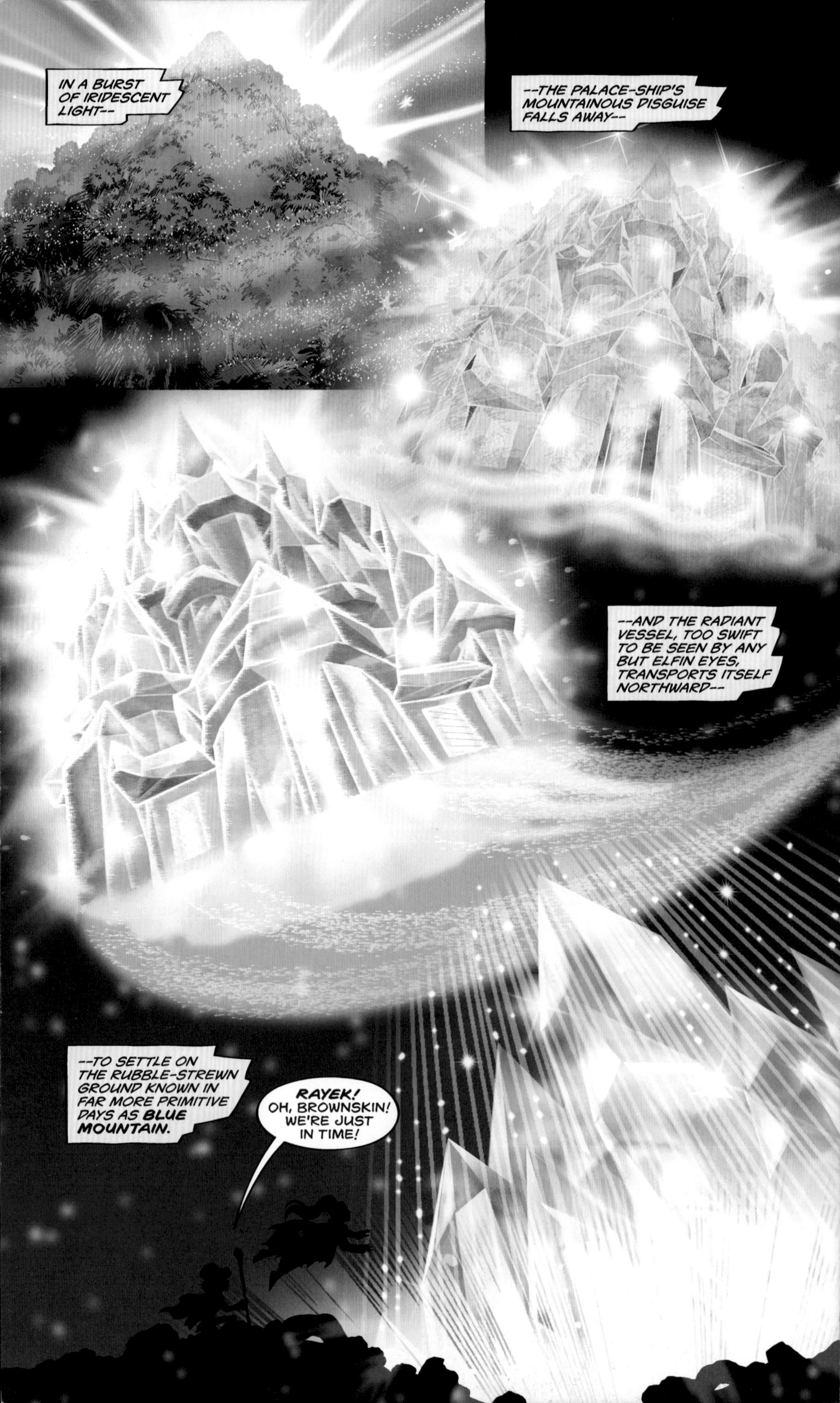
IN A BURST OF IRIDESCENT LIGHT--
--THE PALACE-SHIP'S MOUNTAINOUS DISGUISE FALLS AWAY--
--AND THE RADIANT VESSEL, TOO SWIFT TO BE SEEN BY ANY BUT ELFIN EYES, TRANSPORTS ITSELF NORTHWARD--
--TO SETTLE ON THE RUBBLE-STREWN GROUND KNOWN IN FAR MORE PRIMITIVE DAYS AS BLUE MOUNTAIN.
RAYEK! OH, BROWNSKIN! WE'RE JUST IN TIME!

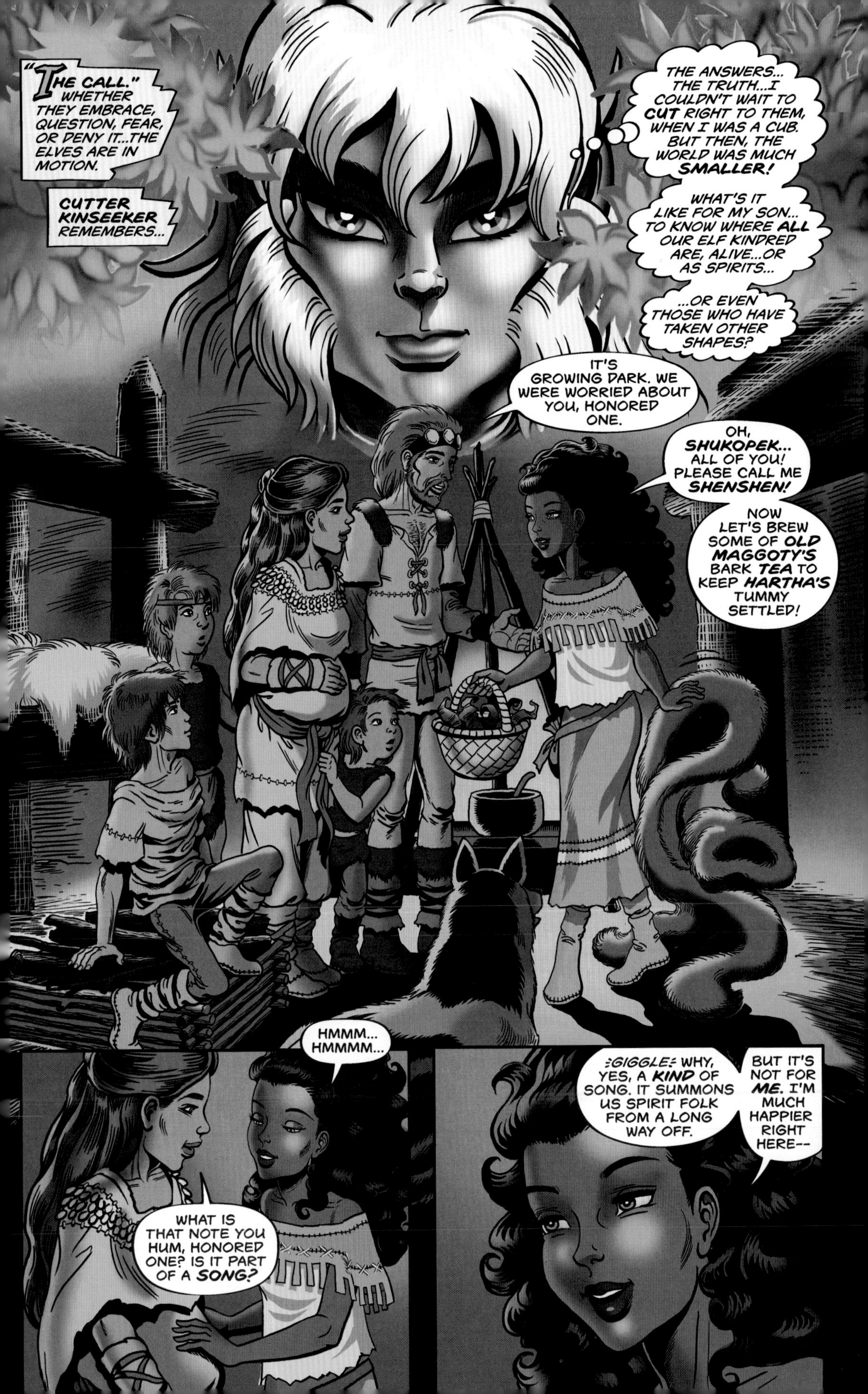
"THE CALL." WHETHER THEY EMBRACE, QUESTION, FEAR, OR DENY IT...THE ELVES ARE IN MOTION.
CUTTER KINSEEKER REMEMBERS...
THE ANSWERS... THE TRUTH...I COULDN'T WAIT TO CUT RIGHT TO THEM, WHEN I WAS A CUB. BUT THEN, THE WORLD WAS MUCH SMALLER!
WHAT'S IT LIKE FOR MY SON... TO KNOW WHERE ALL OUR ELF KINDRED ARE, ALIVE...OR AS SPIRITS...
...OR EVEN THOSE WHO HAVE TAKEN OTHER SHAPES?
IT'S GROWING DARK. WE WERE WORRIED ABOUT YOU, HONORED ONE.
OH, SHUKOPEK... ALL OF YOU! PLEASE CALL ME SHENSHEN!
NOW LET'S BREW SOME OF OLD MAGGOTY'S BARK TEA TO KEEP HARTHA'S TUMMY SETTLED!
HMMM... HMMMM...
WHAT IS THAT NOTE YOU HUM, HONORED ONE? IS IT PART OF A SONG?
:GIGGLE: WHY, YES, A KIND OF SONG. IT SUMMONS US SPIRIT FOLK FROM A LONG WAY OFF.
BUT IT'S NOT FOR ME. I'M MUCH HAPPIER RIGHT HERE--

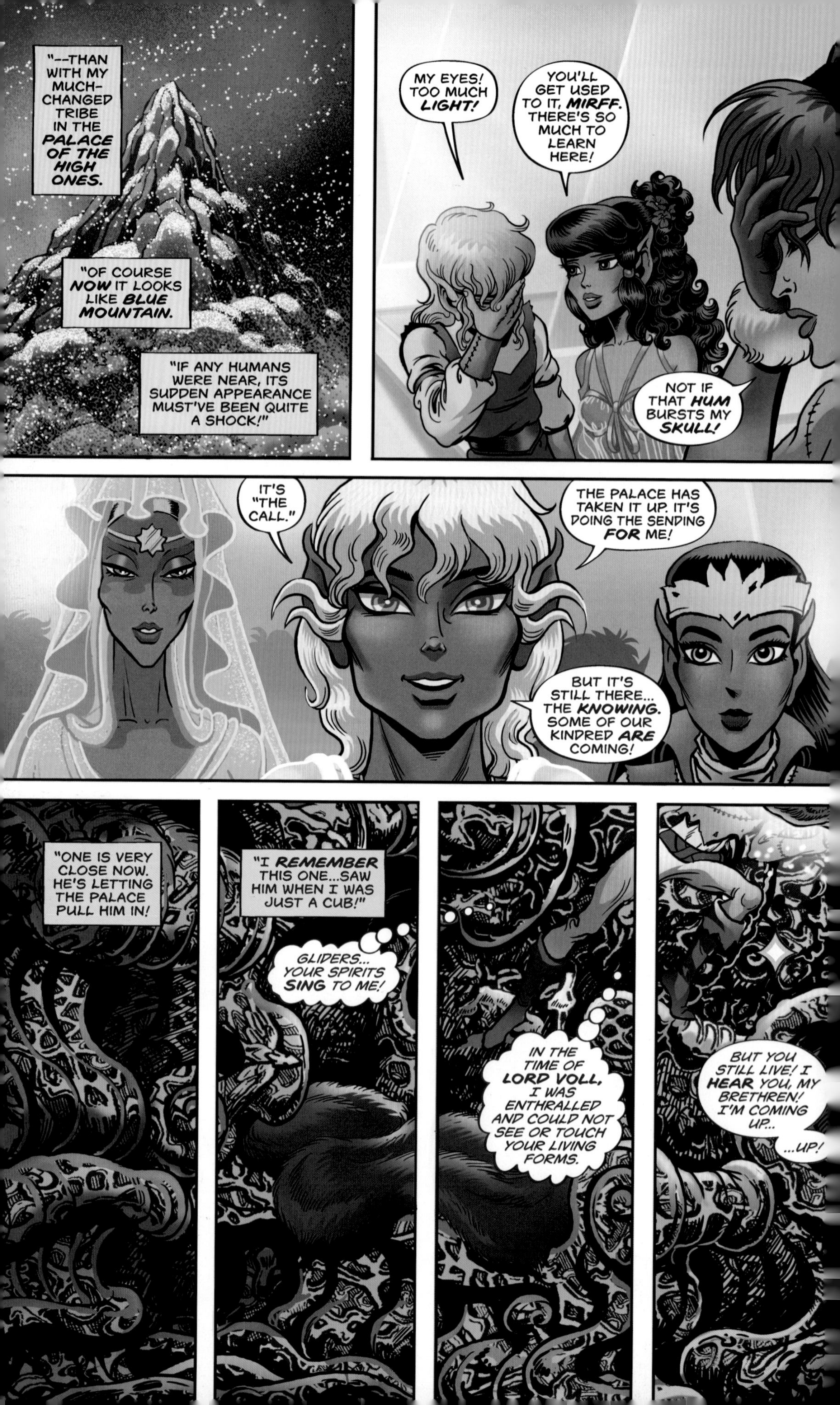
"--THAN WITH MY MUCH-CHANGED TRIBE IN THE PALACE OF THE HIGH ONES.
"OF COURSE NOW IT LOOKS LIKE BLUE MOUNTAIN.
"IF ANY HUMANS WERE NEAR, ITS SUDDEN APPEARANCE MUST'VE BEEN QUITE A SHOCK!"
MY EYES! TOO MUCH LIGHT!
YOU'LL GET USED TO IT, MIRFF. THERE'S SO MUCH TO LEARN HERE!
NOT IF THAT HUM BURSTS MY SKULL!
IT'S "THE CALL."
THE PALACE HAS TAKEN IT UP. IT'S DOING THE SENDING FOR ME!
BUT IT'S STILL THERE... THE KNOWING. SOME OF OUR KINDRED ARE COMING!
"ONE IS VERY CLOSE NOW. HE'S LETTING THE PALACE PULL HIM IN!
"I REMEMBER THIS ONE...SAW HIM WHEN I WAS JUST A CUB!"
GLIDERS... YOUR SPIRITS SING TO ME!
IN THE TIME OF LORD VOLL, I WAS ENTHRALLED AND COULD NOT SEE OR TOUCH YOUR LIVING FORMS.
BUT YOU STILL LIVE! I HEAR YOU, MY BRETHREN! I'M COMING UP...
...UP!

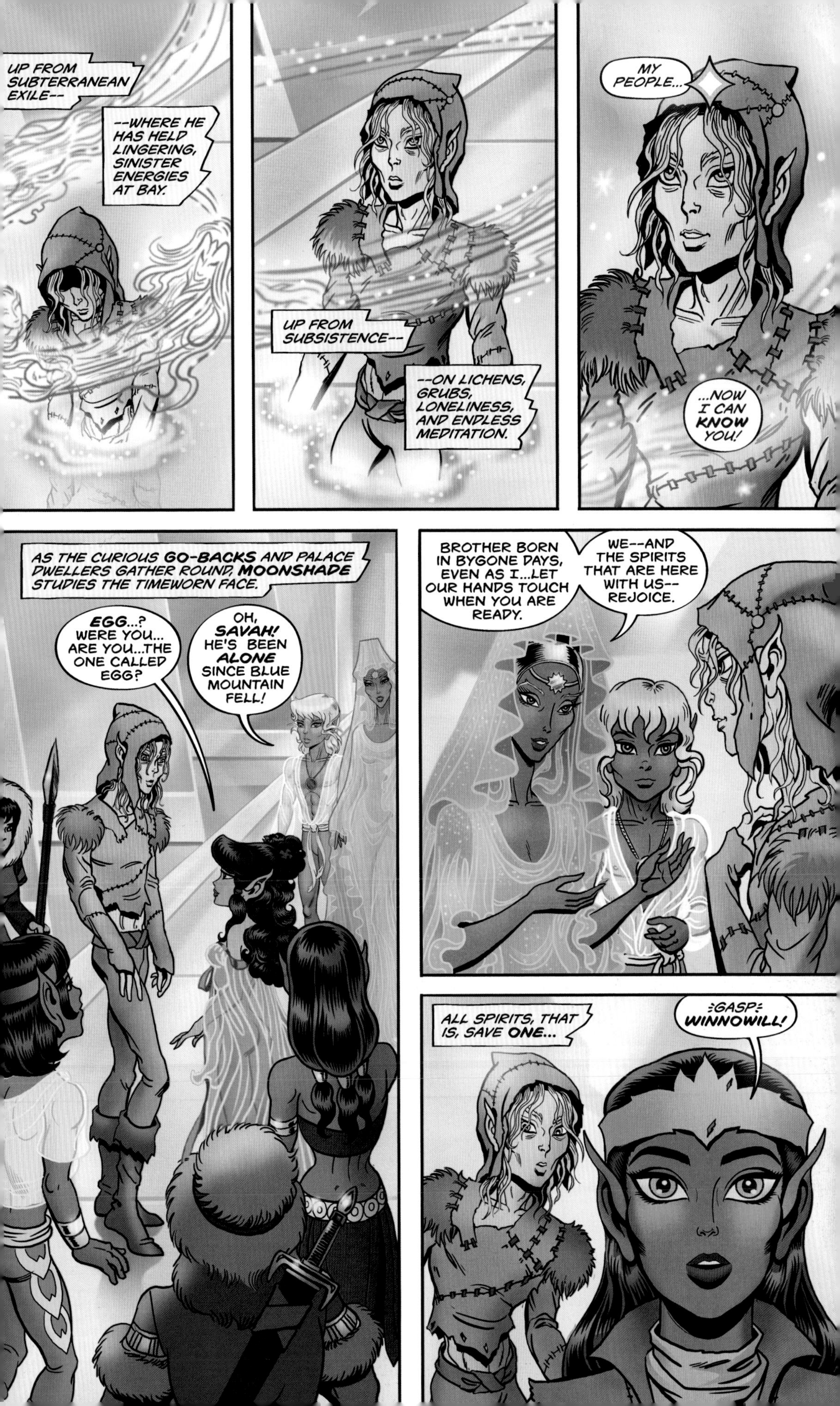
UP FROM SUBTERRANEAN EXILE--
--WHERE HE HAS HELD LINGERING, SINISTER ENERGIES AT BAY.
UP FROM SUBSISTENCE--
--ON LICHENS, GRUBS, LONELINESS, AND ENDLESS MEDITATION.
MY PEOPLE...
...NOW I CAN KNOW YOU!
AS THE CURIOUS GO-BACKS AND PALACE DWELLERS GATHER ROUND, MOONSHADE STUDIES THE TIMEWORN FACE.
EGG...? WERE YOU... ARE YOU...THE ONE CALLED EGG?
OH, SAVAH! HE'S BEEN ALONE SINCE BLUE MOUNTAIN FELL!
BROTHER BORN IN BYGONE DAYS, EVEN AS I...LET OUR HANDS TOUCH WHEN YOU ARE READY.
WE--AND THE SPIRITS THAT ARE HERE WITH US-- REJOICE.
ALL SPIRITS, THAT IS, SAVE ONE...
GASP WINNOWILL!

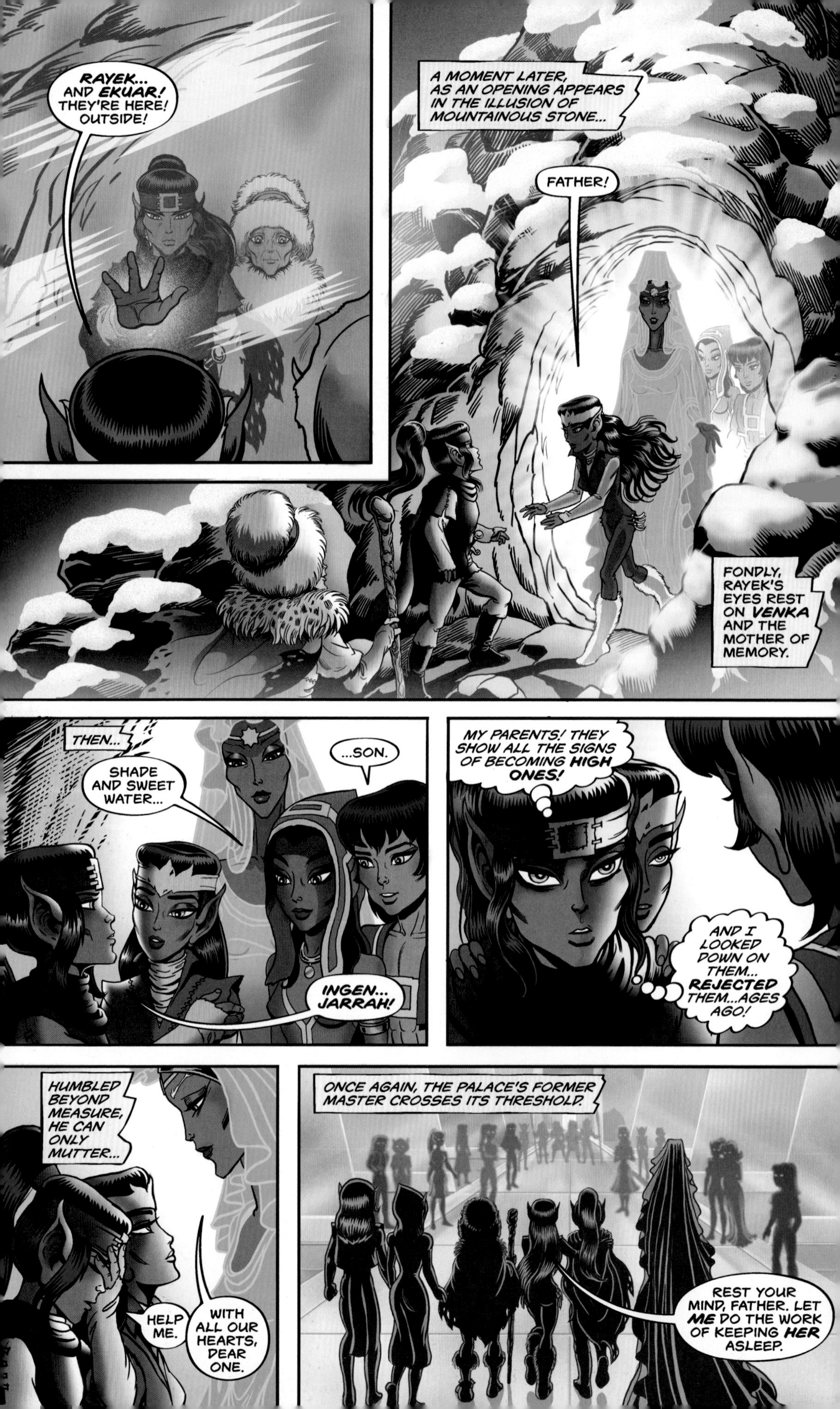

RAYEK... AND EKUAR! THEY'RE HERE! OUTSIDE!
A MOMENT LATER, AS AN OPENING APPEARS IN THE ILLUSION OF MOUNTAINOUS STONE...
FATHER!
FONDLY, RAYEK'S EYES REST ON VENKA AND THE MOTHER OF MEMORY.
THEN...
SHADE AND SWEET WATER...
...SON.
INGEN... JARRAH!
MY PARENTS! THEY SHOW ALL THE SIGNS OF BECOMING HIGH ONES!
AND I LOOKED DOWN ON THEM... REJECTED THEM...AGES AGO!
HUMBLED BEYOND MEASURE, HE CAN ONLY MUTTER...
HELP ME.
WITH ALL OUR HEARTS, DEAR ONE.
ONCE AGAIN, THE PALACE'S FORMER MASTER CROSSES ITS THRESHOLD.
REST YOUR MIND, FATHER. LET ME DO THE WORK OF KEEPING HER ASLEEP.

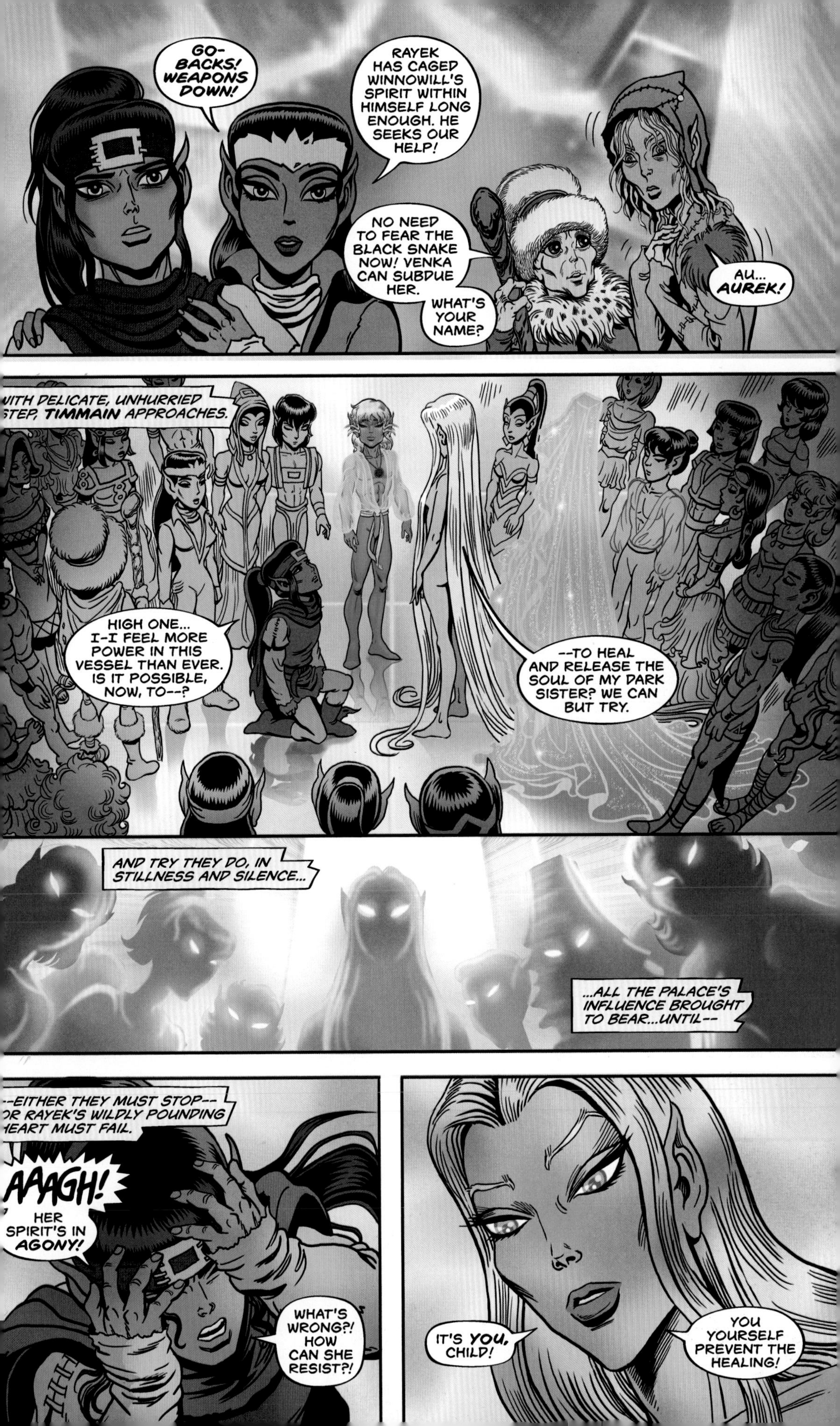
GO-BACKS! WEAPONS DOWN!
RAYEK HAS CAGED WINNOWILL'S SPIRIT WITHIN HIMSELF LONG ENOUGH. HE SEEKS OUR HELP!
NO NEED TO FEAR THE BLACK SNAKE NOW! VENKA CAN SUBDUE HER.
WHAT'S YOUR NAME?
AU... AUREK!
WITH DELICATE, UNHURRIED STEP, TIMMAIN APPROACHES.
HIGH ONE... I-I FEEL MORE POWER IN THIS VESSEL THAN EVER. IS IT POSSIBLE, NOW, TO--?
--TO HEAL AND RELEASE THE SOUL OF MY DARK SISTER? WE CAN BUT TRY.
AND TRY THEY DO, IN STILLNESS AND SILENCE...
...ALL THE PALACE'S INFLUENCE BROUGHT TO BEAR...UNTIL--
--EITHER THEY MUST STOP-- OR RAYEK'S WILDLY POUNDING HEART MUST FAIL.
AAAGH!
HER SPIRIT'S IN AGONY!
WHAT'S WRONG?! HOW CAN SHE RESIST?!
IT'S YOU, CHILD!
YOU YOURSELF PREVENT THE HEALING!

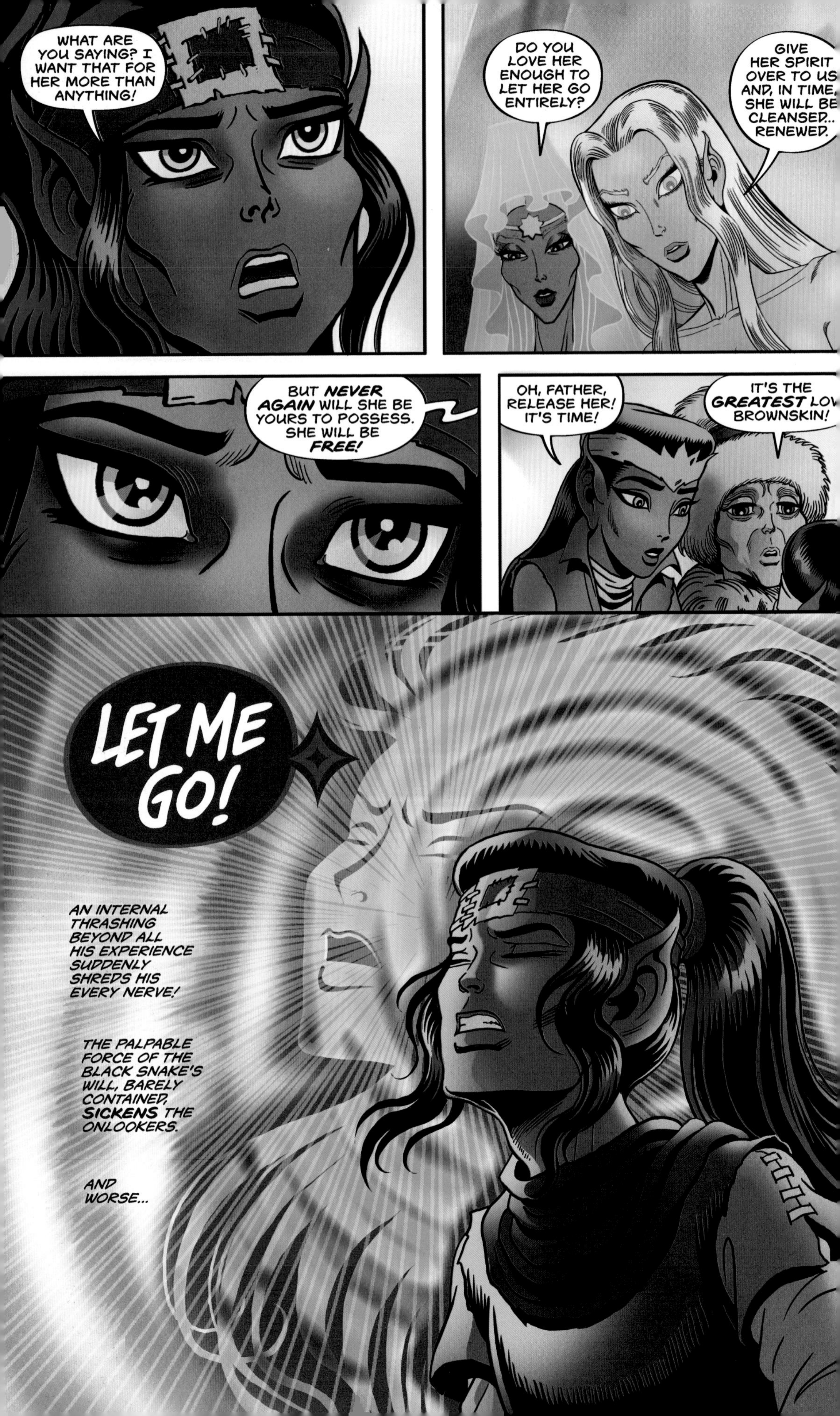
WHAT ARE YOU SAYING? I WANT THAT FOR HER MORE THAN ANYTHING!
DO YOU LOVE HER ENOUGH TO LET HER GO ENTIRELY?
GIVE HER SPIRIT OVER TO US AND, IN TIME, SHE WILL BE CLEANSED... RENEWED.
BUT NEVER AGAIN WILL SHE BE YOURS TO POSSESS. SHE WILL BE FREE!
OH, FATHER, RELEASE HER! IT'S TIME!
IT'S THE GREATEST LOV BROWNSKIN!
LET ME GO!
AN INTERNAL THRASHING BEYOND ALL HIS EXPERIENCE SUDDENLY SHREDS HIS EVERY NERVE!
THE PALPABLE FORCE OF THE BLACK SNAKE'S WILL, BARELY CONTAINED, SICKENS THE ONLOOKERS.
AND WORSE...

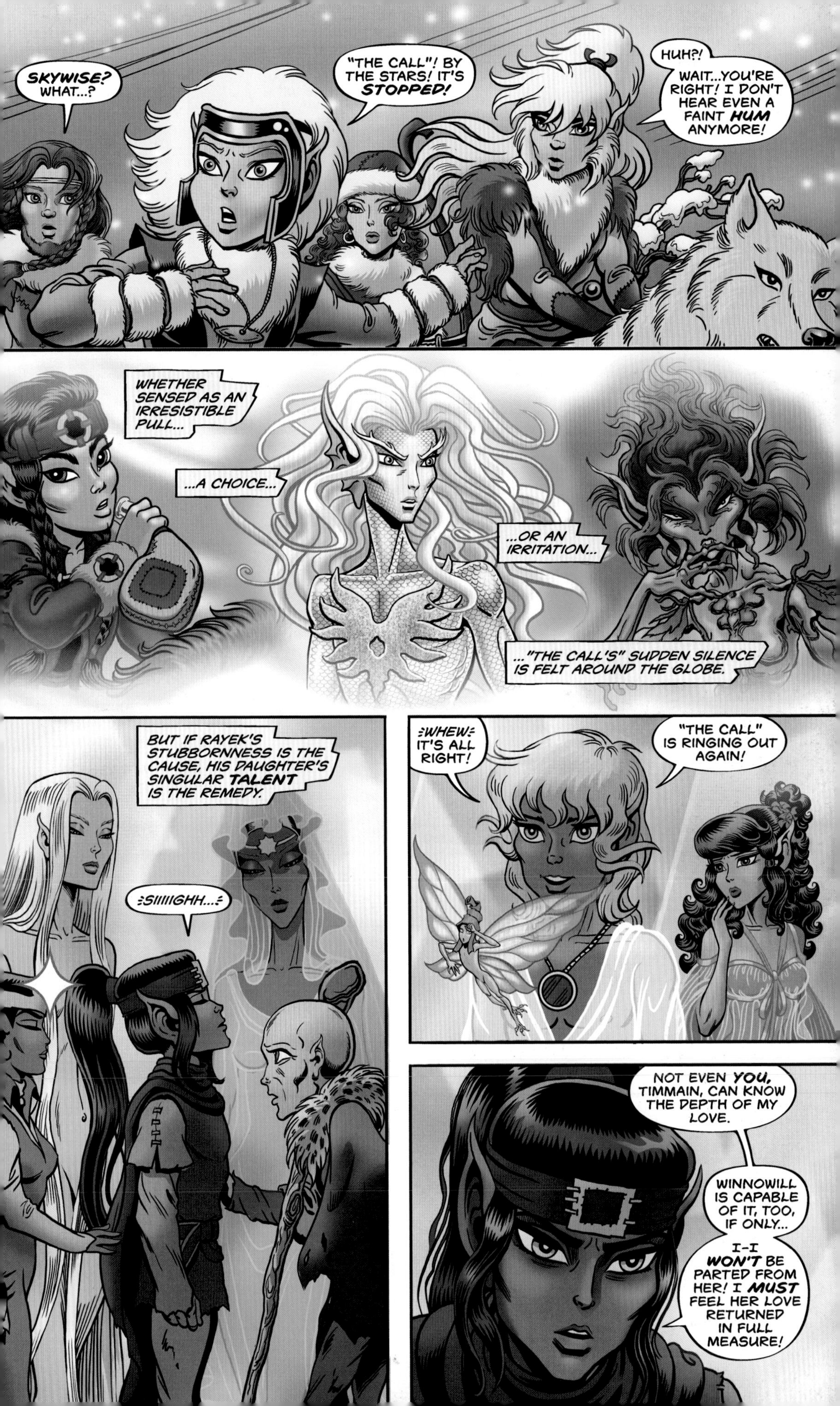
SKYWISE? WHAT...?
"THE CALL"! BY THE STARS! IT'S STOPPED!
HUH?!
WAIT...YOU'RE RIGHT! I DON'T HEAR EVEN A FAINT HUM ANYMORE!
WHETHER SENSED AS AN IRRESISTIBLE PULL...
...A CHOICE...
...OR AN IRRITATION...
..."THE CALL'S" SUDDEN SILENCE IS FELT AROUND THE GLOBE.
BUT IF RAYEK'S STUBBORNNESS IS THE CAUSE, HIS DAUGHTER'S SINGULAR TALENT IS THE REMEDY.
SIIIIGHH...
WHEW! IT'S ALL RIGHT!
"THE CALL" IS RINGING OUT AGAIN!
NOT EVEN YOU, TIMMAIN, CAN KNOW THE DEPTH OF MY LOVE.
WINNOWILL IS CAPABLE OF IT, TOO, IF ONLY...
I-I WON'T BE PARTED FROM HER! I MUST FEEL HER LOVE RETURNED IN FULL MEASURE!

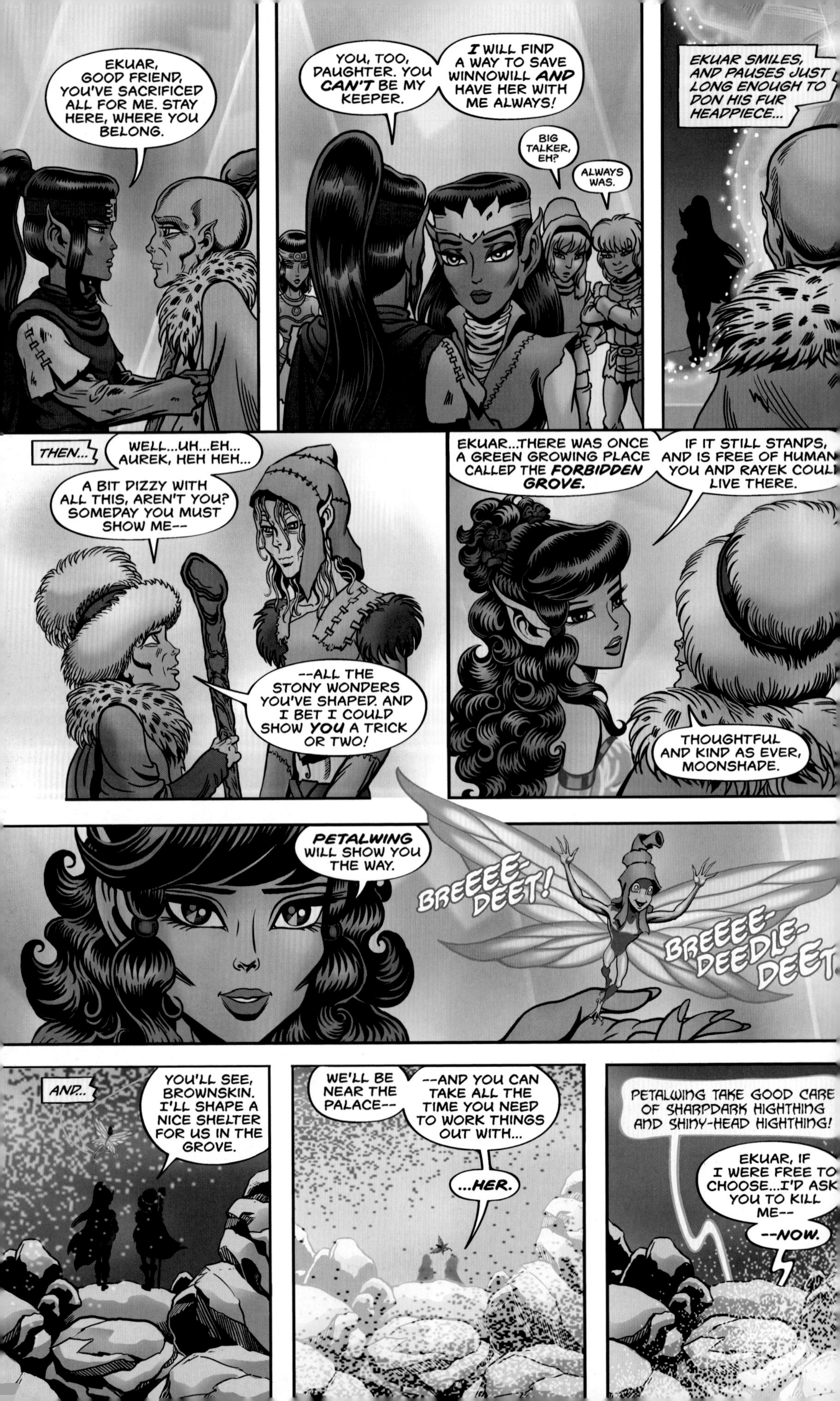

EKUAR, GOOD FRIEND, YOU'VE SACRIFICED ALL FOR ME. STAY HERE, WHERE YOU BELONG.
YOU, TOO, DAUGHTER. YOU CAN'T BE MY KEEPER.
I WILL FIND A WAY TO SAVE WINNOWILL AND HAVE HER WITH ME ALWAYS!
BIG TALKER, EH?
ALWAYS WAS.
EKUAR SMILES, AND PAUSES JUST LONG ENOUGH TO DON HIS FUR HEADPIECE...
THEN...
WELL...UH...EH... AUREK, HEH HEH...
A BIT DIZZY WITH ALL THIS, AREN'T YOU? SOMEDAY YOU MUST SHOW ME--
--ALL THE STONY WONDERS YOU'VE SHAPED. AND I BET I COULD SHOW YOU A TRICK OR TWO!
EKUAR...THERE WAS ONCE A GREEN GROWING PLACE CALLED THE FORBIDDEN GROVE.
IF IT STILL STANDS, AND IS FREE OF HUMAN YOU AND RAYEK COUL LIVE THERE.
THOUGHTFUL AND KIND AS EVER, MOONSHADE.
PETALWING WILL SHOW YOU THE WAY.
BREEEE-DEET!
BREEEE-DEEDLE-DEET
AND...
YOU'LL SEE, BROWNSKIN. I'LL SHAPE A NICE SHELTER FOR US IN THE GROVE.
WE'LL BE NEAR THE PALACE--
--AND YOU CAN TAKE ALL THE TIME YOU NEED TO WORK THINGS OUT WITH...
...HER.
PETALWING TAKE GOOD CARE OF SHARPDARK HIGHTHING AND SHINY-HEAD HIGHTHING!
EKUAR, IF I WERE FREE TO CHOOSE...I'D ASK YOU TO KILL ME--
--NOW.

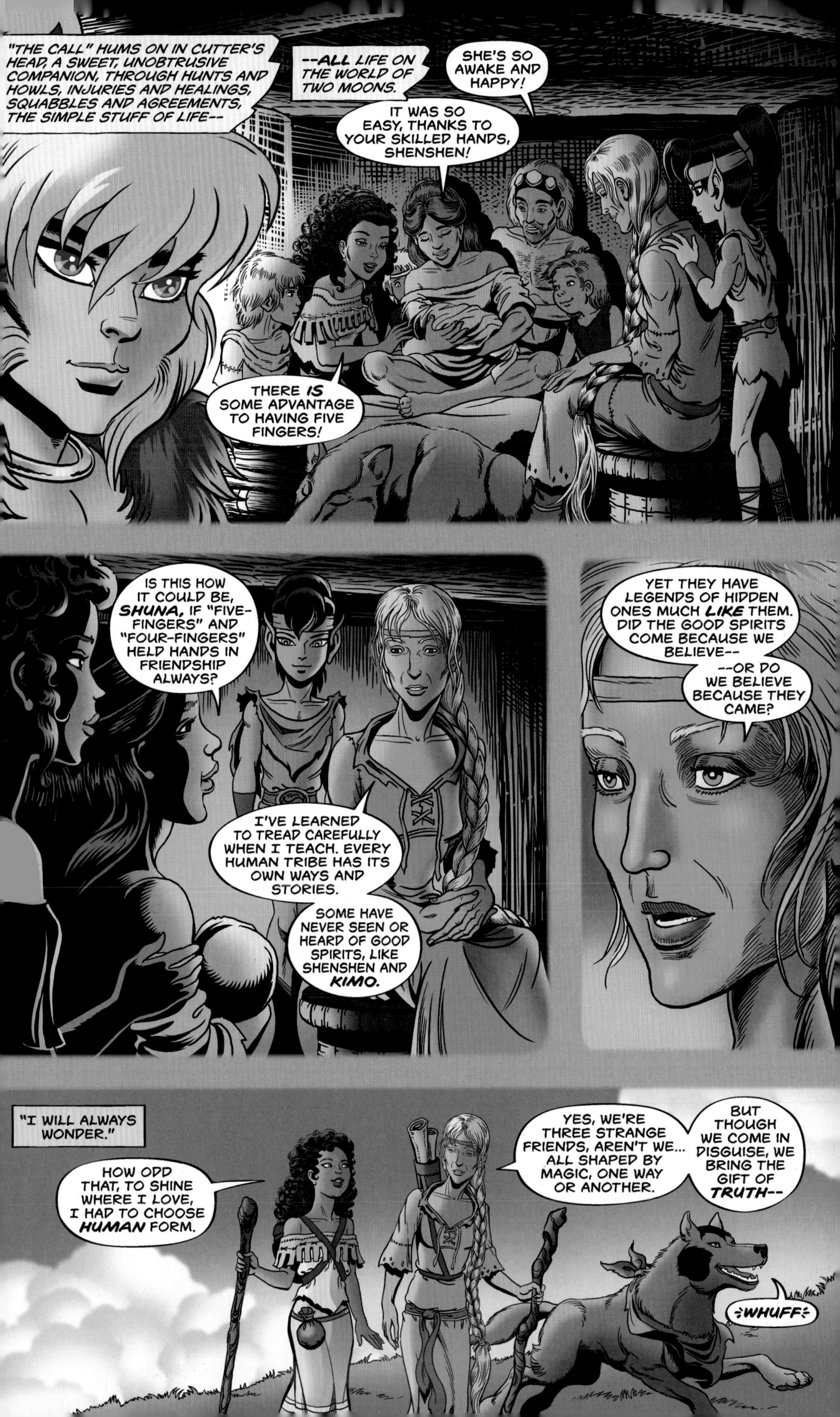
"THE CALL" HUMS ON IN CUTTER'S HEAD, A SWEET, UNOBTRUSIVE COMPANION, THROUGH HUNTS AND HOWLS, INJURIES AND HEALINGS, SQUABBLES AND AGREEMENTS, THE SIMPLE STUFF OF LIFE--
--ALL LIFE ON THE WORLD OF TWO MOONS.
SHE'S SO AWAKE AND HAPPY!
IT WAS SO EASY, THANKS TO YOUR SKILLED HANDS, SHENSHEN!
THERE IS SOME ADVANTAGE TO HAVING FIVE FINGERS!
IS THIS HOW IT COULD BE, SHUNA, IF "FIVE-FINGERS" AND "FOUR-FINGERS" HELD HANDS IN FRIENDSHIP ALWAYS?
I'VE LEARNED TO TREAD CAREFULLY WHEN I TEACH. EVERY HUMAN TRIBE HAS ITS OWN WAYS AND STORIES.
SOME HAVE NEVER SEEN OR HEARD OF GOOD SPIRITS, LIKE SHENSHEN AND KIMO.
YET THEY HAVE LEGENDS OF HIDDEN ONES MUCH LIKE THEM. DID THE GOOD SPIRITS COME BECAUSE WE BELIEVE--
--OR DO WE BELIEVE BECAUSE THEY CAME?
"I WILL ALWAYS WONDER."
HOW ODD THAT, TO SHINE WHERE I LOVE, I HAD TO CHOOSE HUMAN FORM.
YES, WE'RE THREE STRANGE FRIENDS, AREN'T WE... ALL SHAPED BY MAGIC, ONE WAY OR ANOTHER.
BUT THOUGH WE COME IN DISGUISE, WE BRING THE GIFT OF TRUTH--
WHUFF

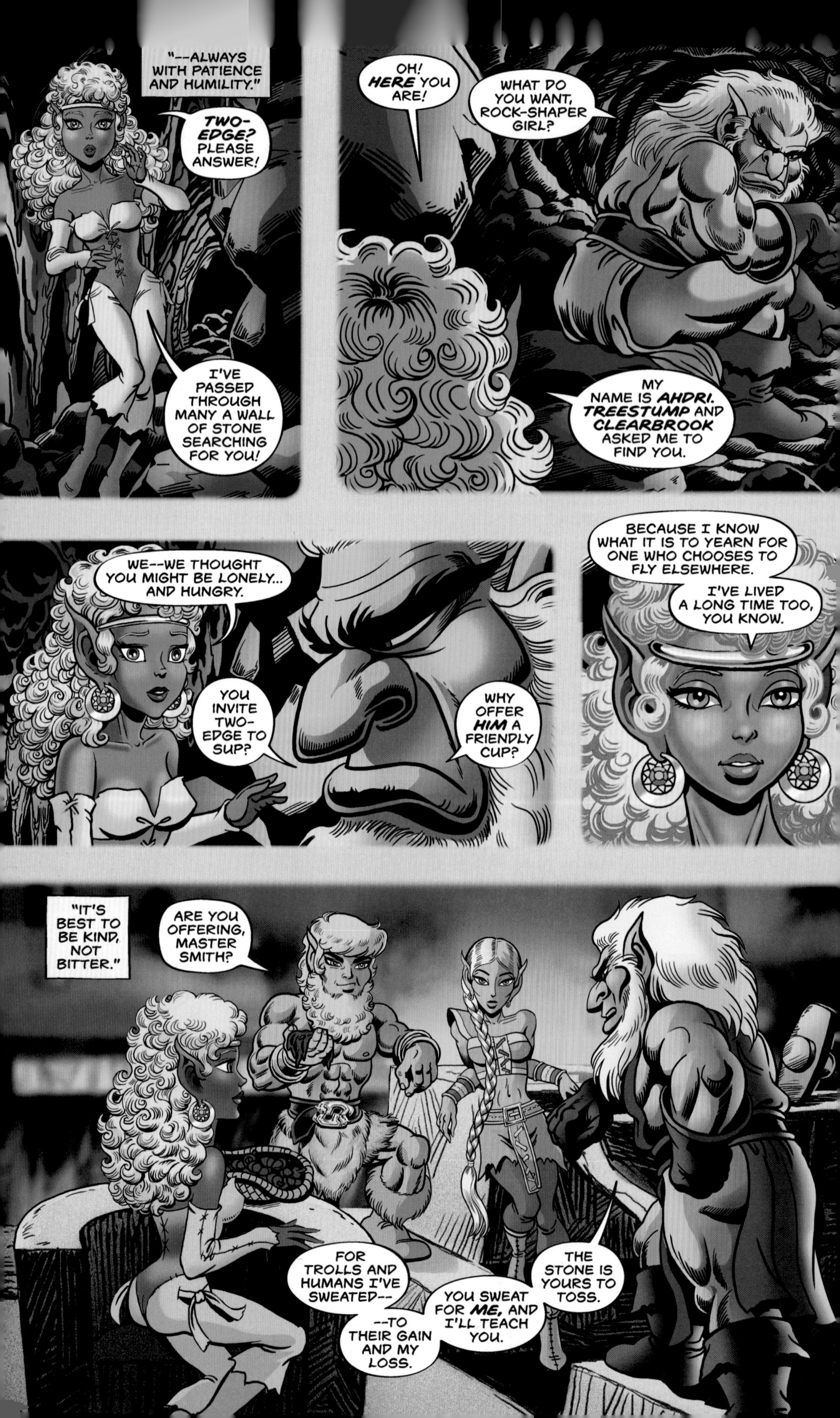
"--ALWAYS WITH PATIENCE AND HUMILITY."
TWO-EDGE? PLEASE ANSWER!
I'VE PASSED THROUGH MANY A WALL OF STONE SEARCHING FOR YOU!
OH! HERE YOU ARE!
WHAT DO YOU WANT, ROCK-SHAPER GIRL?
MY NAME IS AHDRI. TREESTUMP AND CLEARBROOK ASKED ME TO FIND YOU.
WE--WE THOUGHT YOU MIGHT BE LONELY... AND HUNGRY.
YOU INVITE TWO-EDGE TO SUP?
WHY OFFER HIM A FRIENDLY CUP?
BECAUSE I KNOW WHAT IT IS TO YEARN FOR ONE WHO CHOOSES TO FLY ELSEWHERE.
I'VE LIVED A LONG TIME TOO, YOU KNOW.
"IT'S BEST TO BE KIND, NOT BITTER."
ARE YOU OFFERING, MASTER SMITH?
FOR TROLLS AND HUMANS I'VE SWEATED--
--TO THEIR GAIN AND MY LOSS.
YOU SWEAT FOR ME, AND I'LL TEACH YOU.
THE STONE IS YOURS TO TOSS.

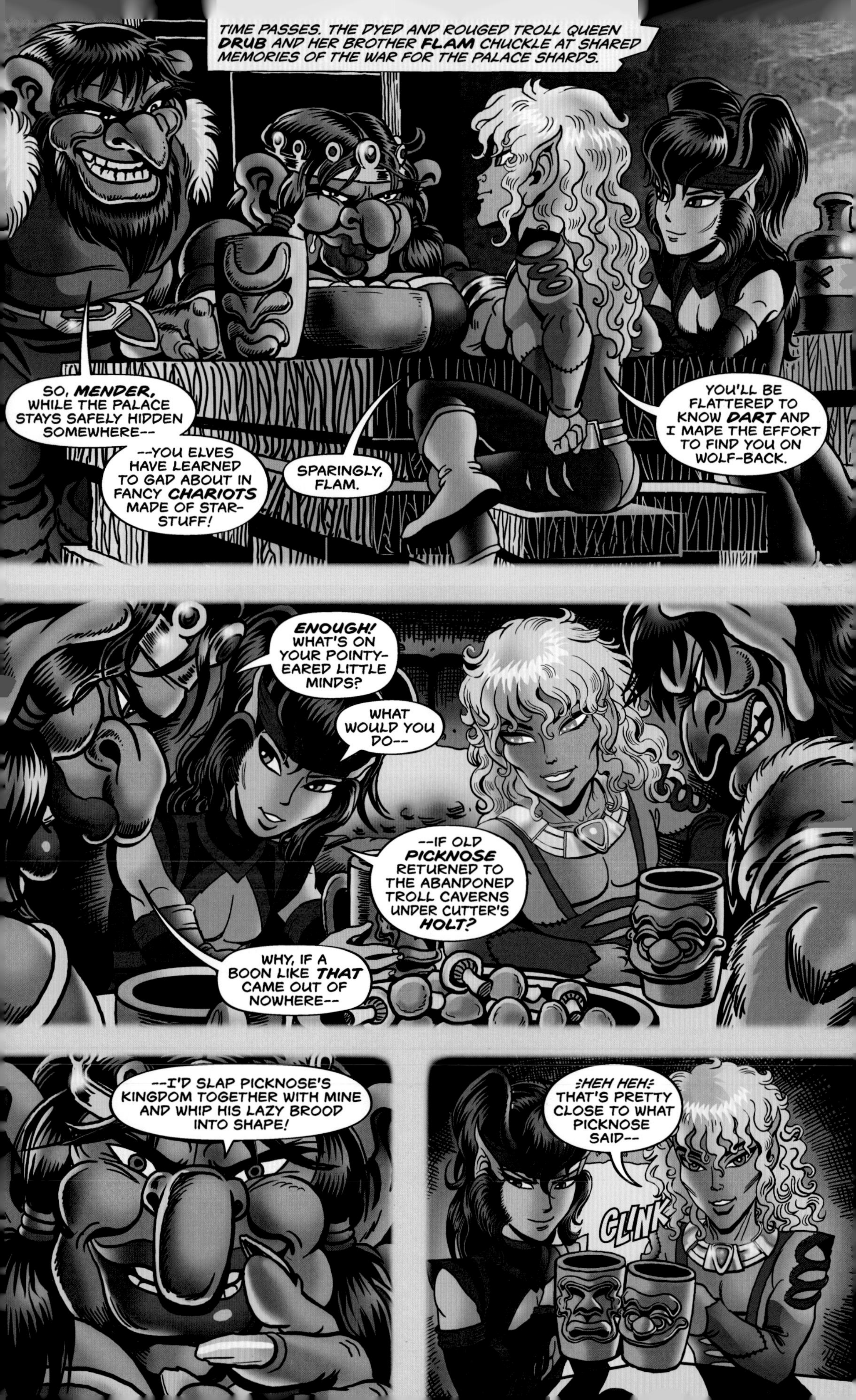
TIME PASSES. THE DYED AND ROUGED TROLL QUEEN DRUB AND HER BROTHER FLAM CHUCKLE AT SHARED MEMORIES OF THE WAR FOR THE PALACE SHARDS.
SO, MENDER, WHILE THE PALACE STAYS SAFELY HIDDEN SOMEWHERE--
--YOU ELVES HAVE LEARNED TO GAD ABOUT IN FANCY CHARIOTS MADE OF STAR-STUFF!
SPARINGLY, FLAM.
YOU'LL BE FLATTERED TO KNOW DART AND I MADE THE EFFORT TO FIND YOU ON WOLF-BACK.
ENOUGH! WHAT'S ON YOUR POINTY-EARED LITTLE MINDS?
WHAT WOULD YOU DO--
--IF OLD PICKNOSE RETURNED TO THE ABANDONED TROLL CAVERNS UNDER CUTTER'S HOLT?
WHY, IF A BOON LIKE THAT CAME OUT OF NOWHERE--
--I'D SLAP PICKNOSE'S KINGDOM TOGETHER WITH MINE AND WHIP HIS LAZY BROOD INTO SHAPE!
:HEH HEH: THAT'S PRETTY CLOSE TO WHAT PICKNOSE SAID--
CLINK

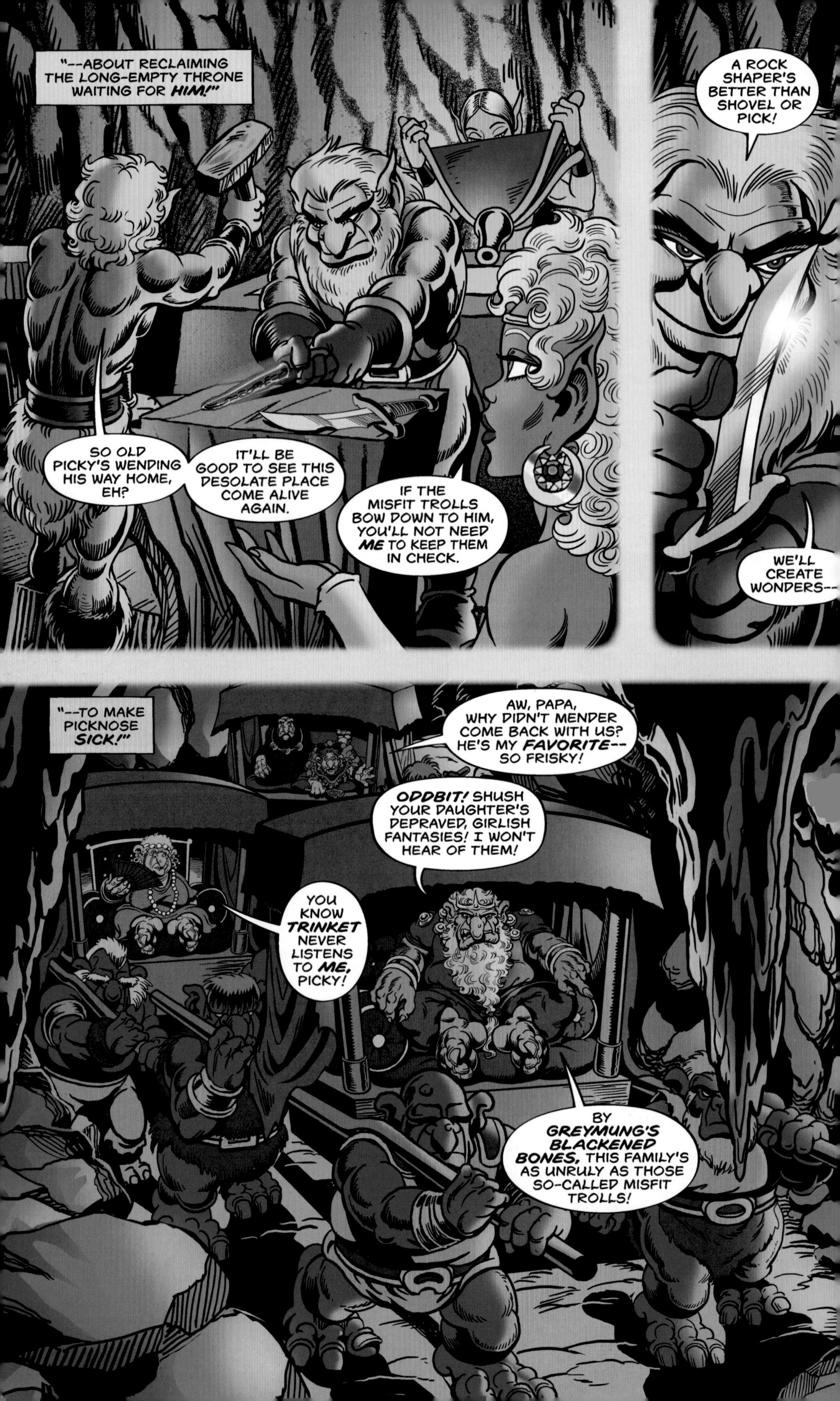

"--ABOUT RECLAIMING THE LONG-EMPTY THRONE WAITING FOR HIM!"
SO OLD PICKY'S WENDING HIS WAY HOME, EH?
IT'LL BE GOOD TO SEE THIS DESOLATE PLACE COME ALIVE AGAIN.
IF THE MISFIT TROLLS BOW DOWN TO HIM, YOU'LL NOT NEED ME TO KEEP THEM IN CHECK.
A ROCK SHAPER'S BETTER THAN SHOVEL OR PICK!
WE'LL CREATE WONDERS--
"--TO MAKE PICKNOSE SICK!"
AW, PAPA, WHY DIDN'T MENDER COME BACK WITH US? HE'S MY FAVORITE-- SO FRISKY!
ODDBIT! SHUSH YOUR DAUGHTER'S DEPRAVED, GIRLISH FANTASIES! I WON'T HEAR OF THEM!
YOU KNOW TRINKET NEVER LISTENS TO ME, PICKY!
BY GREYMUNG'S BLACKENED BONES, THIS FAMILY'S AS UNRULY AS THOSE SO-CALLED MISFIT TROLLS!

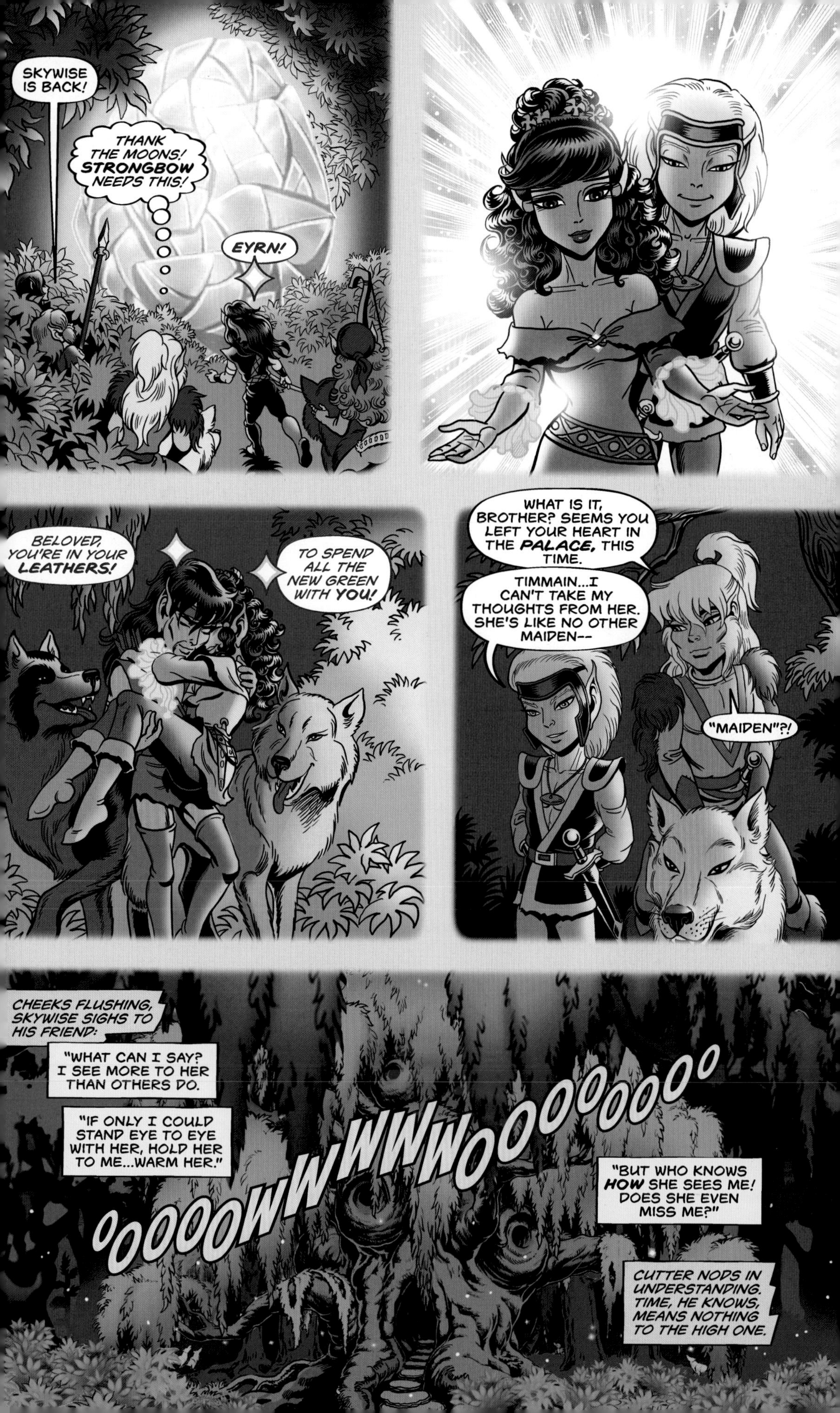

SKYWISE IS BACK!
THANK THE MOONS! **STRONGBOW** NEEDS THIS!
EYRN!
BELOVED, YOU'RE IN YOUR **LEATHERS!**
TO SPEND ALL THE NEW GREEN WITH **YOU!**
WHAT IS IT, BROTHER? SEEMS YOU LEFT YOUR HEART IN THE **PALACE,** THIS TIME.
TIMMAIN...I CAN'T TAKE MY THOUGHTS FROM HER. SHE'S LIKE NO OTHER MAIDEN--
"MAIDEN"?!
CHEEKS FLUSHING, SKYWISE SIGHS TO HIS FRIEND:
"WHAT CAN I SAY? I SEE MORE TO HER THAN OTHERS DO.
"IF ONLY I COULD STAND EYE TO EYE WITH HER, HOLD HER TO ME...WARM HER."
OOOOOWWWWWOOOOOOOOO
"BUT WHO KNOWS **HOW** SHE SEES ME! DOES SHE EVEN MISS ME?"
CUTTER NODS IN UNDERSTANDING. TIME, HE KNOWS, MEANS NOTHING TO THE HIGH ONE.

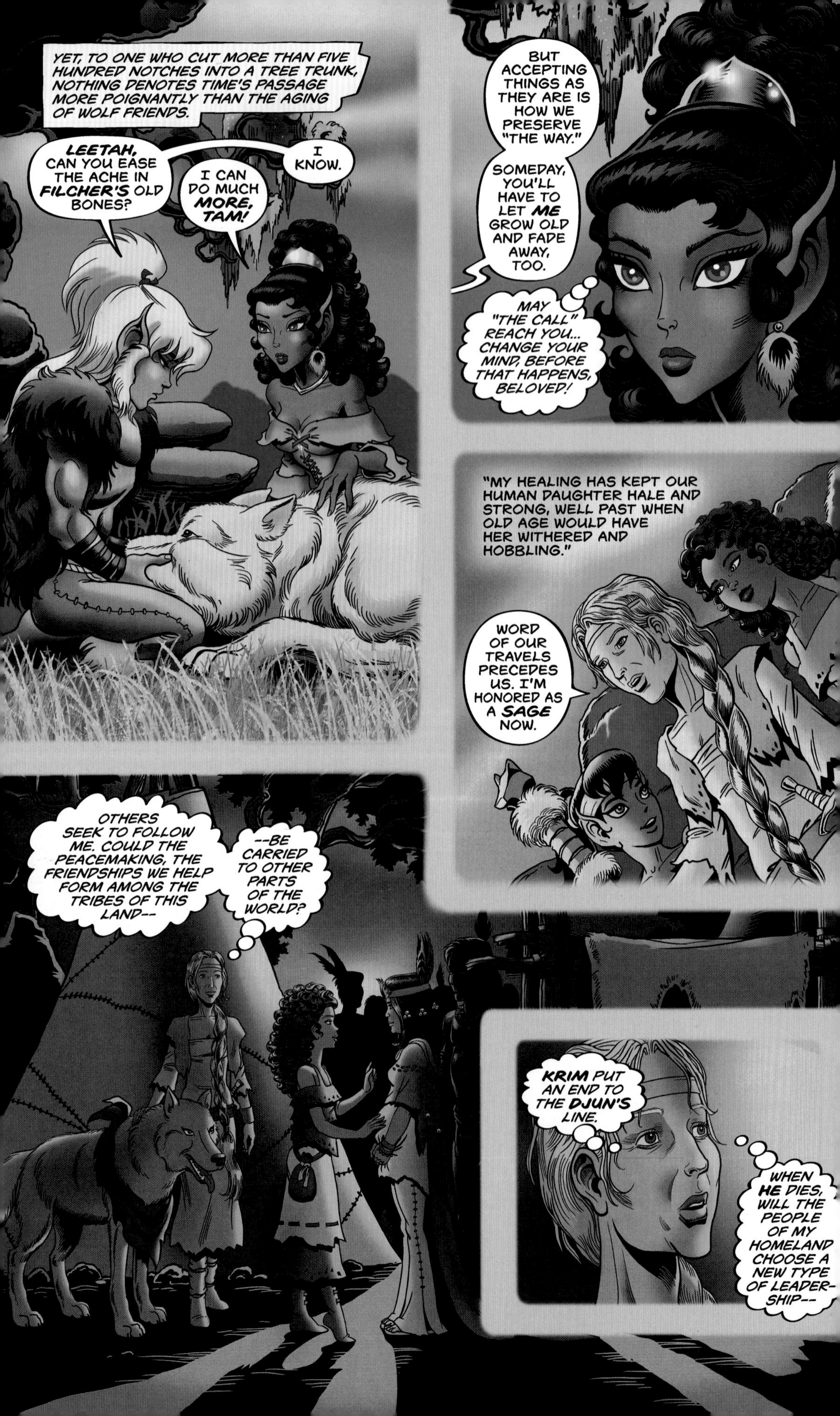
YET, TO ONE WHO CUT MORE THAN FIVE HUNDRED NOTCHES INTO A TREE TRUNK, NOTHING DENOTES TIME'S PASSAGE MORE POIGNANTLY THAN THE AGING OF WOLF FRIENDS.
LEETAH, CAN YOU EASE THE ACHE IN FILCHER'S OLD BONES?
I CAN DO MUCH MORE, TAM!
I KNOW.
BUT ACCEPTING THINGS AS THEY ARE IS HOW WE PRESERVE "THE WAY."
SOMEDAY, YOU'LL HAVE TO LET ME GROW OLD AND FADE AWAY, TOO.
MAY "THE CALL" REACH YOU... CHANGE YOUR MIND, BEFORE THAT HAPPENS, BELOVED!
"MY HEALING HAS KEPT OUR HUMAN DAUGHTER HALE AND STRONG, WELL PAST WHEN OLD AGE WOULD HAVE HER WITHERED AND HOBBLING."
WORD OF OUR TRAVELS PRECEDES US. I'M HONORED AS A SAGE NOW.
OTHERS SEEK TO FOLLOW ME. COULD THE PEACEMAKING, THE FRIENDSHIPS WE HELP FORM AMONG THE TRIBES OF THIS LAND--
--BE CARRIED TO OTHER PARTS OF THE WORLD?
KRIM PUT AN END TO THE DJUN'S LINE.
WHEN HE DIES, WILL THE PEOPLE OF MY HOMELAND CHOOSE A NEW TYPE OF LEADER-SHIP--

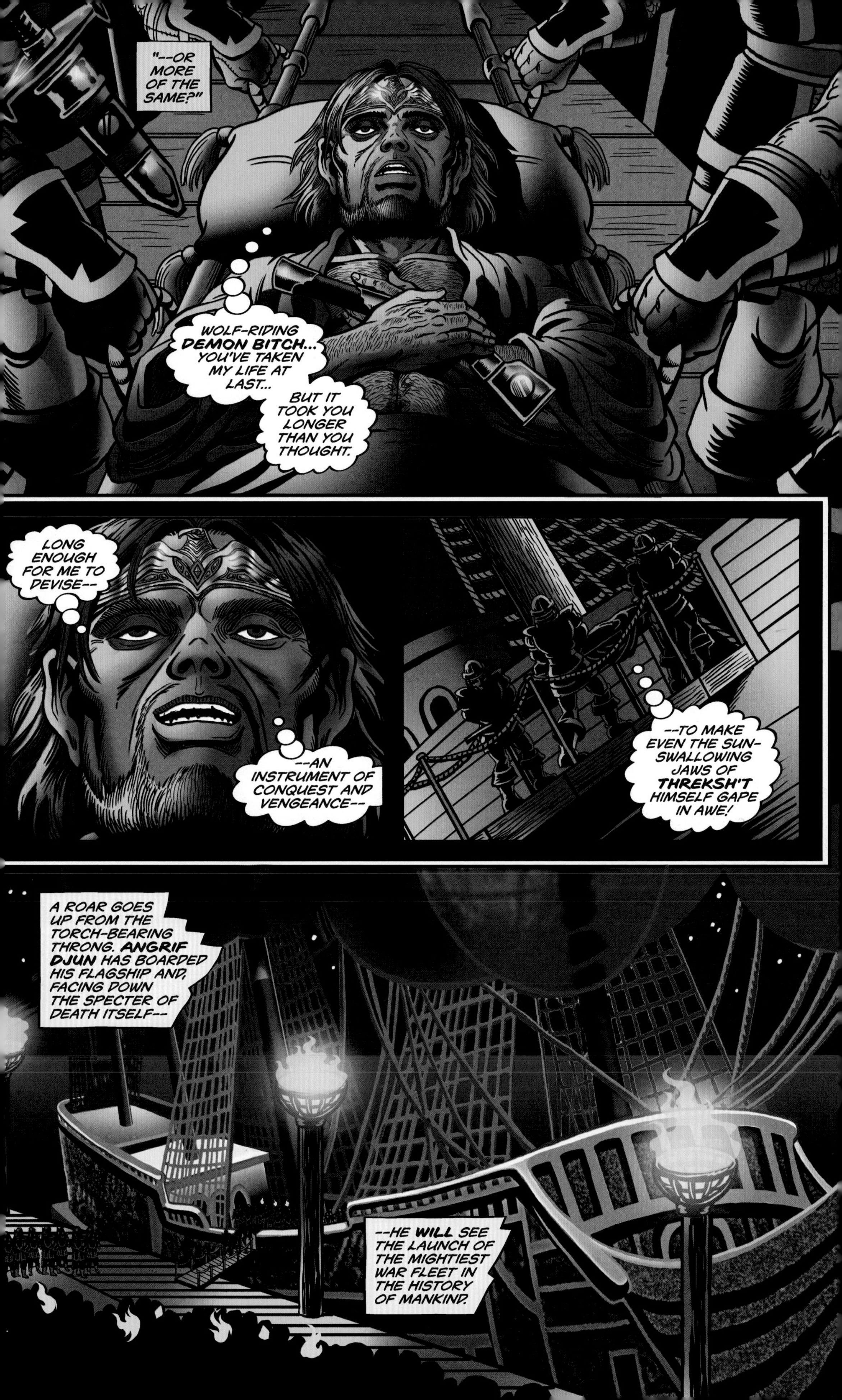
"--OR MORE OF THE SAME?"
WOLF-RIDING DEMON BITCH... YOU'VE TAKEN MY LIFE AT LAST...
BUT IT TOOK YOU LONGER THAN YOU THOUGHT.
LONG ENOUGH FOR ME TO DEVISE--
--AN INSTRUMENT OF CONQUEST AND VENGEANCE--
--TO MAKE EVEN THE SUN-SWALLOWING JAWS OF THREKSH'T HIMSELF GAPE IN AWE!
A ROAR GOES UP FROM THE TORCH-BEARING THRONG. ANGRIF DJUN HAS BOARDED HIS FLAGSHIP AND, FACING DOWN THE SPECTER OF DEATH ITSELF--
--HE WILL SEE THE LAUNCH OF THE MIGHTIEST WAR FLEET IN THE HISTORY OF MANKIND.

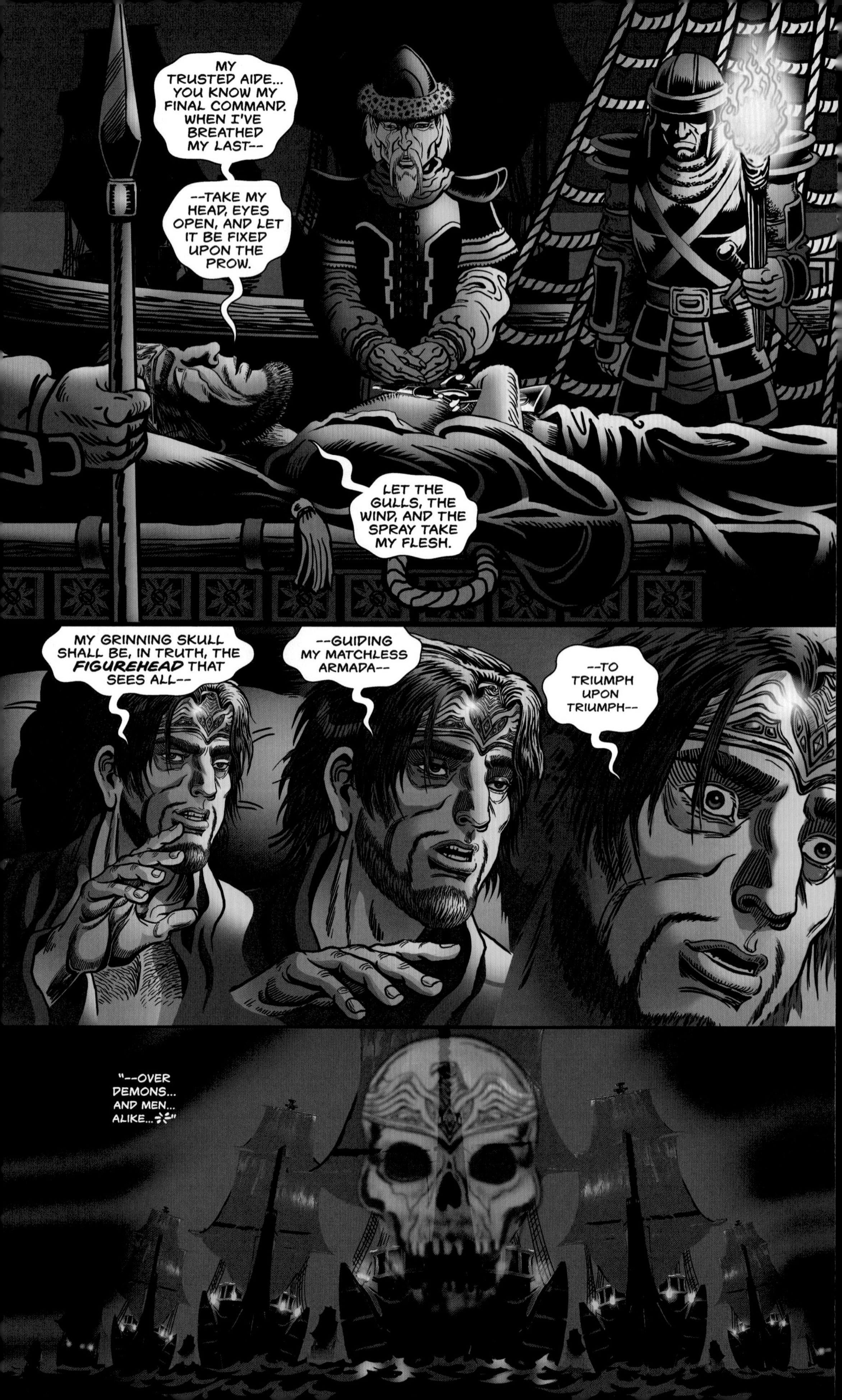
MY TRUSTED AIDE... YOU KNOW MY FINAL COMMAND. WHEN I'VE BREATHED MY LAST--
--TAKE MY HEAD, EYES OPEN, AND LET IT BE FIXED UPON THE PROW.
LET THE GULLS, THE WIND, AND THE SPRAY TAKE MY FLESH.
MY GRINNING SKULL SHALL BE, IN TRUTH, THE FIGUREHEAD THAT SEES ALL--
--GUIDING MY MATCHLESS ARMADA--
--TO TRIUMPH UPON TRIUMPH--
"--OVER DEMONS... AND MEN... ALIKE..."

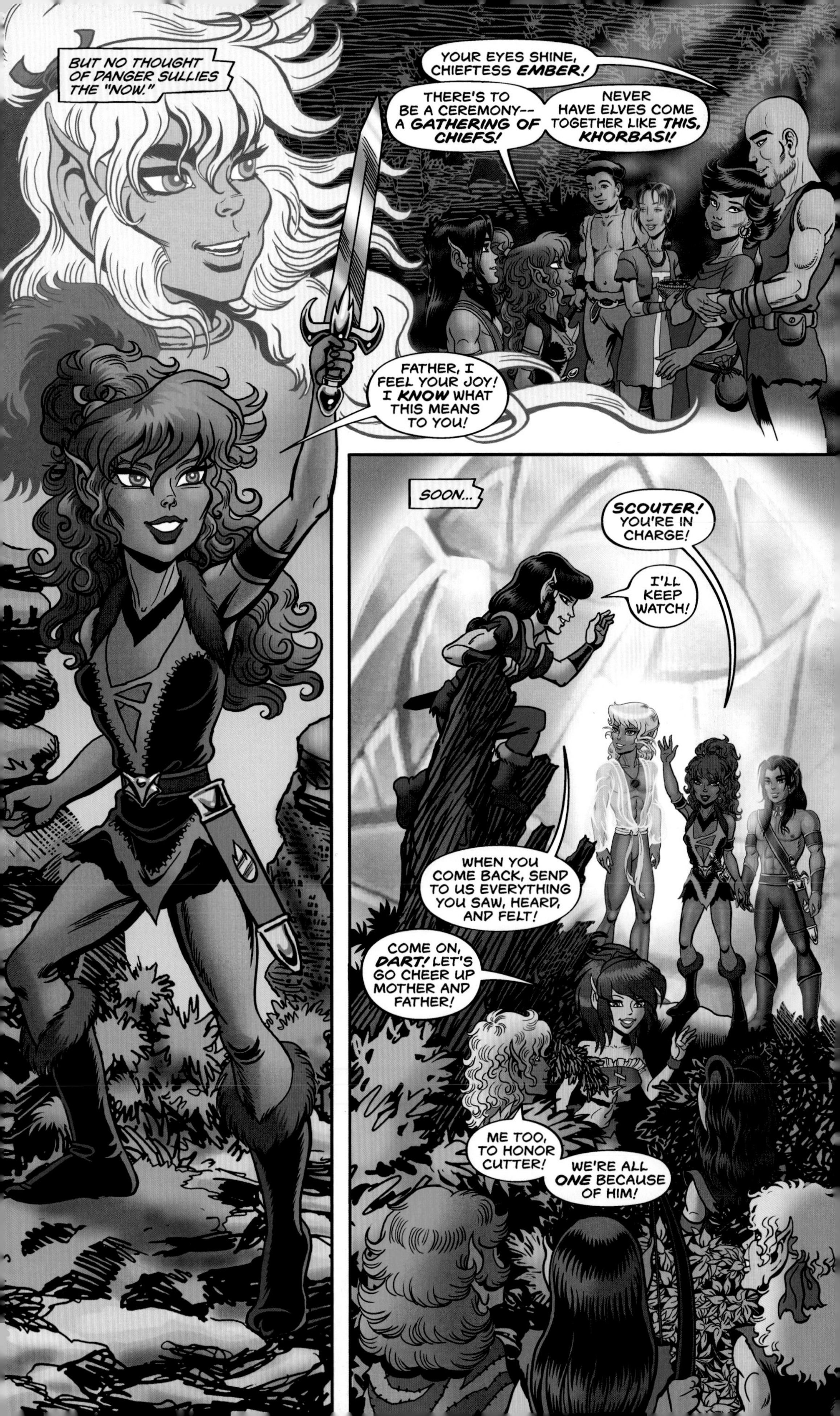
BUT NO THOUGHT OF DANGER SULLIES THE "NOW."
YOUR EYES SHINE, CHIEFTESS EMBER!
THERE'S TO BE A CEREMONY-- A GATHERING OF CHIEFS!
NEVER HAVE ELVES COME TOGETHER LIKE THIS, KHORBAS!!
FATHER, I FEEL YOUR JOY! I KNOW WHAT THIS MEANS TO YOU!
SOON...
SCOUTER! YOU'RE IN CHARGE!
I'LL KEEP WATCH!
WHEN YOU COME BACK, SEND TO US EVERYTHING YOU SAW, HEARD, AND FELT!
COME ON, DART! LET'S GO CHEER UP MOTHER AND FATHER!
ME TOO, TO HONOR CUTTER!
WE'RE ALL ONE BECAUSE OF HIM!

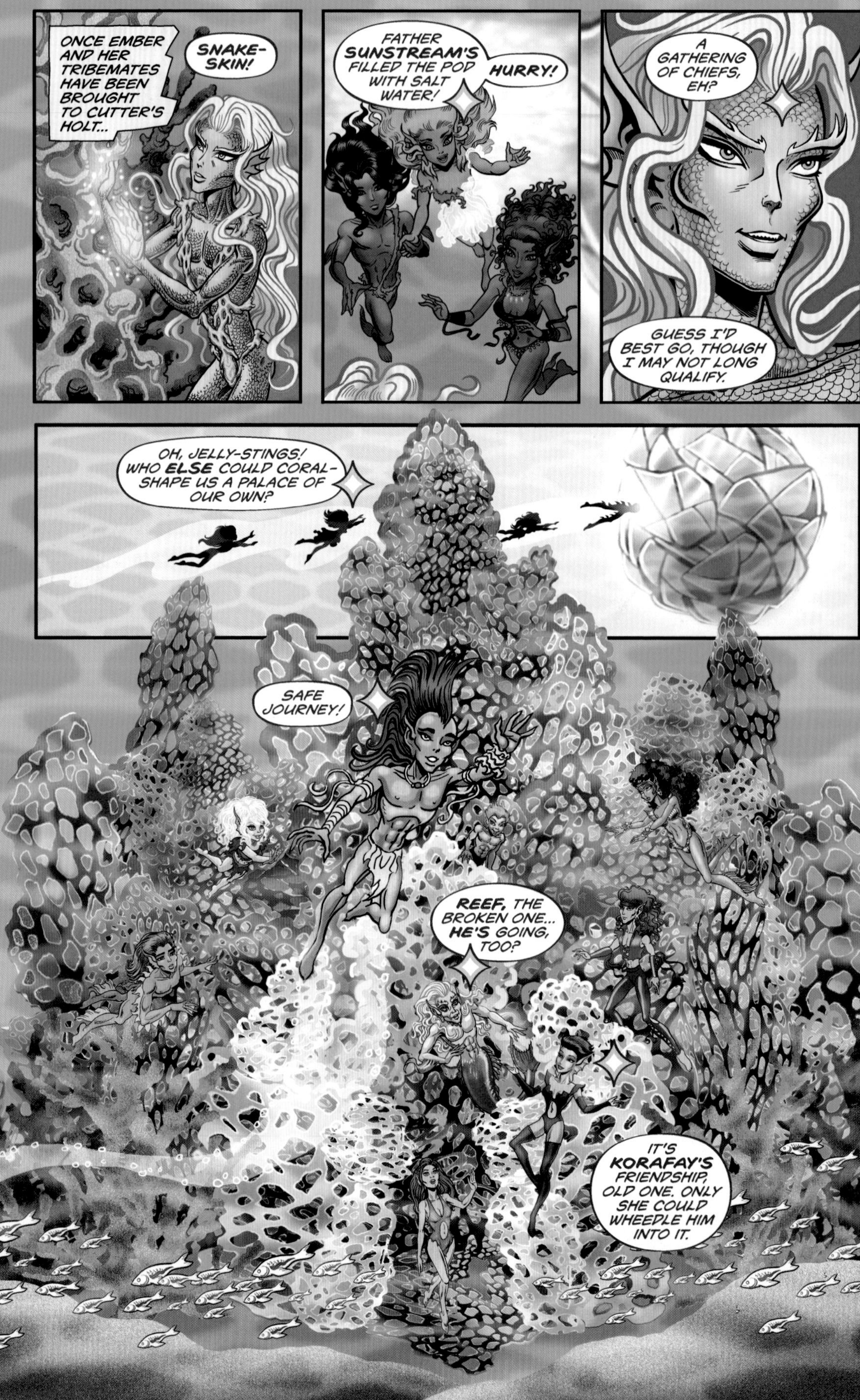

ONCE EMBER AND HER TRIBEMATES HAVE BEEN BROUGHT TO CUTTER'S HOLT...
SNAKE-SKIN!
FATHER SUNSTREAM'S FILLED THE POD WITH SALT WATER!
HURRY!
A GATHERING OF CHIEFS, EH?
GUESS I'D BEST GO, THOUGH I MAY NOT LONG QUALIFY.
OH, JELLY-STINGS! WHO ELSE COULD CORAL-SHAPE US A PALACE OF OUR OWN?
SAFE JOURNEY!
REEF, THE BROKEN ONE... HE'S GOING, TOO?
IT'S KORAFAY'S FRIENDSHIP, OLD ONE. ONLY SHE COULD WHEEDLE HIM INTO IT.

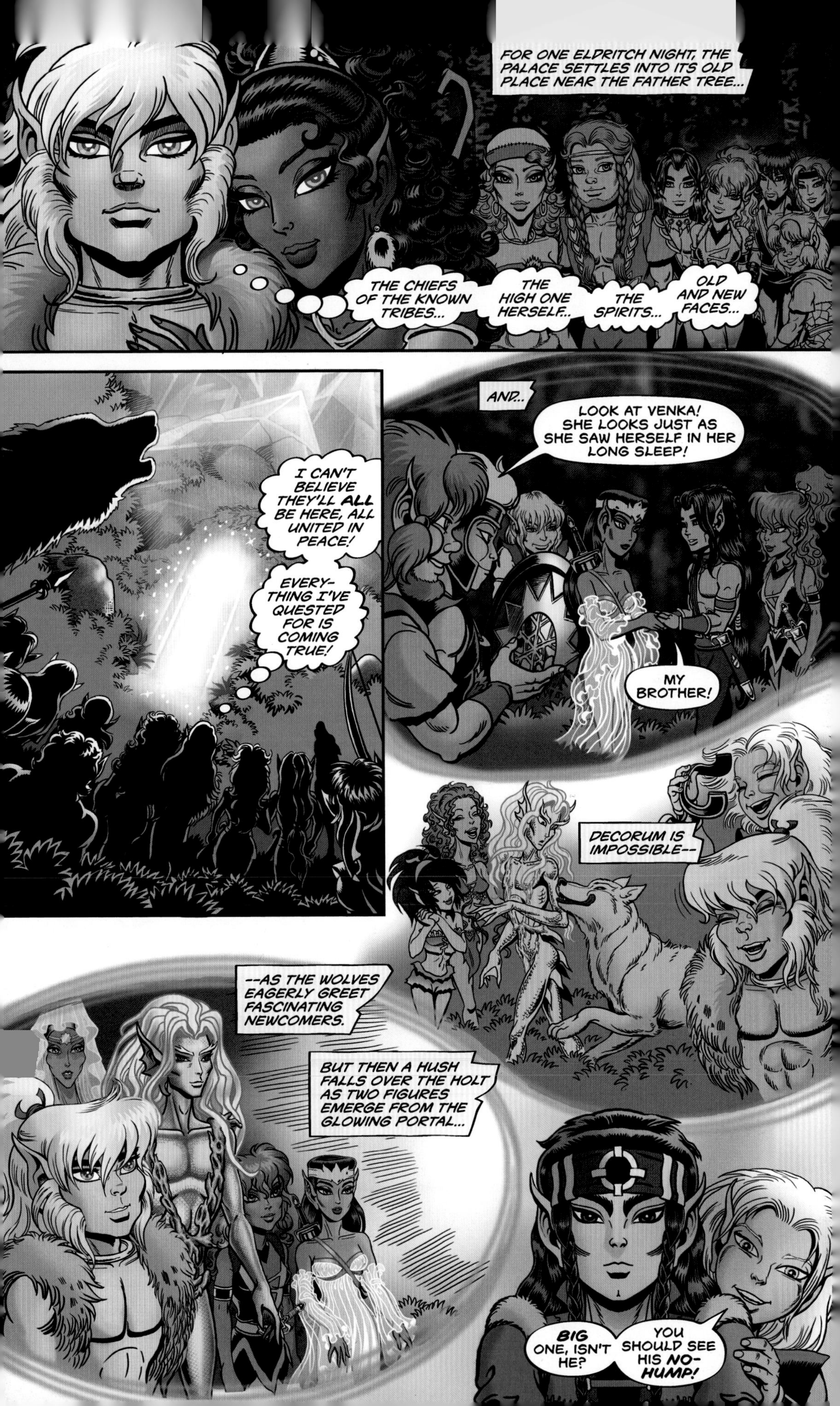

FOR ONE ELDRITCH NIGHT, THE PALACE SETTLES INTO ITS OLD PLACE NEAR THE FATHER TREE...
THE CHIEFS OF THE KNOWN TRIBES...
THE HIGH ONE HERSELF...
THE SPIRITS...
OLD AND NEW FACES...
I CAN'T BELIEVE THEY'LL ALL BE HERE, ALL UNITED IN PEACE!
EVERY-THING I'VE QUESTED FOR IS COMING TRUE!
AND...
LOOK AT VENKA! SHE LOOKS JUST AS SHE SAW HERSELF IN HER LONG SLEEP!
MY BROTHER!
DECORUM IS IMPOSSIBLE--
--AS THE WOLVES EAGERLY GREET FASCINATING NEWCOMERS.
BUT THEN A HUSH FALLS OVER THE HOLT AS TWO FIGURES EMERGE FROM THE GLOWING PORTAL...
BIG ONE, ISN'T HE?
YOU SHOULD SEE HIS NO-HUMP!

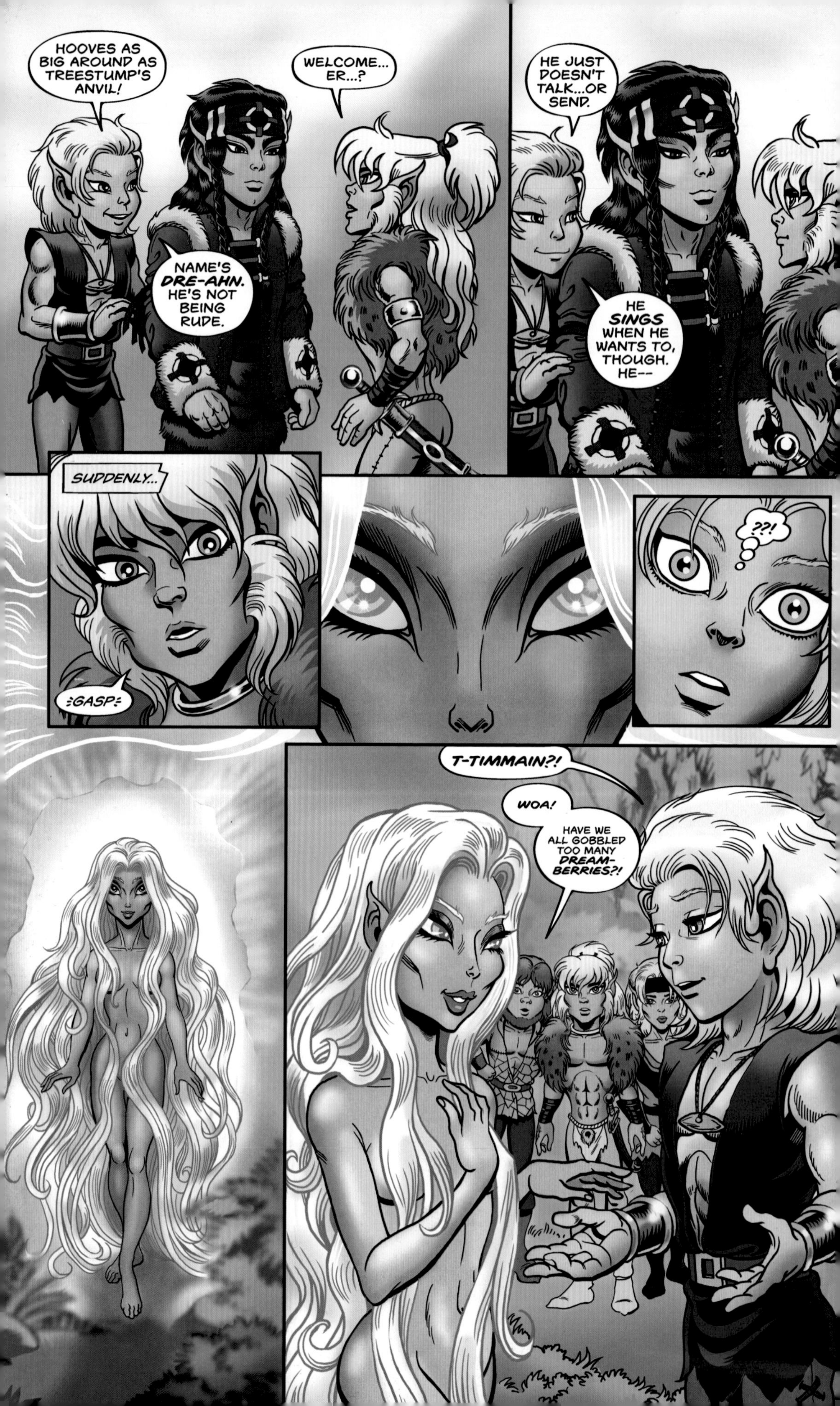

HOOVES AS BIG AROUND AS TREESTUMP'S ANVIL!
WELCOME... ER...?
NAME'S DRE-AHN. HE'S NOT BEING RUDE.
HE JUST DOESN'T TALK...OR SEND.
HE SINGS WHEN HE WANTS TO, THOUGH. HE--
SUDDENLY...
:GASP:
??!
T-TIMMAIN?!
WOA!
HAVE WE ALL GOBBLED TOO MANY DREAM-BERRIES?!

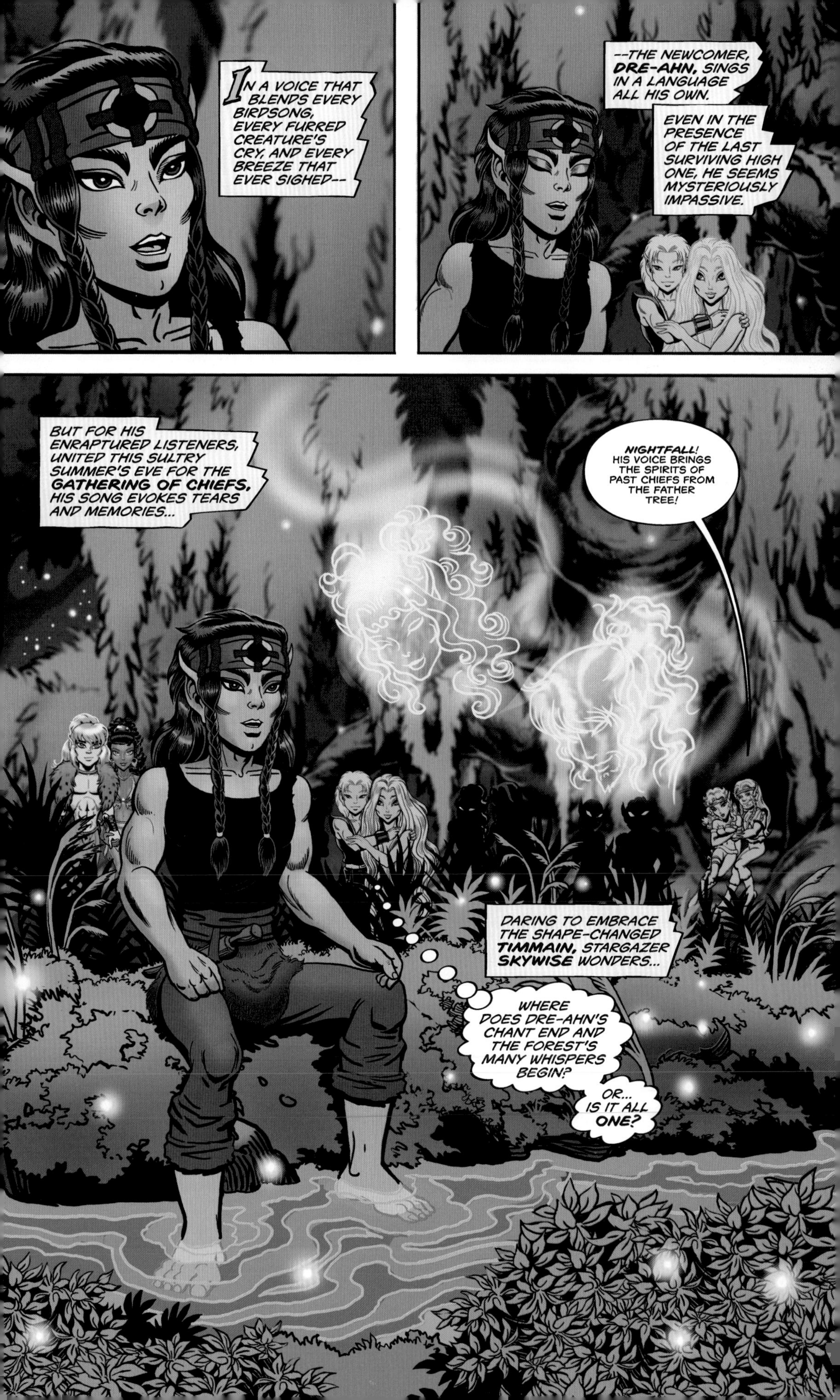
IN A VOICE THAT BLENDS EVERY BIRDSONG, EVERY FURRED CREATURE'S CRY, AND EVERY BREEZE THAT EVER SIGHED--
--THE NEWCOMER, DRE-AHN, SINGS IN A LANGUAGE ALL HIS OWN.
EVEN IN THE PRESENCE OF THE LAST SURVIVING HIGH ONE, HE SEEMS MYSTERIOUSLY IMPASSIVE.
BUT FOR HIS ENRAPTURED LISTENERS, UNITED THIS SULTRY SUMMER'S EVE FOR THE GATHERING OF CHIEFS, HIS SONG EVOKES TEARS AND MEMORIES...
NIGHTFALL! HIS VOICE BRINGS THE SPIRITS OF PAST CHIEFS FROM THE FATHER TREE!
DARING TO EMBRACE THE SHAPE-CHANGED TIMMAIN, STARGAZER SKYWISE WONDERS...
WHERE DOES DRE-AHN'S CHANT END AND THE FOREST'S MANY WHISPERS BEGIN?
OR... IS IT ALL ONE?

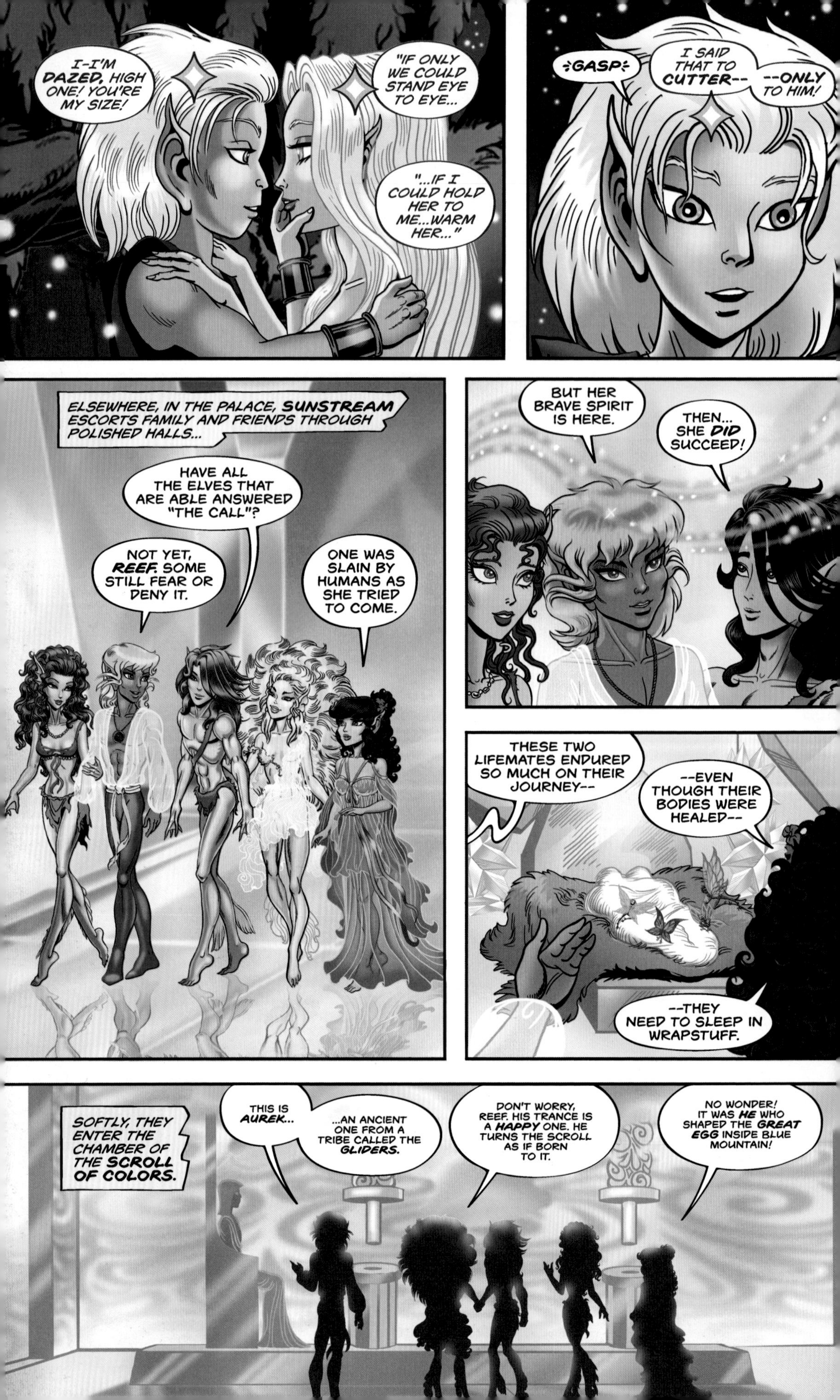
I-I'M DAZED, HIGH ONE! YOU'RE MY SIZE!
"IF ONLY WE COULD STAND EYE TO EYE...
"...IF I COULD HOLD HER TO ME...WARM HER..."
GASP
I SAID THAT TO CUTTER--
--ONLY TO HIM!
ELSEWHERE, IN THE PALACE, SUNSTREAM ESCORTS FAMILY AND FRIENDS THROUGH POLISHED HALLS...
HAVE ALL THE ELVES THAT ARE ABLE ANSWERED "THE CALL"?
NOT YET, REEF. SOME STILL FEAR OR DENY IT.
ONE WAS SLAIN BY HUMANS AS SHE TRIED TO COME.
BUT HER BRAVE SPIRIT IS HERE.
THEN... SHE DID SUCCEED!
THESE TWO LIFEMATES ENDURED SO MUCH ON THEIR JOURNEY--
--EVEN THOUGH THEIR BODIES WERE HEALED--
--THEY NEED TO SLEEP IN WRAPSTUFF.
SOFTLY, THEY ENTER THE CHAMBER OF THE SCROLL OF COLORS.
THIS IS AUREK...
...AN ANCIENT ONE FROM A TRIBE CALLED THE GLIDERS.
DON'T WORRY, REEF. HIS TRANCE IS A HAPPY ONE. HE TURNS THE SCROLL AS IF BORN TO IT.
NO WONDER! IT WAS HE WHO SHAPED THE GREAT EGG INSIDE BLUE MOUNTAIN!

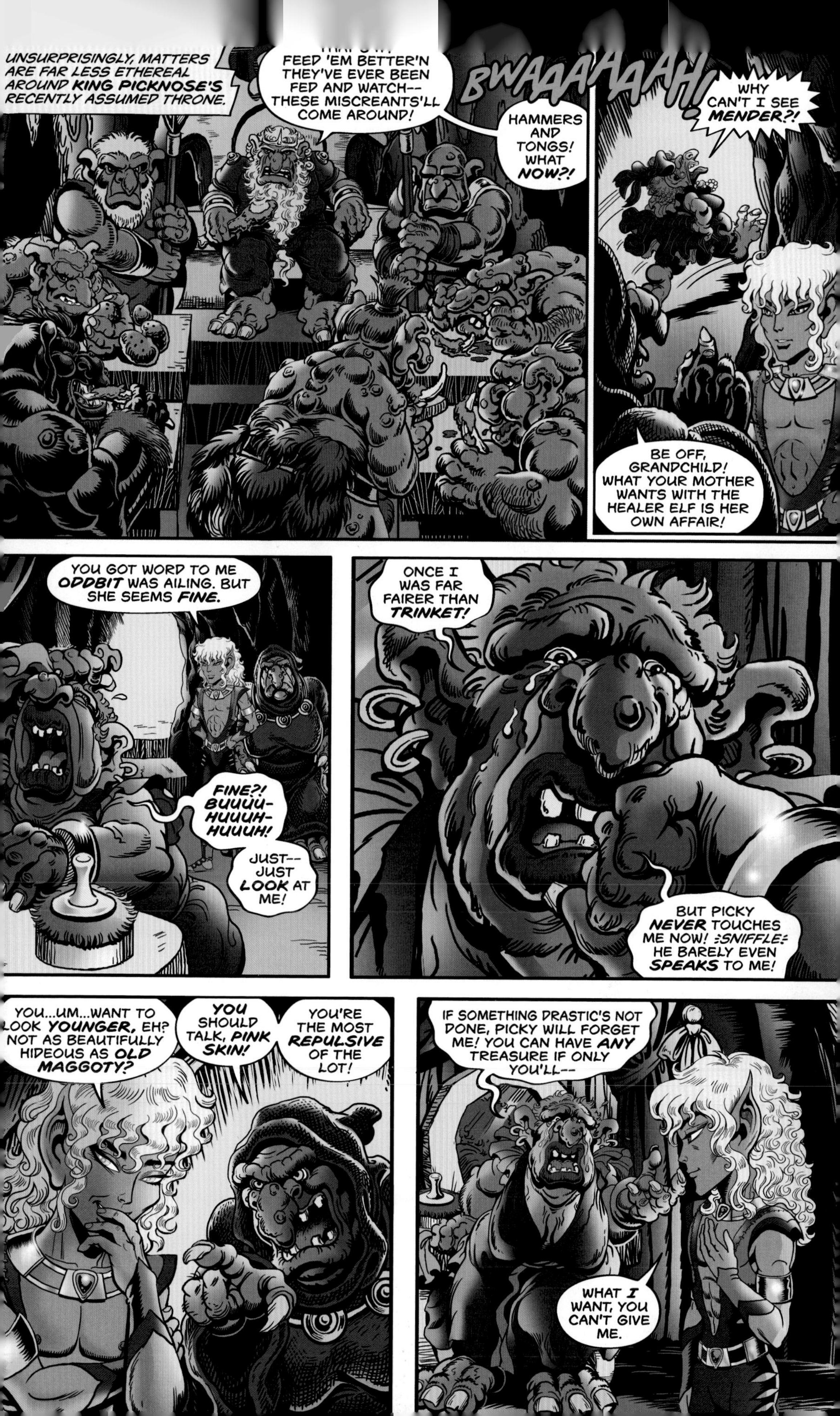

UNSURPRISINGLY, MATTERS ARE FAR LESS ETHEREAL AROUND KING PICKNOSE'S RECENTLY ASSUMED THRONE.
FEED 'EM BETTER'N THEY'VE EVER BEEN FED AND WATCH-- THESE MISCREANTS'LL COME AROUND!
BWAAAAHAAAH!
HAMMERS AND TONGS! WHAT NOW?!
WHY CAN'T I SEE MENDER?!
BE OFF, GRANDCHILD! WHAT YOUR MOTHER WANTS WITH THE HEALER ELF IS HER OWN AFFAIR!
YOU GOT WORD TO ME ODDBIT WAS AILING. BUT SHE SEEMS FINE.
FINE?! BUUUU-HUUUH-HUUUH!
JUST-- JUST LOOK AT ME!
ONCE I WAS FAR FAIRER THAN TRINKET!
BUT PICKY NEVER TOUCHES ME NOW! :SNIFFLE: HE BARELY EVEN SPEAKS TO ME!
YOU...UM...WANT TO LOOK YOUNGER, EH? NOT AS BEAUTIFULLY HIDEOUS AS OLD MAGGOTY?
YOU SHOULD TALK, PINK SKIN!
YOU'RE THE MOST REPULSIVE OF THE LOT!
IF SOMETHING DRASTIC'S NOT DONE, PICKY WILL FORGET ME! YOU CAN HAVE ANY TREASURE IF ONLY YOU'LL--
WHAT I WANT, YOU CAN'T GIVE ME.

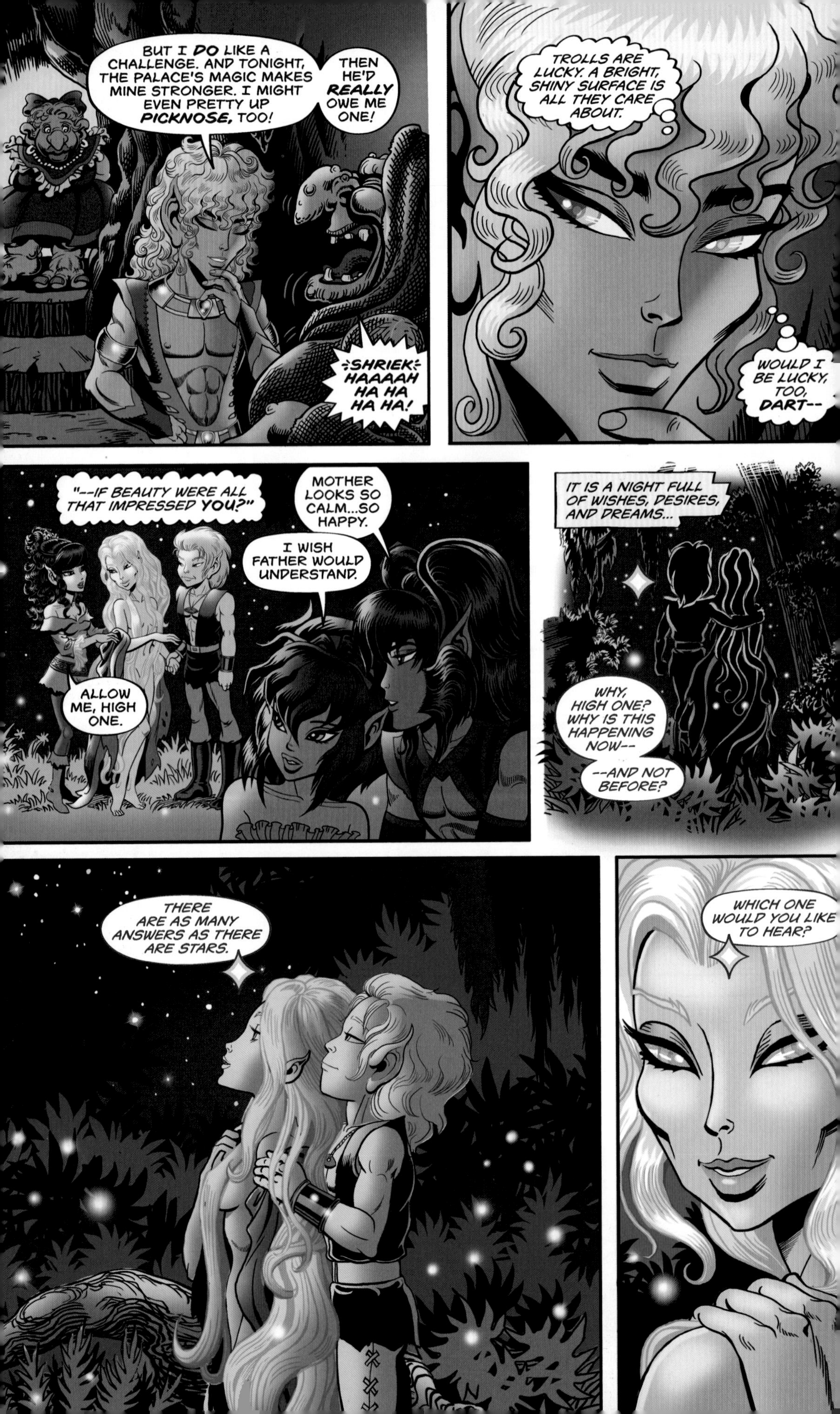
BUT I DO LIKE A CHALLENGE. AND TONIGHT, THE PALACE'S MAGIC MAKES MINE STRONGER. I MIGHT EVEN PRETTY UP PICKNOSE, TOO!
THEN HE'D REALLY OWE ME ONE!
SHRIEK HAAAAH HA HA HA HA!
TROLLS ARE LUCKY. A BRIGHT, SHINY SURFACE IS ALL THEY CARE ABOUT.
WOULD I BE LUCKY, TOO, DART--
"--IF BEAUTY WERE ALL THAT IMPRESSED YOU?"
MOTHER LOOKS SO CALM...SO HAPPY.
I WISH FATHER WOULD UNDERSTAND.
ALLOW ME, HIGH ONE.
IT IS A NIGHT FULL OF WISHES, DESIRES, AND DREAMS...
WHY, HIGH ONE? WHY IS THIS HAPPENING NOW--
--AND NOT BEFORE?
THERE ARE AS MANY ANSWERS AS THERE ARE STARS.
WHICH ONE WOULD YOU LIKE TO HEAR?

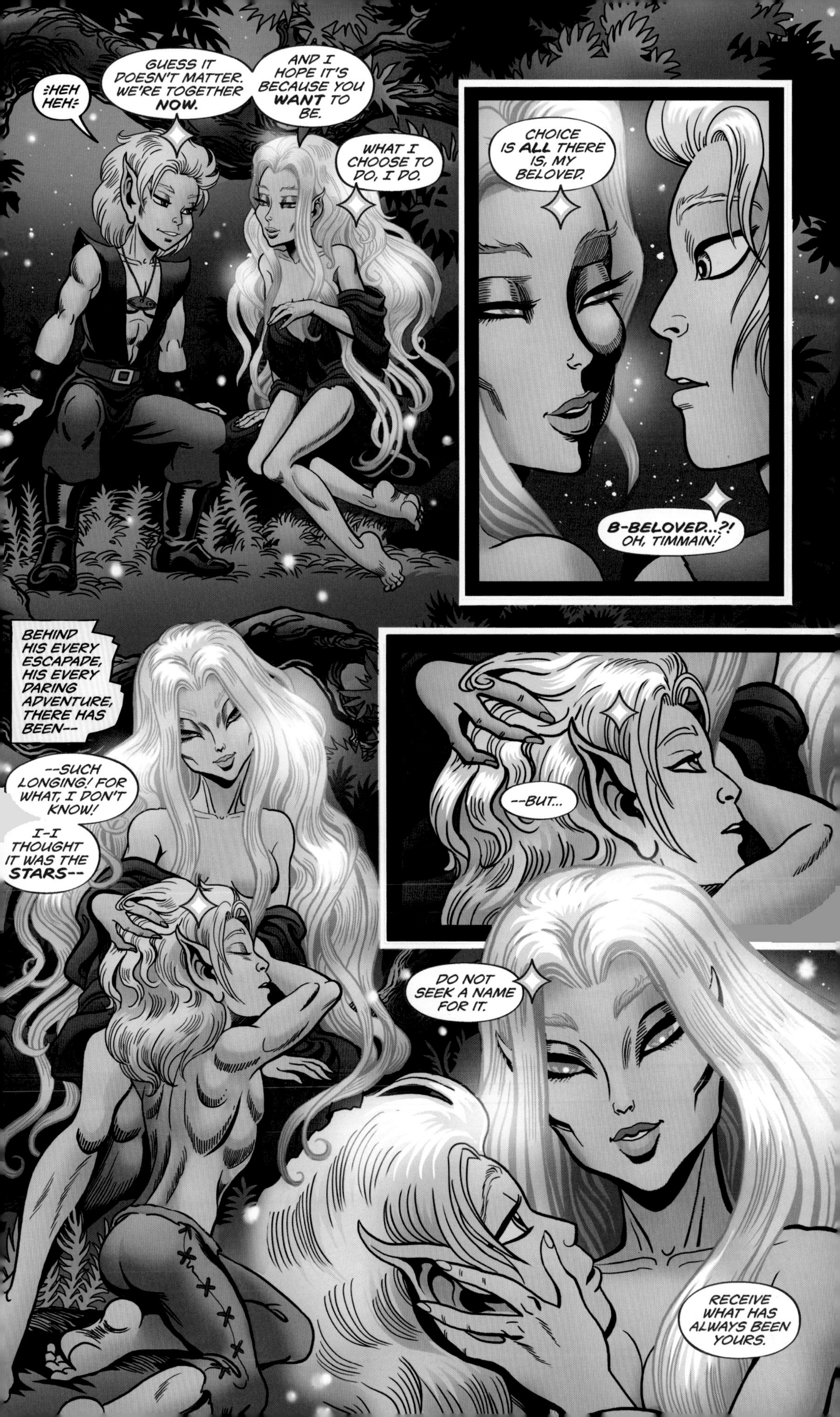

HEH HEH
GUESS IT DOESN'T MATTER. WE'RE TOGETHER **NOW.**
AND I HOPE IT'S BECAUSE YOU **WANT** TO BE.
WHAT I CHOOSE TO DO, I DO.
CHOICE IS **ALL** THERE IS, MY BELOVED.
B-BELOVED...?! OH, TIMMAIN!
BEHIND HIS EVERY ESCAPADE, HIS EVERY DARING ADVENTURE, THERE HAS BEEN--
--SUCH LONGING! FOR WHAT, I DON'T KNOW!
I-I THOUGHT IT WAS THE **STARS**--
--BUT...
DO NOT SEEK A NAME FOR IT.
RECEIVE WHAT HAS ALWAYS BEEN YOURS.

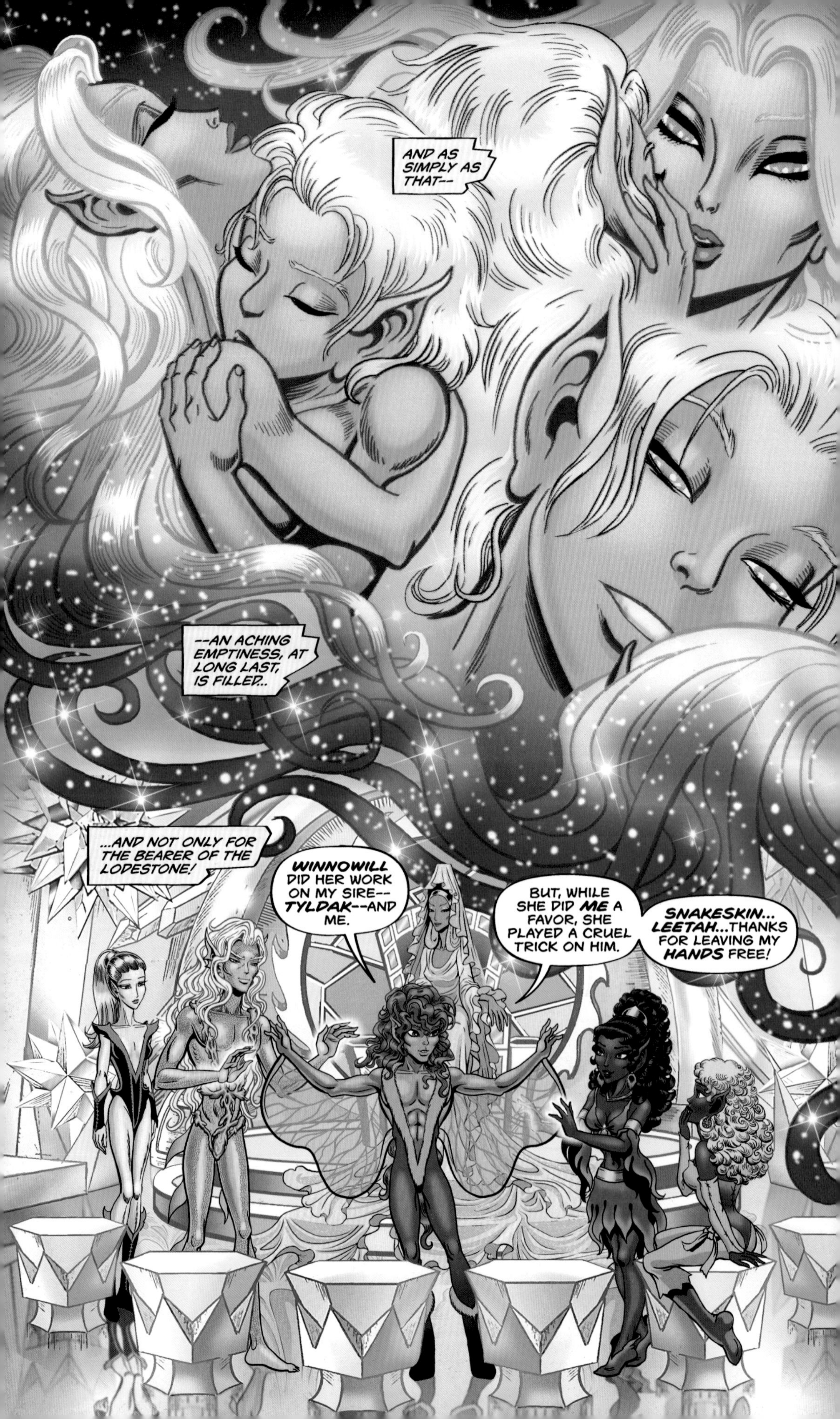
AND AS SIMPLY AS THAT--
--AN ACHING EMPTINESS, AT LONG LAST, IS FILLED...
...AND NOT ONLY FOR THE BEARER OF THE LODESTONE!
WINNOWILL DID HER WORK ON MY SIRE--TYLDAK--AND ME.
BUT, WHILE SHE DID ME A FAVOR, SHE PLAYED A CRUEL TRICK ON HIM.
SNAKESKIN... LEETAH...THANKS FOR LEAVING MY HANDS FREE!

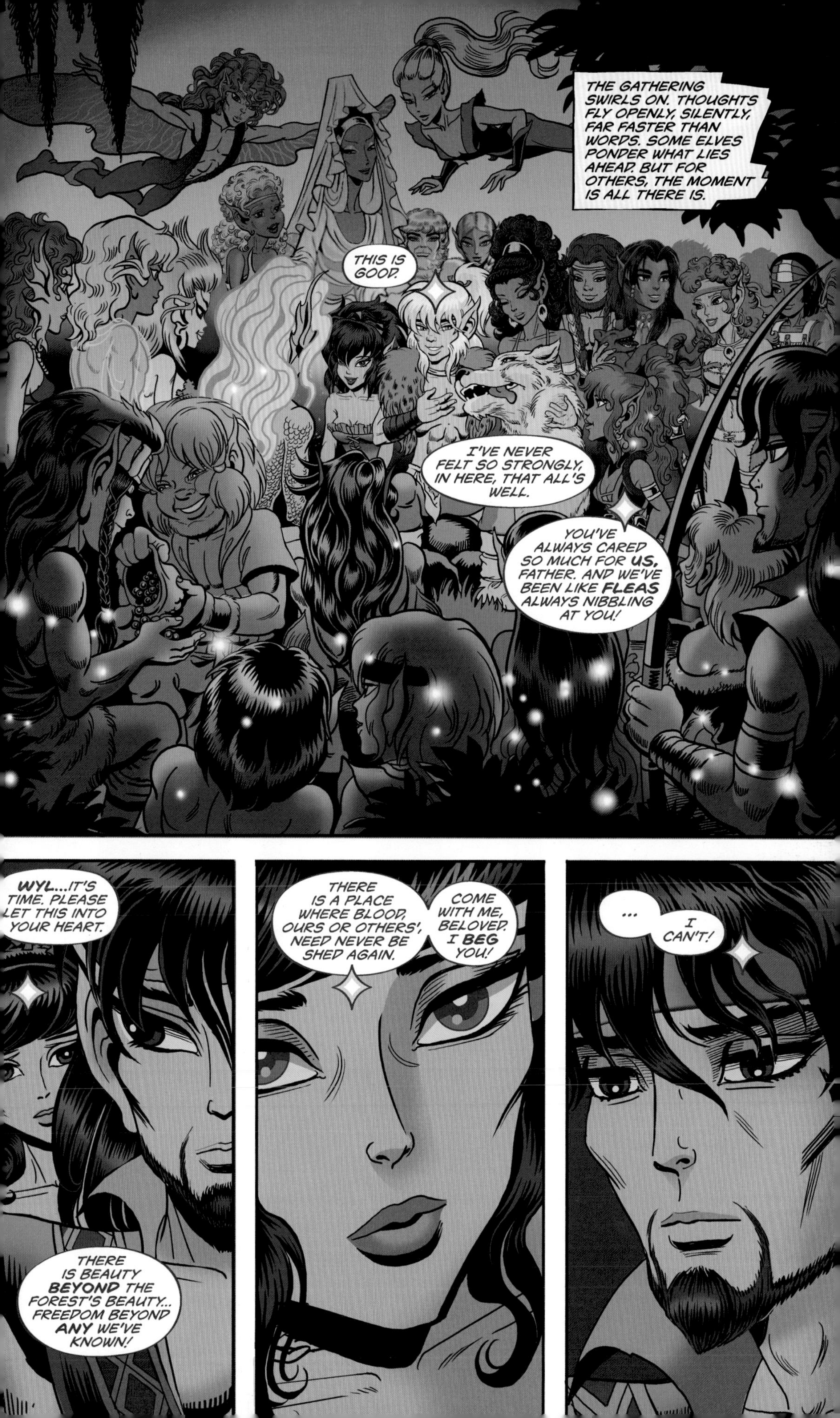

THE GATHERING SWIRLS ON. THOUGHTS FLY OPENLY, SILENTLY, FAR FASTER THAN WORDS. SOME ELVES PONDER WHAT LIES AHEAD. BUT FOR OTHERS, THE MOMENT IS ALL THERE IS.
THIS IS GOOD.
I'VE NEVER FELT SO STRONGLY, IN HERE, THAT ALL'S WELL.
YOU'VE ALWAYS CARED SO MUCH FOR US, FATHER. AND WE'VE BEEN LIKE FLEAS ALWAYS NIBBLING AT YOU!
WYL...IT'S TIME. PLEASE LET THIS INTO YOUR HEART.
THERE IS BEAUTY BEYOND THE FOREST'S BEAUTY... FREEDOM BEYOND ANY WE'VE KNOWN!
THERE IS A PLACE WHERE BLOOD, OURS OR OTHERS', NEED NEVER BE SHED AGAIN.
COME WITH ME, BELOVED. I BEG YOU!
...
I CAN'T!

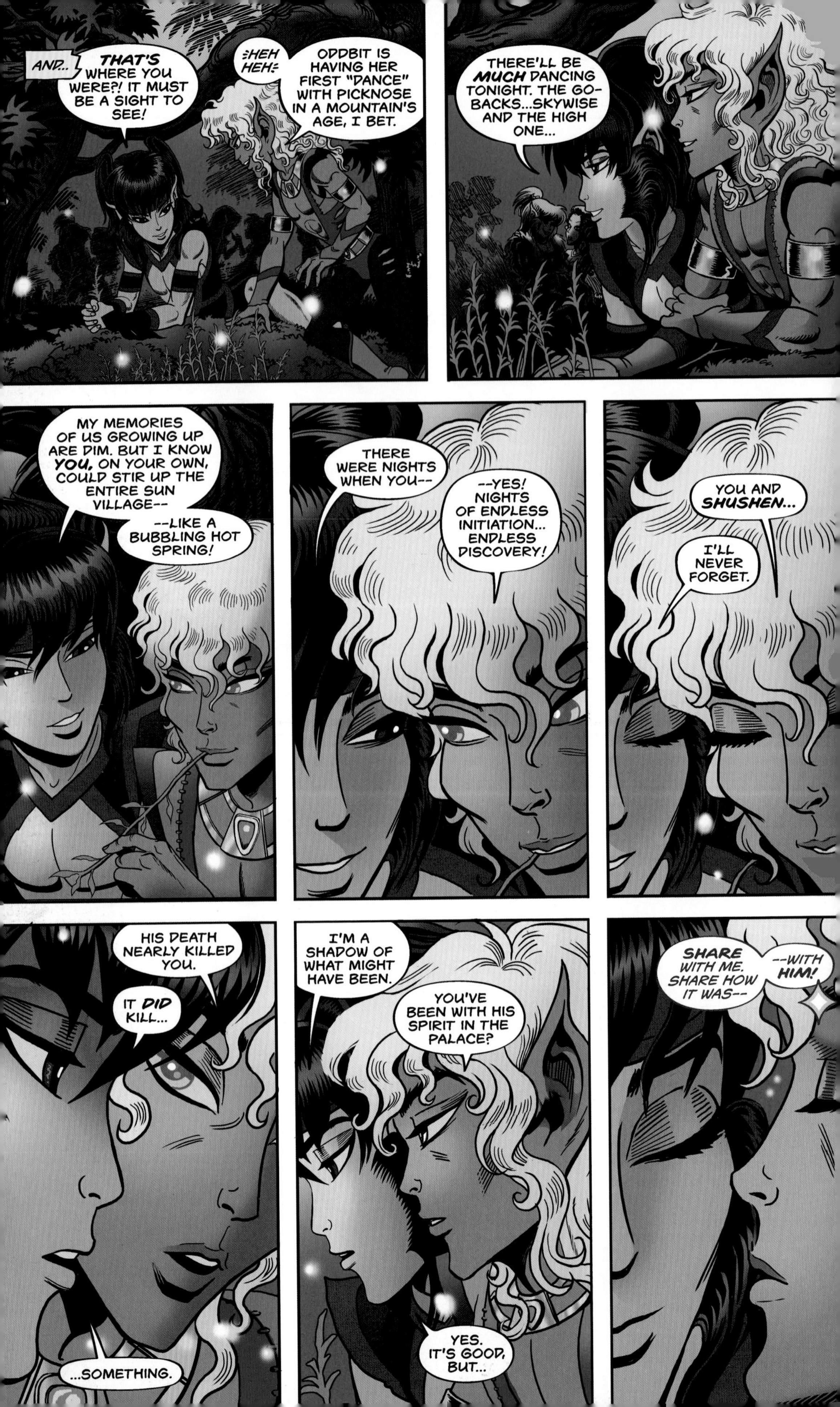
AND...
THAT'S WHERE YOU WERE?! IT MUST BE A SIGHT TO SEE!
:HEH HEH:
ODDBIT IS HAVING HER FIRST "DANCE" WITH PICKNOSE IN A MOUNTAIN'S AGE, I BET.
THERE'LL BE MUCH DANCING TONIGHT. THE GO-BACKS...SKYWISE AND THE HIGH ONE...
MY MEMORIES OF US GROWING UP ARE DIM. BUT I KNOW YOU, ON YOUR OWN, COULD STIR UP THE ENTIRE SUN VILLAGE--
--LIKE A BUBBLING HOT SPRING!
THERE WERE NIGHTS WHEN YOU--
--YES! NIGHTS OF ENDLESS INITIATION... ENDLESS DISCOVERY!
YOU AND SHUSHEN...
I'LL NEVER FORGET.
HIS DEATH NEARLY KILLED YOU.
IT DID KILL...
...SOMETHING.
I'M A SHADOW OF WHAT MIGHT HAVE BEEN.
YOU'VE BEEN WITH HIS SPIRIT IN THE PALACE?
YES. IT'S GOOD, BUT...
SHARE WITH ME. SHARE HOW IT WAS--
--WITH HIM!

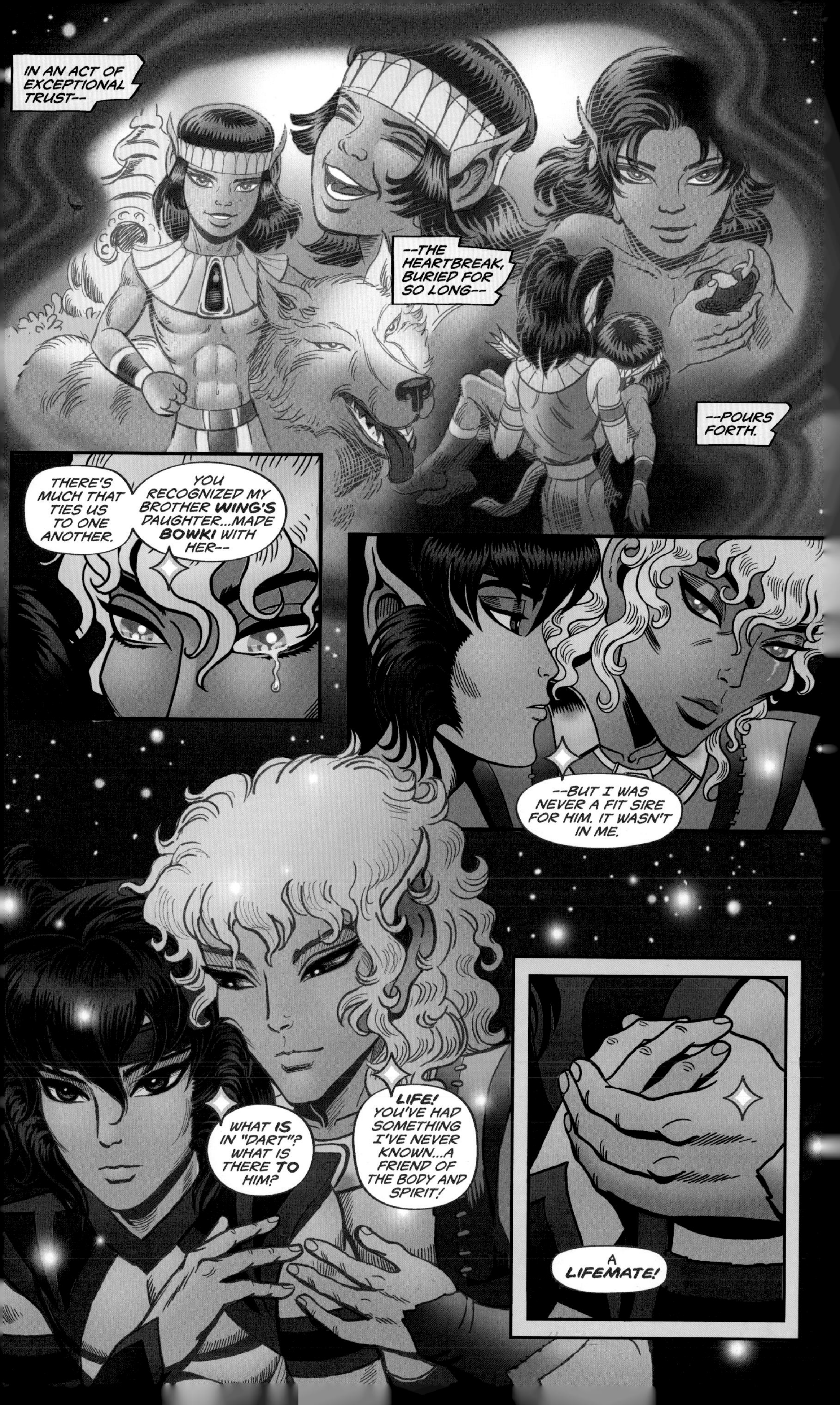
IN AN ACT OF EXCEPTIONAL TRUST--
--THE HEARTBREAK, BURIED FOR SO LONG--
--POURS FORTH.
THERE'S MUCH THAT TIES US TO ONE ANOTHER.
YOU RECOGNIZED MY BROTHER WING'S DAUGHTER...MADE BOWKI WITH HER--
--BUT I WAS NEVER A FIT SIRE FOR HIM. IT WASN'T IN ME.
WHAT IS IN "DART"? WHAT IS THERE TO HIM?
LIFE! YOU'VE HAD SOMETHING I'VE NEVER KNOWN...A FRIEND OF THE BODY AND SPIRIT!
A LIFEMATE!

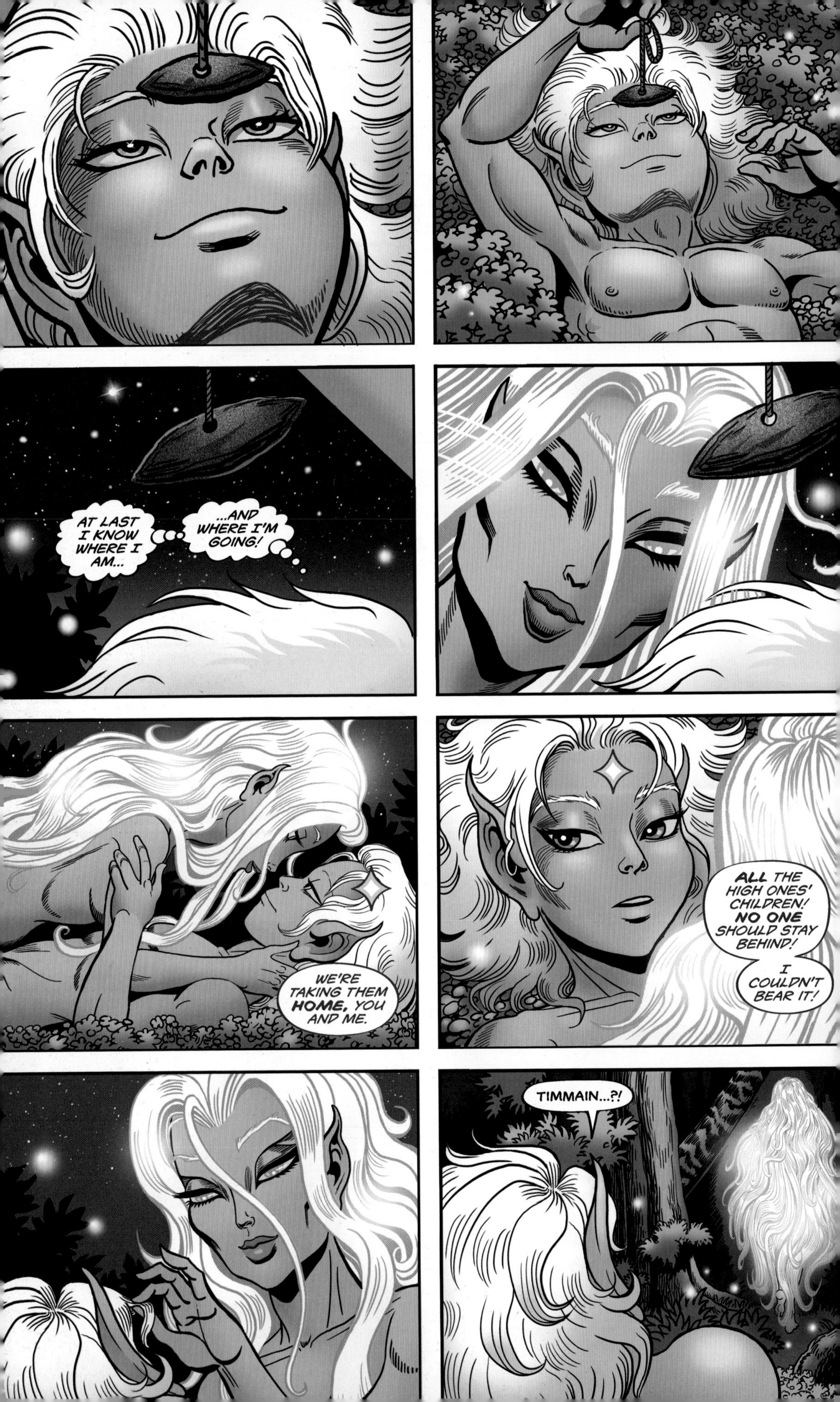
AT LAST I KNOW WHERE I AM...
...AND WHERE I'M GOING!
WE'RE TAKING THEM **HOME,** YOU AND ME.
ALL THE HIGH ONES' CHILDREN! **NO ONE** SHOULD STAY BEHIND!
I COULDN'T BEAR IT!
TIMMAIN...?!

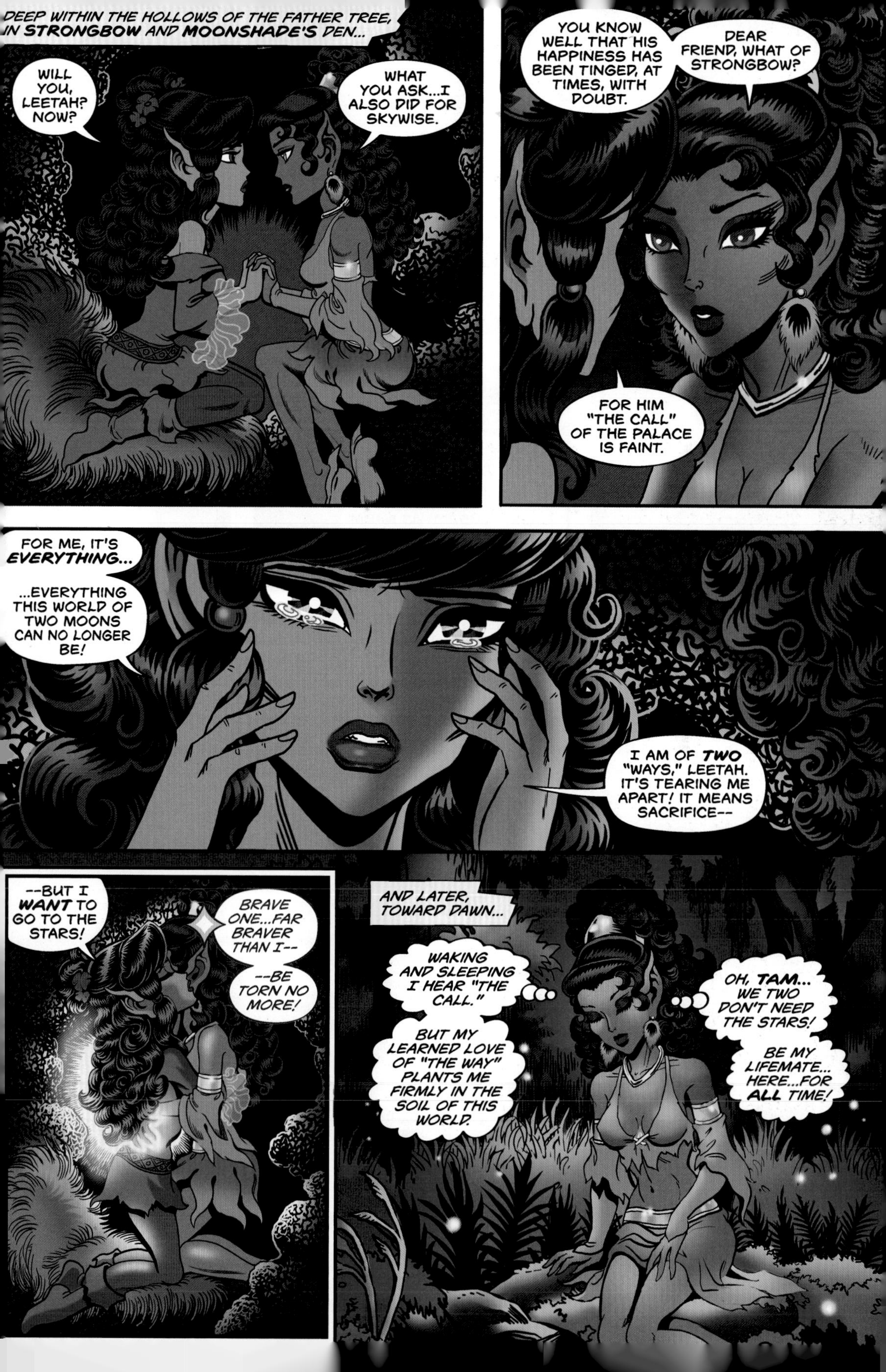
DEEP WITHIN THE HOLLOWS OF THE FATHER TREE, IN STRONGBOW AND MOONSHADE'S DEN...
WILL YOU, LEETAH? NOW?
WHAT YOU ASK...I ALSO DID FOR SKYWISE.
DEAR FRIEND, WHAT OF STRONGBOW?
YOU KNOW WELL THAT HIS HAPPINESS HAS BEEN TINGED, AT TIMES, WITH DOUBT.
FOR HIM "THE CALL" OF THE PALACE IS FAINT.
FOR ME, IT'S EVERYTHING...
...EVERYTHING THIS WORLD OF TWO MOONS CAN NO LONGER BE!
I AM OF TWO "WAYS," LEETAH. IT'S TEARING ME APART! IT MEANS SACRIFICE--
--BUT I WANT TO GO TO THE STARS!
BRAVE ONE...FAR BRAVER THAN I--
--BE TORN NO MORE!
AND LATER, TOWARD DAWN...
WAKING AND SLEEPING I HEAR "THE CALL."
BUT MY LEARNED LOVE OF "THE WAY" PLANTS ME FIRMLY IN THE SOIL OF THIS WORLD.
OH, TAM... WE TWO DON'T NEED THE STARS!
BE MY LIFEMATE... HERE...FOR ALL TIME!

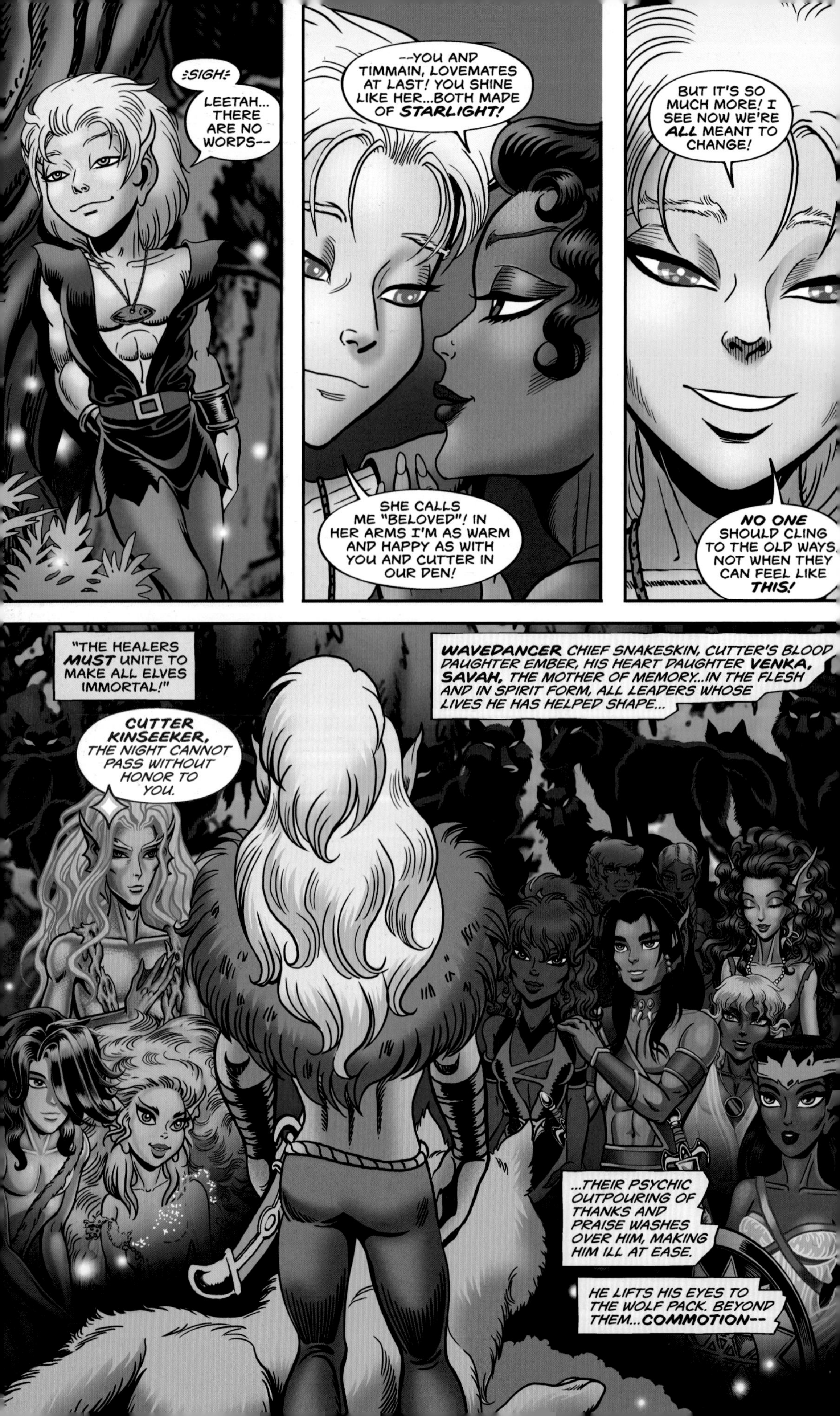
:SIGH:
LEETAH... THERE ARE NO WORDS--
--YOU AND TIMMAIN, LOVEMATES AT LAST! YOU SHINE LIKE HER...BOTH MADE OF STARLIGHT!
SHE CALLS ME "BELOVED"! IN HER ARMS I'M AS WARM AND HAPPY AS WITH YOU AND CUTTER IN OUR DEN!
BUT IT'S SO MUCH MORE! I SEE NOW WE'RE ALL MEANT TO CHANGE!
NO ONE SHOULD CLING TO THE OLD WAYS NOT WHEN THEY CAN FEEL LIKE THIS!
"THE HEALERS MUST UNITE TO MAKE ALL ELVES IMMORTAL!"
CUTTER KINSEEKER, THE NIGHT CANNOT PASS WITHOUT HONOR TO YOU.
WAVEDANCER CHIEF SNAKESKIN, CUTTER'S BLOOD DAUGHTER EMBER, HIS HEART DAUGHTER VENKA, SAVAH, THE MOTHER OF MEMORY...IN THE FLESH AND IN SPIRIT FORM, ALL LEADERS WHOSE LIVES HE HAS HELPED SHAPE...
...THEIR PSYCHIC OUTPOURING OF THANKS AND PRAISE WASHES OVER HIM, MAKING HIM ILL AT EASE.
HE LIFTS HIS EYES TO THE WOLF PACK. BEYOND THEM...COMMOTION--

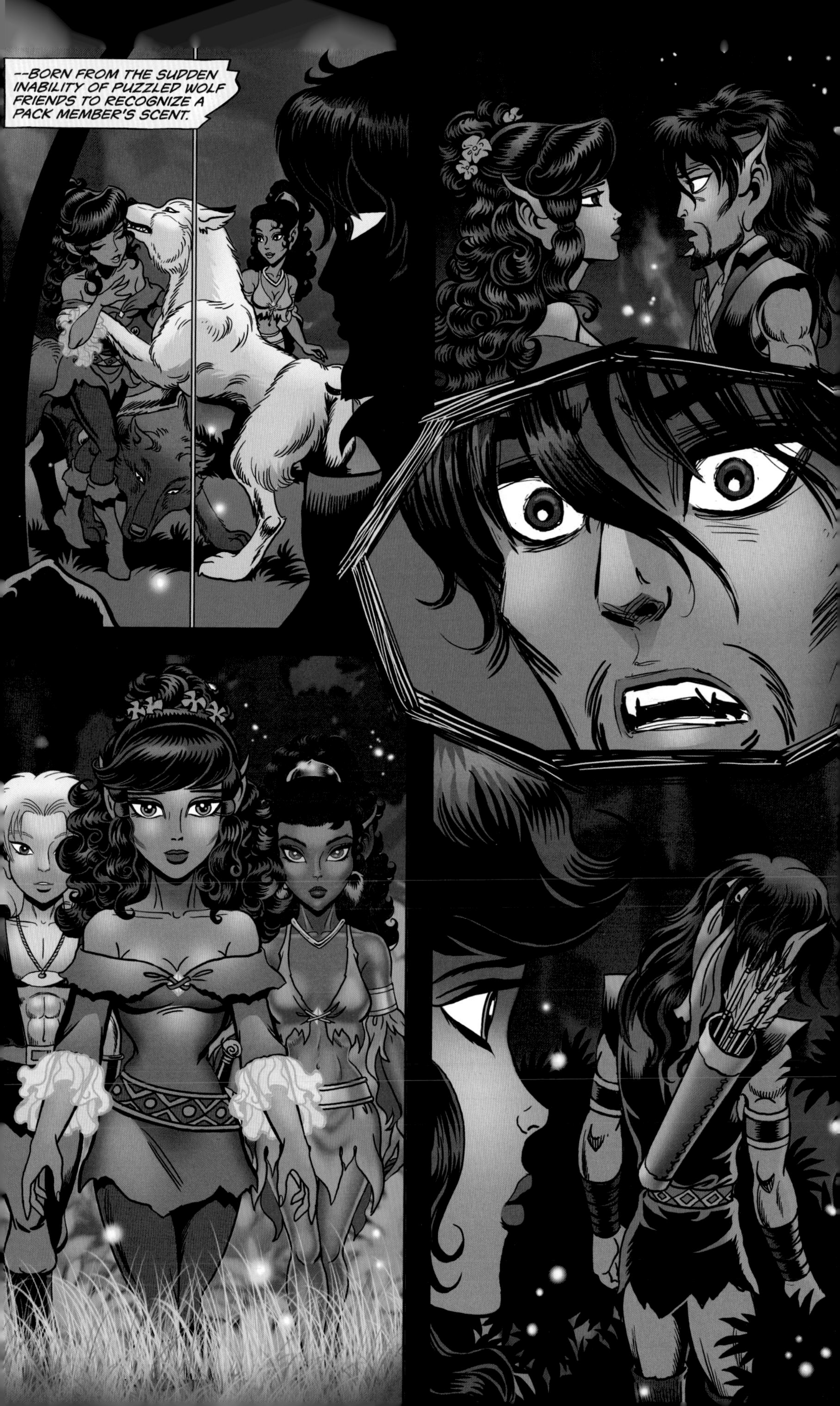
--BORN FROM THE SUDDEN INABILITY OF PUZZLED WOLF FRIENDS TO RECOGNIZE A PACK MEMBER'S SCENT.

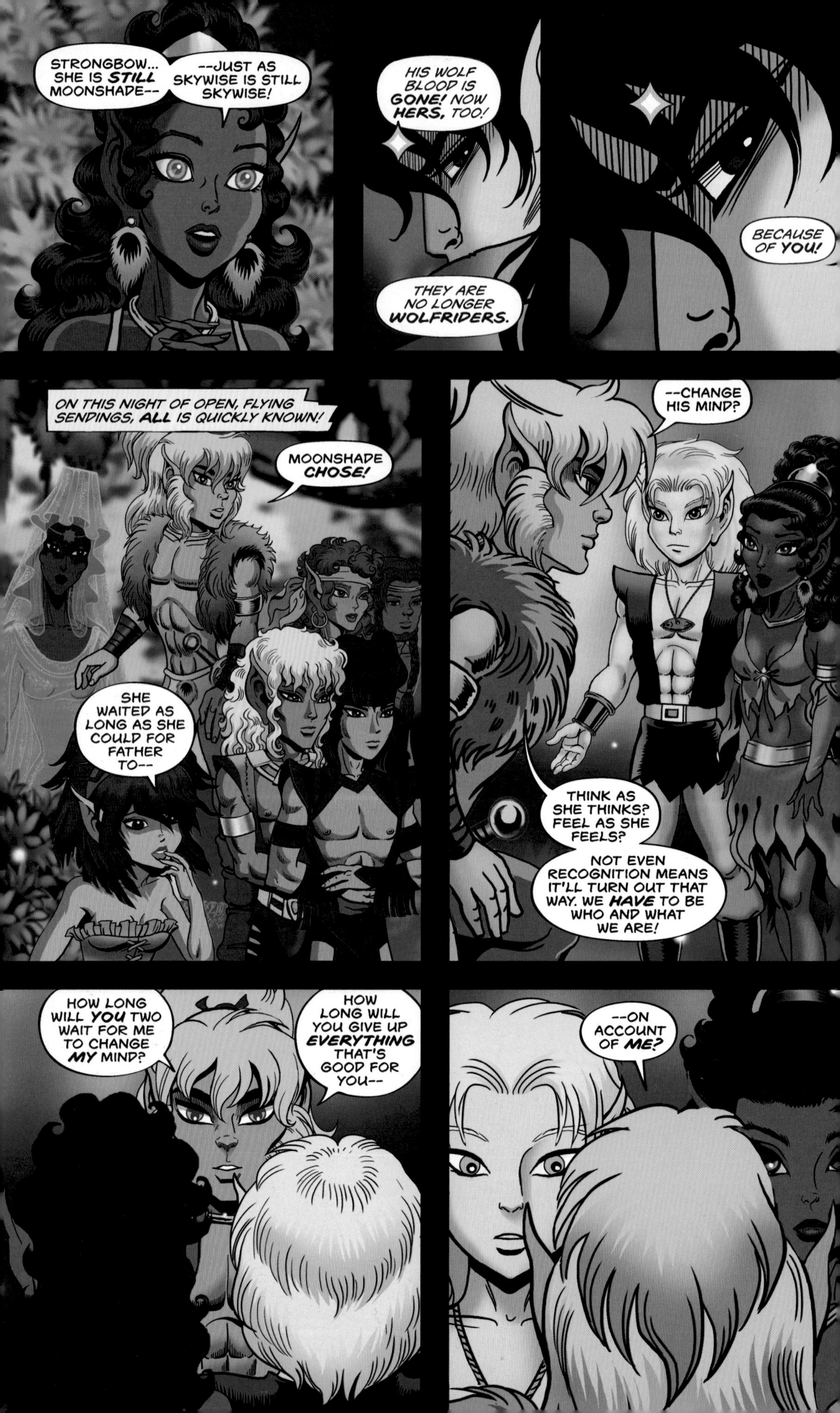
STRONGBOW... SHE IS STILL MOONSHADE--
--JUST AS SKYWISE IS STILL SKYWISE!
HIS WOLF BLOOD IS GONE! NOW HERS, TOO!
THEY ARE NO LONGER WOLFRIDERS.
BECAUSE OF YOU!
ON THIS NIGHT OF OPEN, FLYING SENDINGS, ALL IS QUICKLY KNOWN!
MOONSHADE CHOSE!
SHE WAITED AS LONG AS SHE COULD FOR FATHER TO--
--CHANGE HIS MIND?
THINK AS SHE THINKS? FEEL AS SHE FEELS?
NOT EVEN RECOGNITION MEANS IT'LL TURN OUT THAT WAY. WE HAVE TO BE WHO AND WHAT WE ARE!
HOW LONG WILL YOU TWO WAIT FOR ME TO CHANGE MY MIND?
HOW LONG WILL YOU GIVE UP EVERYTHING THAT'S GOOD FOR YOU--
--ON ACCOUNT OF ME?

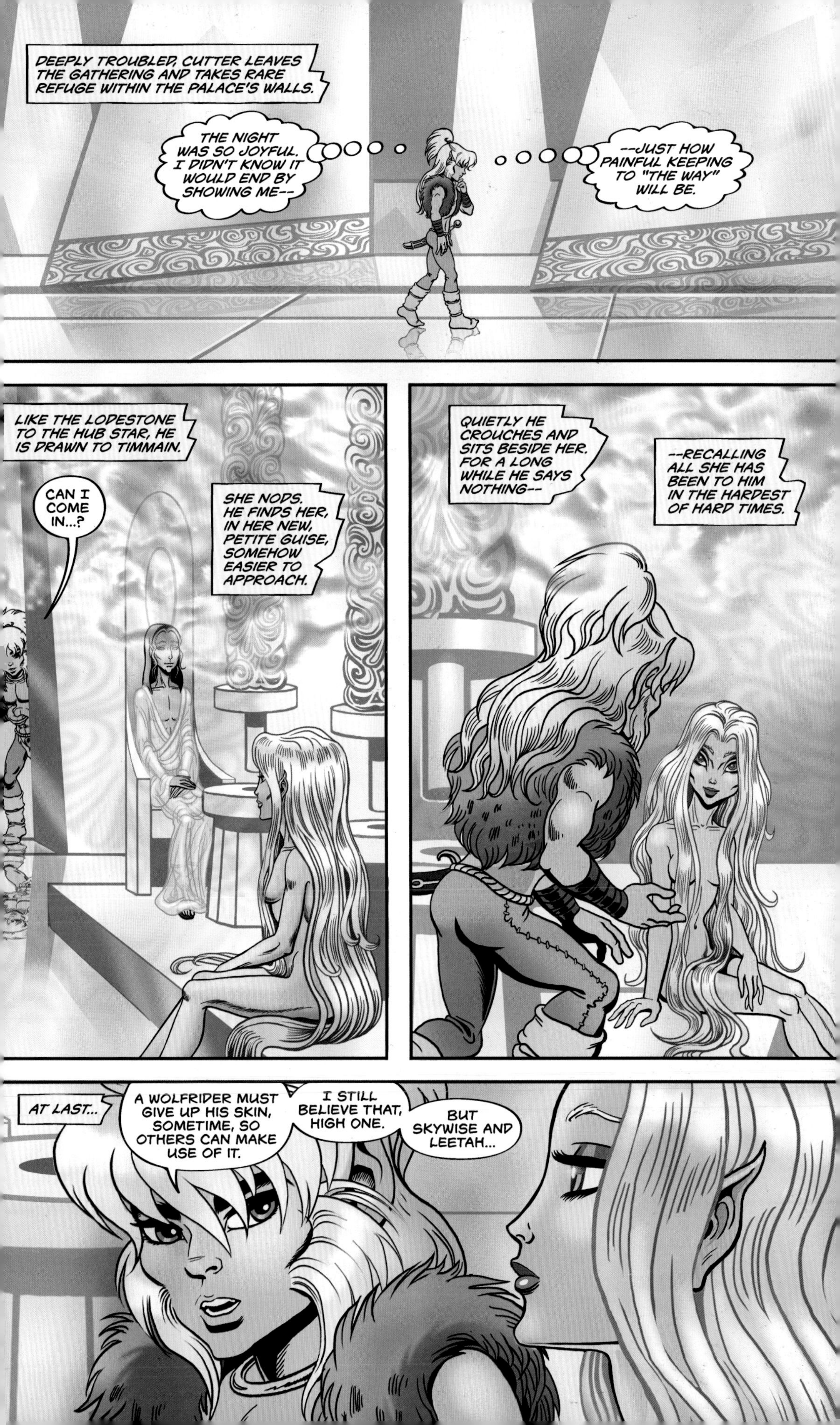
DEEPLY TROUBLED, CUTTER LEAVES THE GATHERING AND TAKES RARE REFUGE WITHIN THE PALACE'S WALLS.
THE NIGHT WAS SO JOYFUL. I DIDN'T KNOW IT WOULD END BY SHOWING ME--
--JUST HOW PAINFUL KEEPING TO "THE WAY" WILL BE.
LIKE THE LODESTONE TO THE HUB STAR, HE IS DRAWN TO TIMMAIN.
CAN I COME IN...?
SHE NODS. HE FINDS HER, IN HER NEW, PETITE GUISE, SOMEHOW EASIER TO APPROACH.
QUIETLY HE CROUCHES AND SITS BESIDE HER. FOR A LONG WHILE HE SAYS NOTHING--
--RECALLING ALL SHE HAS BEEN TO HIM IN THE HARDEST OF HARD TIMES.
AT LAST...
A WOLFRIDER MUST GIVE UP HIS SKIN, SOMETIME, SO OTHERS CAN MAKE USE OF IT.
I STILL BELIEVE THAT, HIGH ONE.
BUT SKYWISE AND LEETAH...

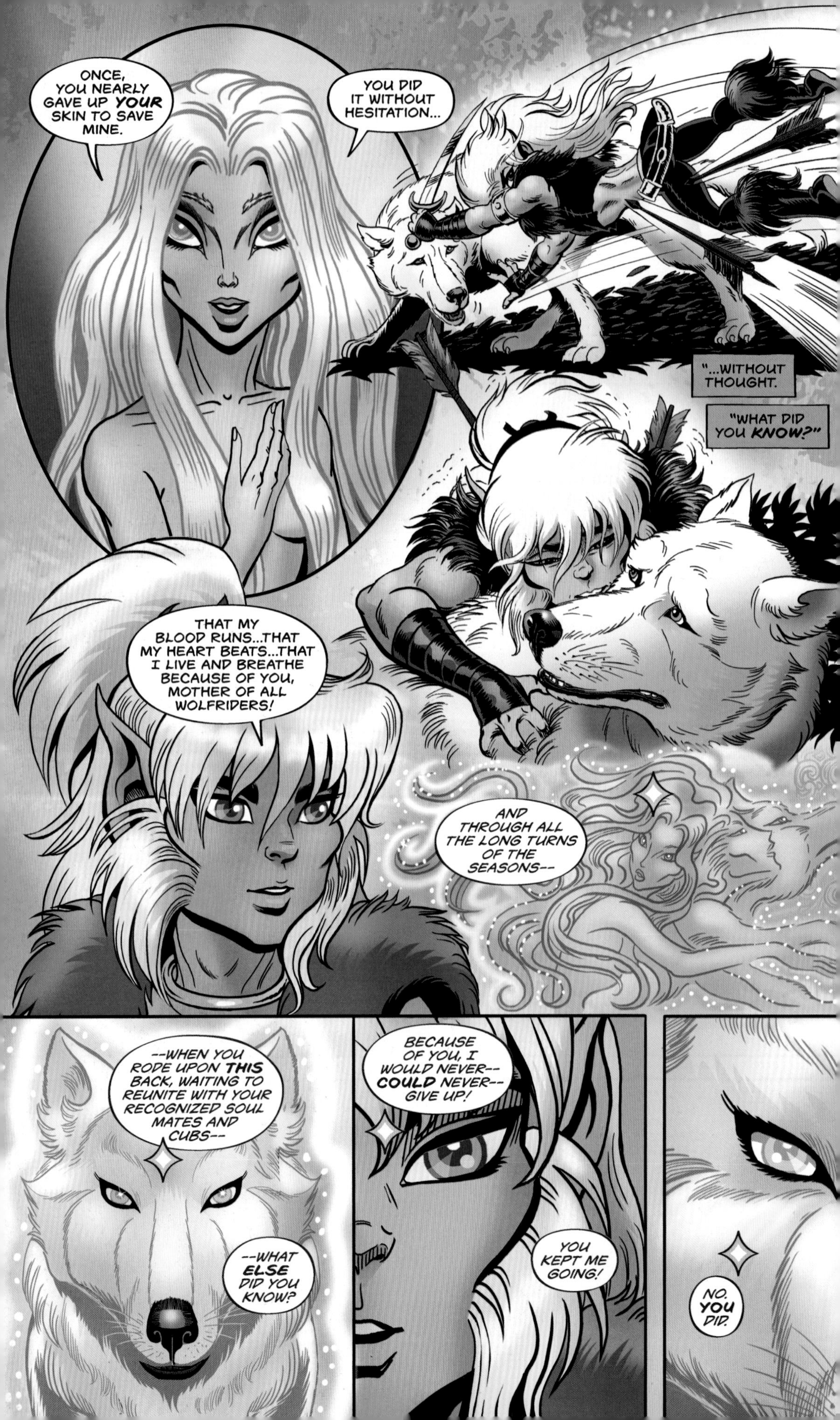
ONCE, YOU NEARLY GAVE UP YOUR SKIN TO SAVE MINE.
YOU DID IT WITHOUT HESITATION...
"...WITHOUT THOUGHT.
"WHAT DID YOU KNOW?"
THAT MY BLOOD RUNS...THAT MY HEART BEATS...THAT I LIVE AND BREATHE BECAUSE OF YOU, MOTHER OF ALL WOLFRIDERS!
AND THROUGH ALL THE LONG TURNS OF THE SEASONS--
--WHEN YOU RODE UPON THIS BACK, WAITING TO REUNITE WITH YOUR RECOGNIZED SOUL MATES AND CUBS--
--WHAT ELSE DID YOU KNOW?
BECAUSE OF YOU, I WOULD NEVER--COULD NEVER--GIVE UP!
YOU KEPT ME GOING!
NO. YOU DID.

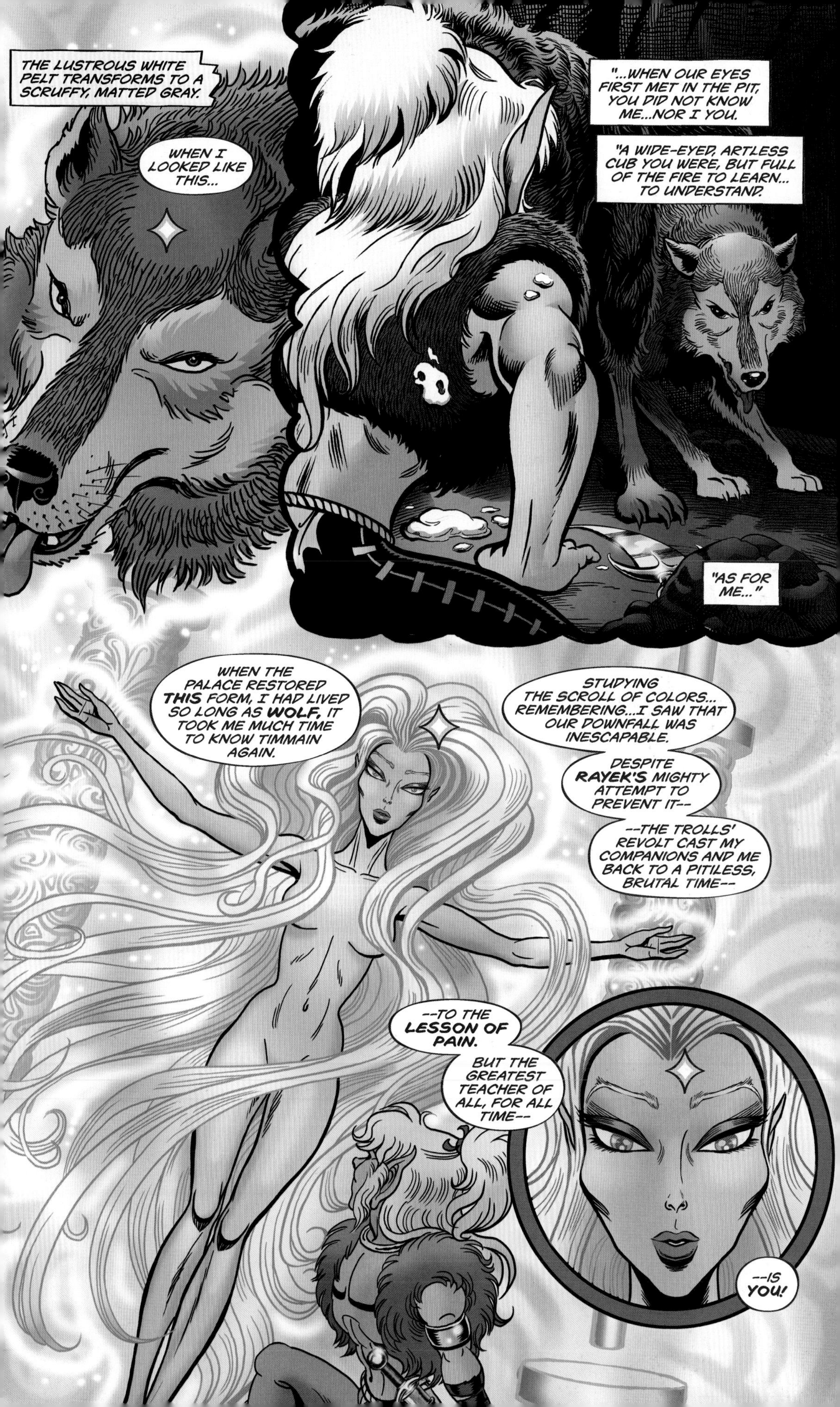
THE LUSTROUS WHITE PELT TRANSFORMS TO A SCRUFFY, MATTED GRAY.
WHEN I LOOKED LIKE THIS...
"...WHEN OUR EYES FIRST MET IN THE PIT, YOU DID NOT KNOW ME...NOR I YOU.
"A WIDE-EYED, ARTLESS CUB YOU WERE, BUT FULL OF THE FIRE TO LEARN... TO UNDERSTAND.
"AS FOR ME..."
WHEN THE PALACE RESTORED THIS FORM, I HAD LIVED SO LONG AS WOLF, IT TOOK ME MUCH TIME TO KNOW TIMMAIN AGAIN.
STUDYING THE SCROLL OF COLORS... REMEMBERING...I SAW THAT OUR DOWNFALL WAS INESCAPABLE.
DESPITE RAYEK'S MIGHTY ATTEMPT TO PREVENT IT--
--THE TROLLS' REVOLT CAST MY COMPANIONS AND ME BACK TO A PITILESS, BRUTAL TIME--
--TO THE LESSON OF PAIN.
BUT THE GREATEST TEACHER OF ALL, FOR ALL TIME--
--IS YOU!

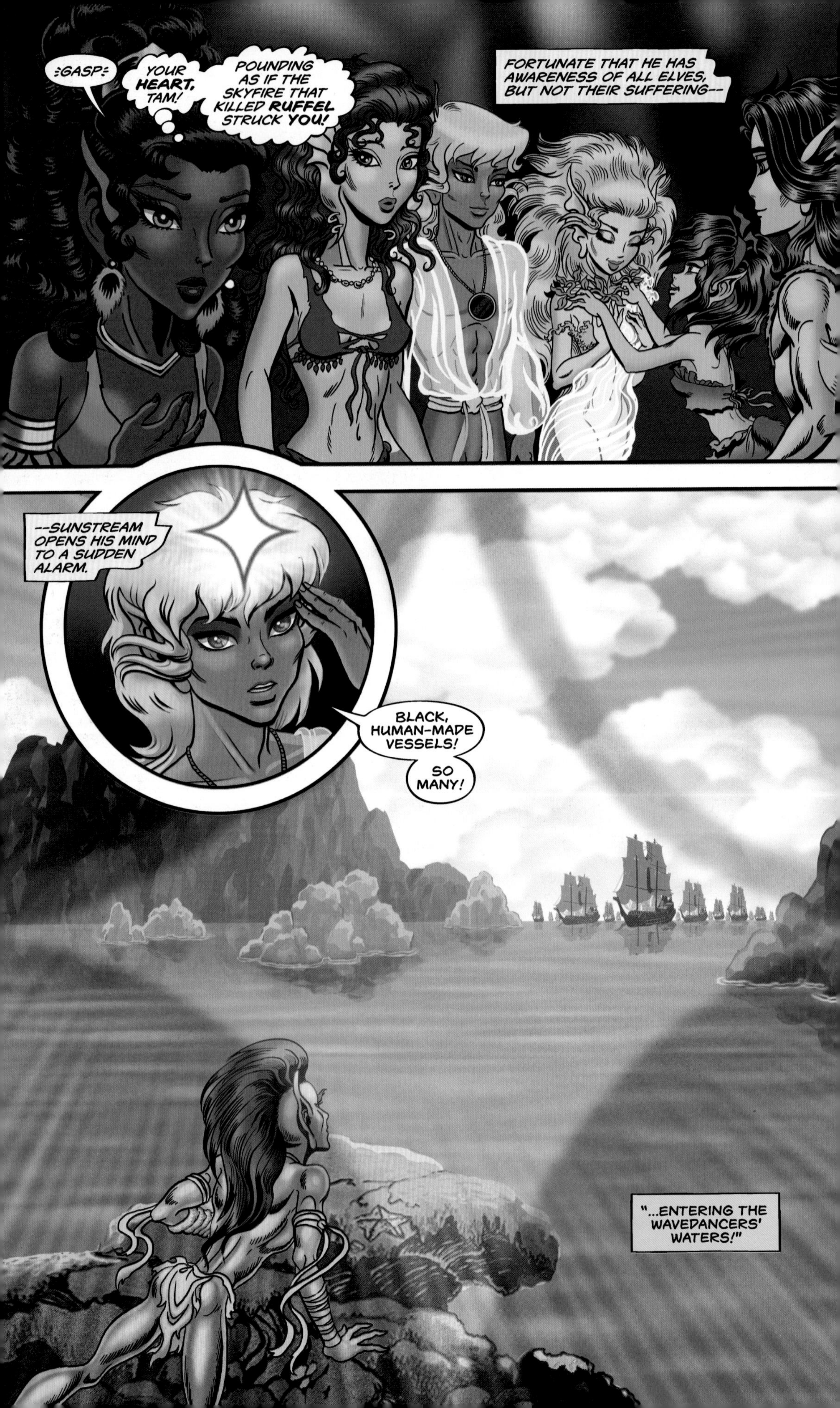

:GASP:
YOUR HEART, TAM!
POUNDING AS IF THE SKYFIRE THAT KILLED RUFFEL STRUCK YOU!
FORTUNATE THAT HE HAS AWARENESS OF ALL ELVES, BUT NOT THEIR SUFFERING--
--SUNSTREAM OPENS HIS MIND TO A SUDDEN ALARM.
BLACK, HUMAN-MADE VESSELS!
SO MANY!
"...ENTERING THE WAVEDANCERS' WATERS!"

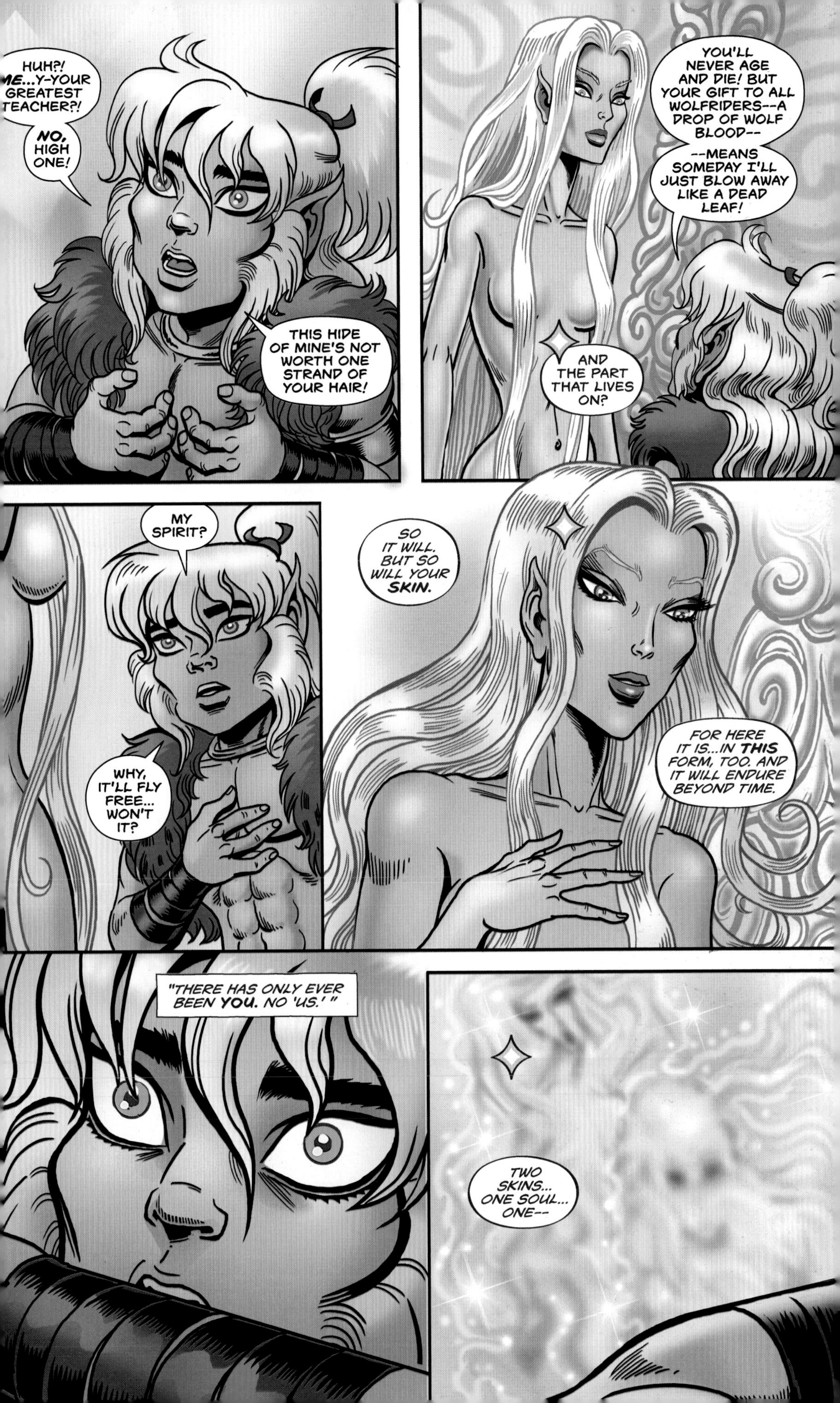

HUH?! ME...Y-YOUR GREATEST TEACHER?!
NO, HIGH ONE!
THIS HIDE OF MINE'S NOT WORTH ONE STRAND OF YOUR HAIR!
YOU'LL NEVER AGE AND DIE! BUT YOUR GIFT TO ALL WOLFRIDERS--A DROP OF WOLF BLOOD--
--MEANS SOMEDAY I'LL JUST BLOW AWAY LIKE A DEAD LEAF!
AND THE PART THAT LIVES ON?
MY SPIRIT?
WHY, IT'LL FLY FREE... WON'T IT?
SO IT WILL. BUT SO WILL YOUR SKIN.
FOR HERE IT IS...IN THIS FORM, TOO. AND IT WILL ENDURE BEYOND TIME.
"THERE HAS ONLY EVER BEEN YOU. NO 'US.' "
TWO SKINS... ONE SOUL... ONE--

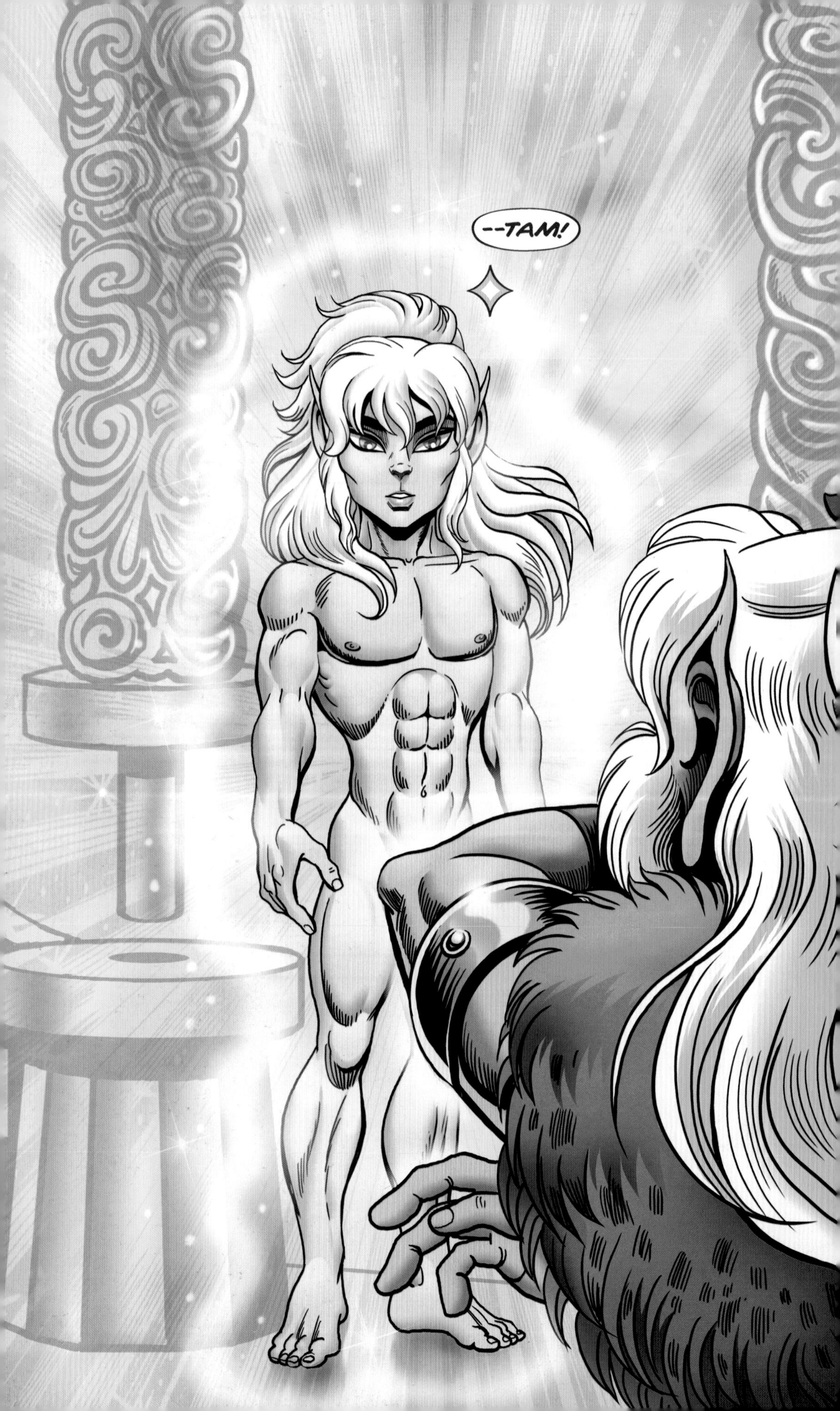
--TAM!

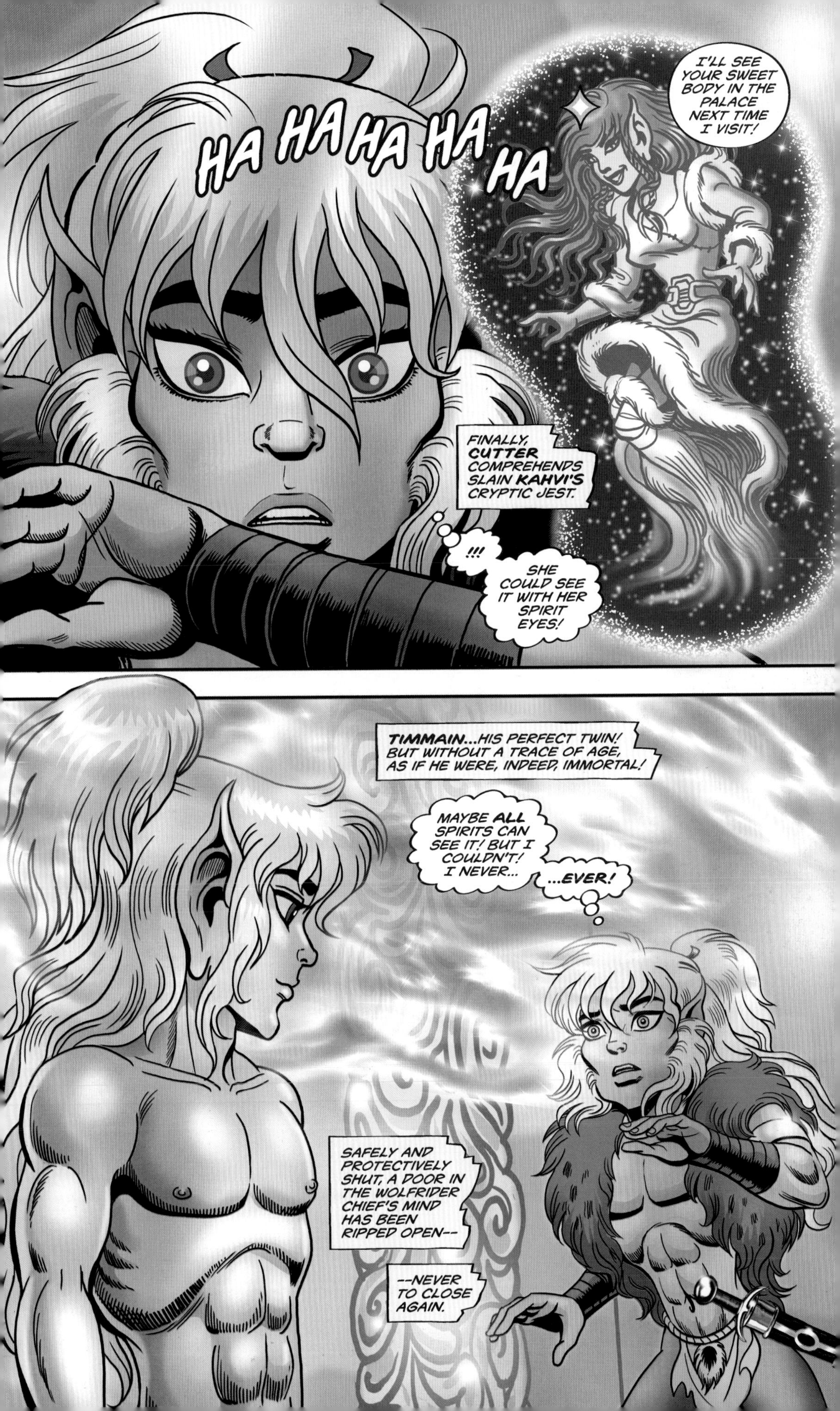
HA HA HA HA HA HA
I'LL SEE YOUR SWEET BODY IN THE PALACE NEXT TIME I VISIT!
FINALLY, CUTTER COMPREHENDS SLAIN KAHVI'S CRYPTIC JEST.
!!!
SHE COULD SEE IT WITH HER SPIRIT EYES!
TIMMAIN...HIS PERFECT TWIN! BUT WITHOUT A TRACE OF AGE, AS IF HE WERE, INDEED, IMMORTAL!
MAYBE ALL SPIRITS CAN SEE IT! BUT I COULDN'T! I NEVER...
...EVER!
SAFELY AND PROTECTIVELY SHUT, A DOOR IN THE WOLFRIDER CHIEF'S MIND HAS BEEN RIPPED OPEN--
--NEVER TO CLOSE AGAIN.

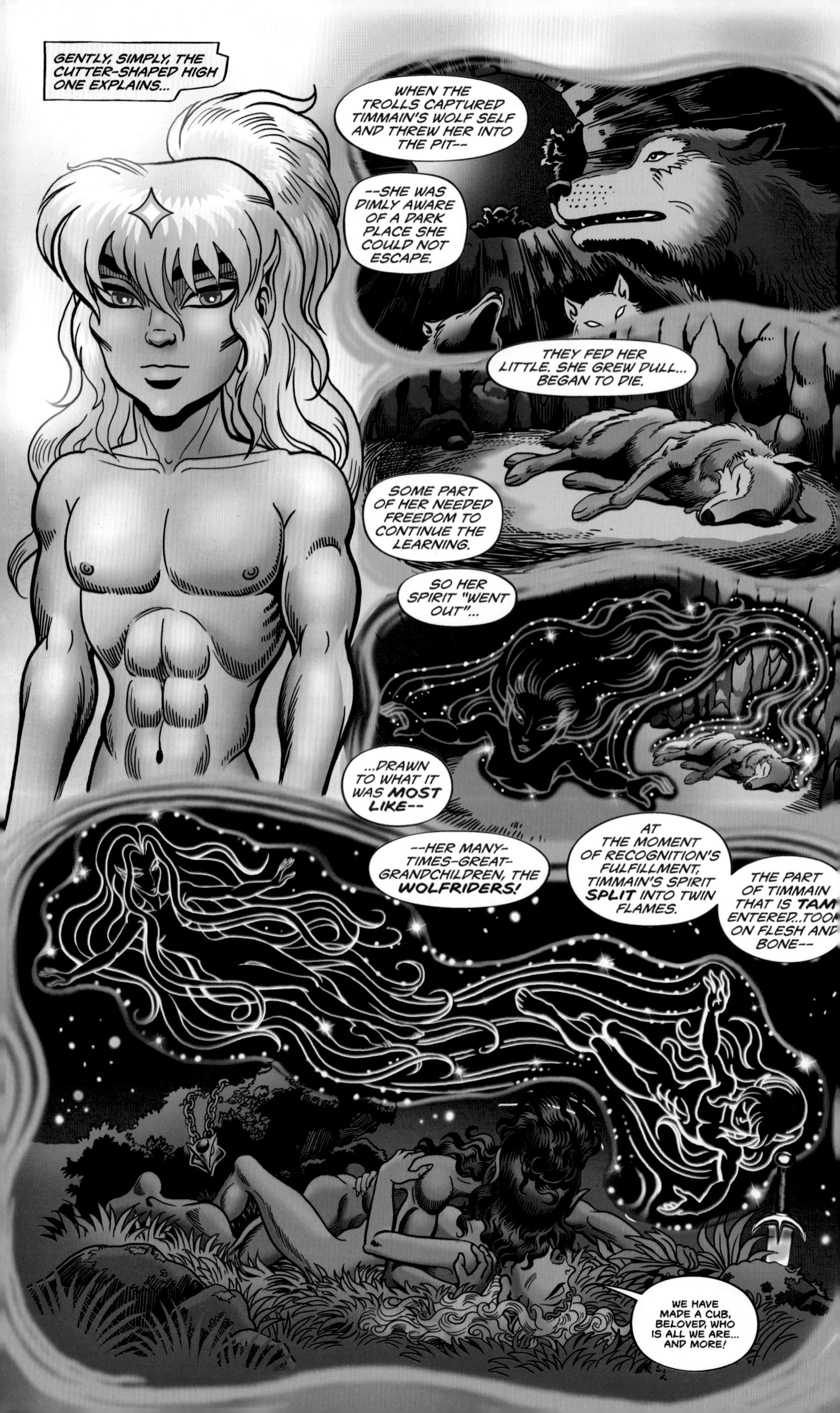
GENTLY, SIMPLY, THE CUTTER-SHAPED HIGH ONE EXPLAINS...
WHEN THE TROLLS CAPTURED TIMMAIN'S WOLF SELF AND THREW HER INTO THE PIT--
--SHE WAS DIMLY AWARE OF A DARK PLACE SHE COULD NOT ESCAPE.
THEY FED HER LITTLE. SHE GREW DULL... BEGAN TO DIE.
SOME PART OF HER NEEDED FREEDOM TO CONTINUE THE LEARNING.
SO HER SPIRIT "WENT OUT"...
...DRAWN TO WHAT IT WAS **MOST LIKE**--
--HER MANY-TIMES-GREAT-GRANDCHILDREN, THE **WOLFRIDERS!**
AT THE MOMENT OF RECOGNITION'S FULFILLMENT, TIMMAIN'S SPIRIT **SPLIT** INTO TWIN FLAMES.
THE PART OF TIMMAIN THAT IS **TAM** ENTERED...TOO ON FLESH AND BONE--
WE HAVE MADE A CUB, BELOVED, WHO IS ALL WE ARE... AND MORE!

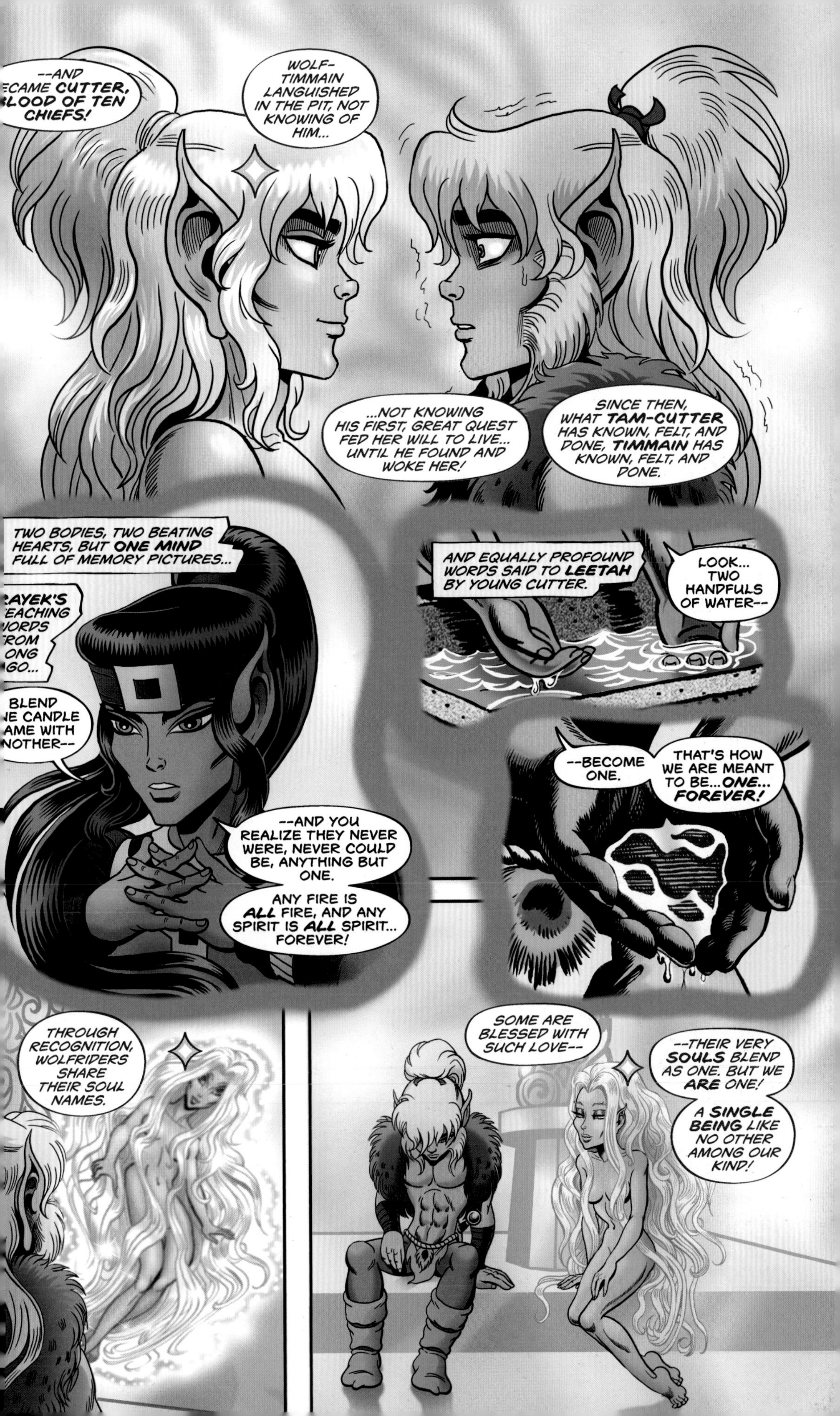
--AND
ECAME **CUTTER, BLOOD OF TEN CHIEFS!**
WOLF-TIMMAIN LANGUISHED IN THE PIT, NOT KNOWING OF HIM...
...NOT KNOWING HIS FIRST, GREAT QUEST FED HER WILL TO LIVE... UNTIL HE FOUND AND WOKE HER!
SINCE THEN, WHAT **TAM-CUTTER** HAS KNOWN, FELT, AND DONE, **TIMMAIN** HAS KNOWN, FELT, AND DONE.
TWO BODIES, TWO BEATING HEARTS, BUT **ONE MIND** FULL OF MEMORY PICTURES...
RAYEK'S EACHING ORDS FROM ONG GO...
BLEND NE CANDLE AME WITH NOTHER--
--AND YOU REALIZE THEY NEVER WERE, NEVER COULD BE, ANYTHING BUT ONE.
ANY FIRE IS **ALL** FIRE, AND ANY SPIRIT IS **ALL** SPIRIT... FOREVER!
AND EQUALLY PROFOUND WORDS SAID TO **LEETAH** BY YOUNG CUTTER.
LOOK... TWO HANDFULS OF WATER--
--BECOME ONE.
THAT'S HOW WE ARE MEANT TO BE...**ONE... FOREVER!**
THROUGH RECOGNITION, WOLFRIDERS SHARE THEIR SOUL NAMES.
SOME ARE BLESSED WITH SUCH LOVE--
--THEIR VERY **SOULS** BLEND AS ONE. BUT WE **ARE** ONE!
A **SINGLE BEING** LIKE NO OTHER AMONG OUR KIND!

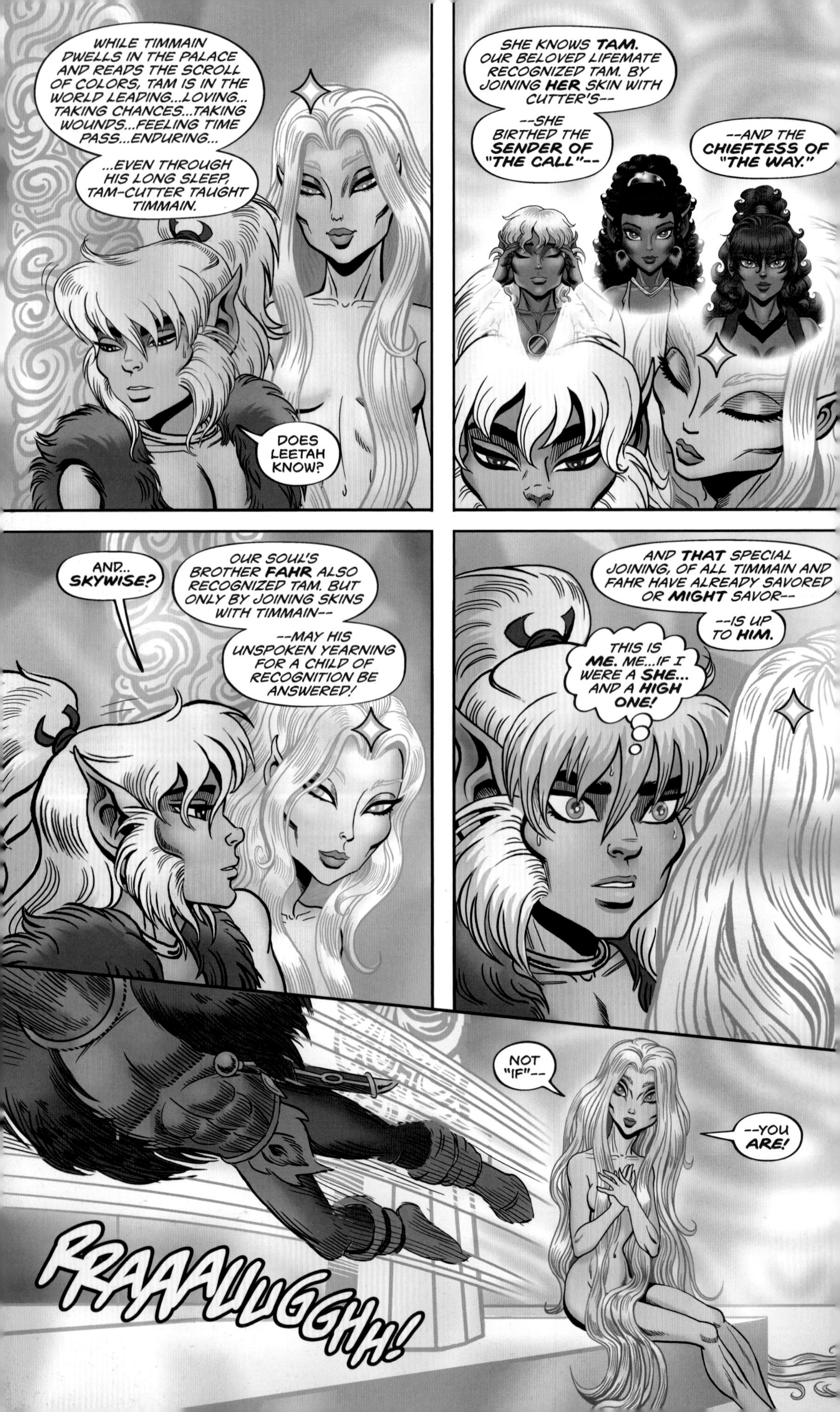

WHILE TIMMAIN DWELLS IN THE PALACE AND READS THE SCROLL OF COLORS, TAM IS IN THE WORLD LEADING...LOVING... TAKING CHANCES...TAKING WOUNDS...FEELING TIME PASS...ENDURING...
...EVEN THROUGH HIS LONG SLEEP, TAM-CUTTER TAUGHT TIMMAIN.
DOES LEETAH KNOW?
SHE KNOWS TAM. OUR BELOVED LIFEMATE RECOGNIZED TAM. BY JOINING HER SKIN WITH CUTTER'S--
--SHE BIRTHED THE SENDER OF "THE CALL"--
--AND THE CHIEFTESS OF "THE WAY."
AND... SKYWISE?
OUR SOUL'S BROTHER FAHR ALSO RECOGNIZED TAM. BUT ONLY BY JOINING SKINS WITH TIMMAIN--
--MAY HIS UNSPOKEN YEARNING FOR A CHILD OF RECOGNITION BE ANSWERED!
AND THAT SPECIAL JOINING, OF ALL TIMMAIN AND FAHR HAVE ALREADY SAVORED OR MIGHT SAVOR--
--IS UP TO HIM.
THIS IS ME. ME...IF I WERE A SHE... AND A HIGH ONE!
NOT "IF"--
--YOU ARE!
RRAAAUUGHH!

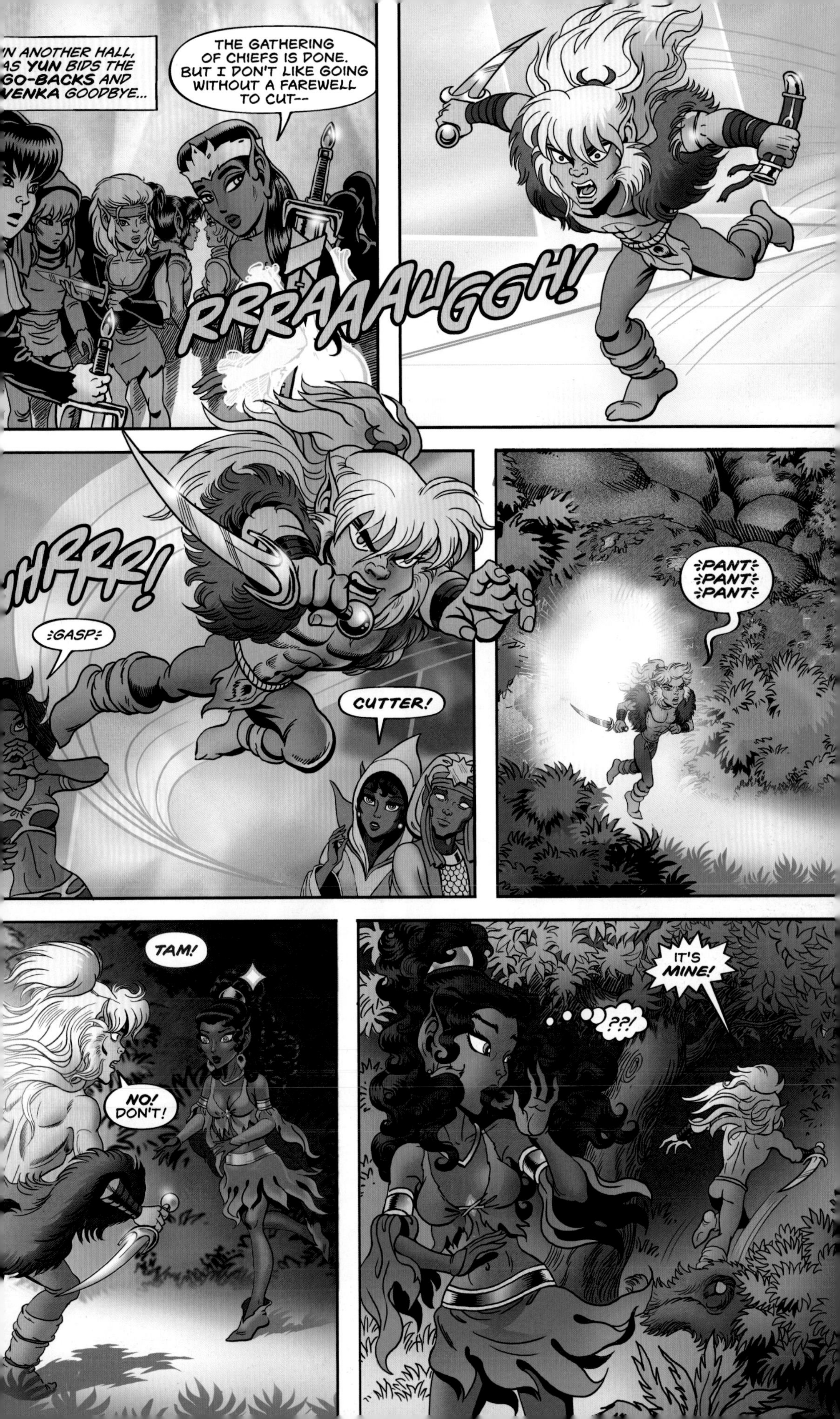

'N ANOTHER HALL, AS YUN BIDS THE GO-BACKS AND VENKA GOODBYE...
THE GATHERING OF CHIEFS IS DONE. BUT I DON'T LIKE GOING WITHOUT A FAREWELL TO CUT--
RRRAAAAUGGH!
HRRR!
GASP
CUTTER!
PANT PANT PANT
TAM!
NO! DON'T!
IT'S MINE!
??!

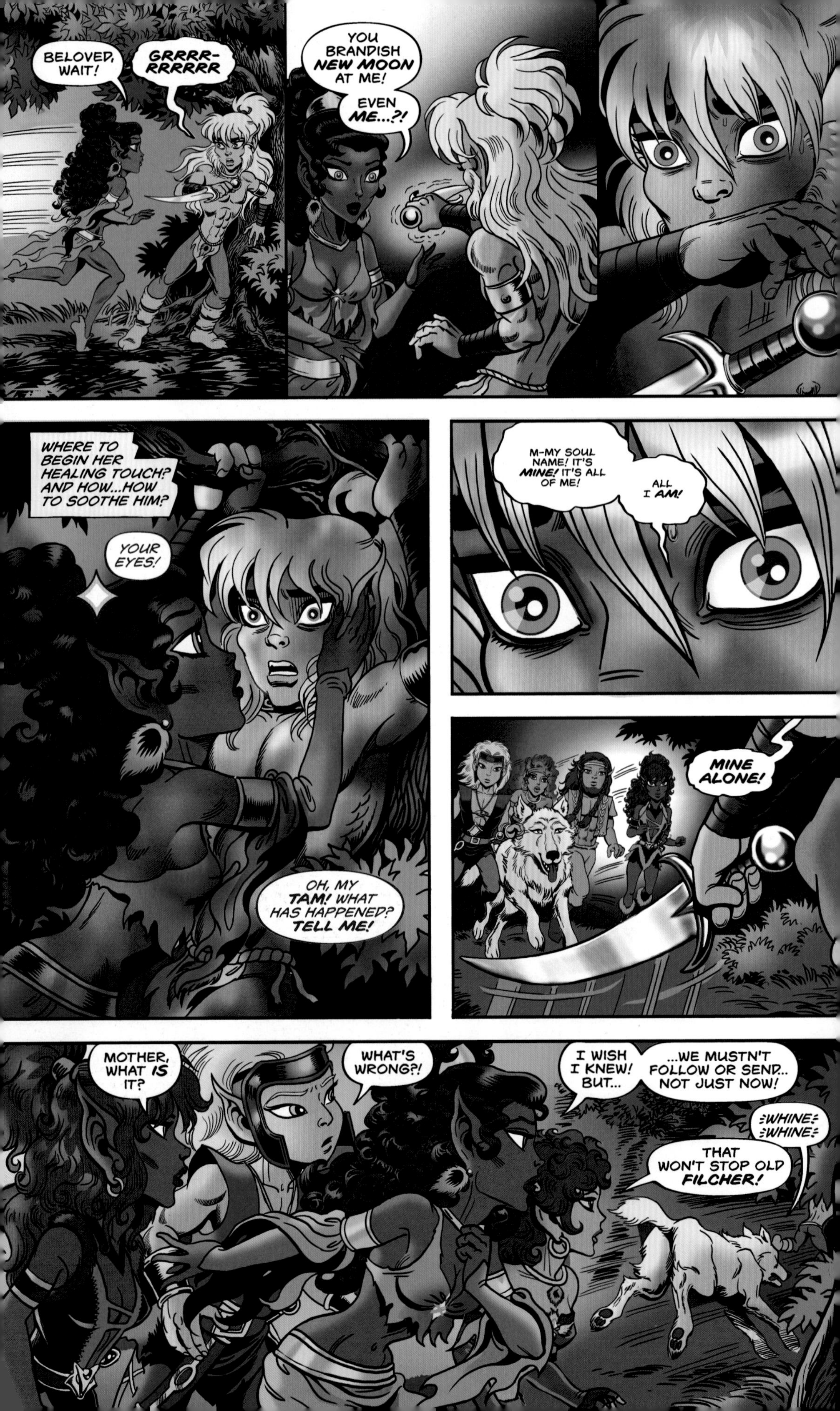
BELOVED, WAIT!
GRRRR-RRRRRR
YOU BRANDISH NEW MOON AT ME!
EVEN ME...?!
WHERE TO BEGIN HER HEALING TOUCH? AND HOW...HOW TO SOOTHE HIM?
YOUR EYES!
OH, MY TAM! WHAT HAS HAPPENED? TELL ME!
M-MY SOUL NAME! IT'S MINE! IT'S ALL OF ME!
ALL I AM!
MINE ALONE!
MOTHER, WHAT IS IT?
WHAT'S WRONG?!
I WISH I KNEW! BUT...
...WE MUSTN'T FOLLOW OR SEND.. NOT JUST NOW!
WHINE WHINE
THAT WON'T STOP OLD FILCHER!

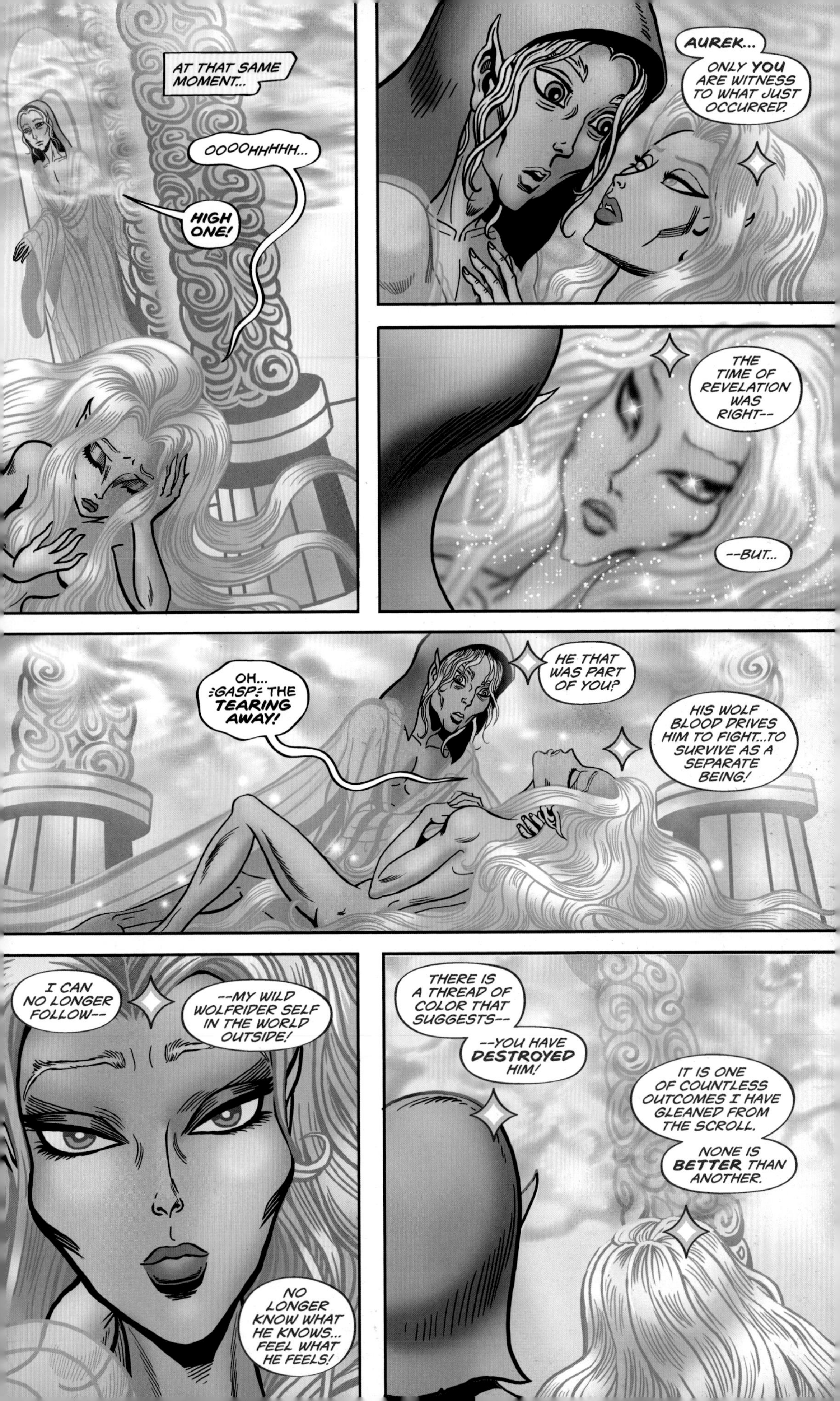
AT THAT SAME MOMENT...
OOOOHHHHH...
HIGH ONE!
AUREK... ONLY YOU ARE WITNESS TO WHAT JUST OCCURRED.
THE TIME OF REVELATION WAS RIGHT--
--BUT...
OH... GASP THE TEARING AWAY!
HE THAT WAS PART OF YOU?
HIS WOLF BLOOD DRIVES HIM TO FIGHT...TO SURVIVE AS A SEPARATE BEING!
I CAN NO LONGER FOLLOW--
--MY WILD WOLFRIDER SELF IN THE WORLD OUTSIDE!
NO LONGER KNOW WHAT HE KNOWS... FEEL WHAT HE FEELS!
THERE IS A THREAD OF COLOR THAT SUGGESTS--
--YOU HAVE DESTROYED HIM!
IT IS ONE OF COUNTLESS OUTCOMES I HAVE GLEANED FROM THE SCROLL.
NONE IS BETTER THAN ANOTHER.

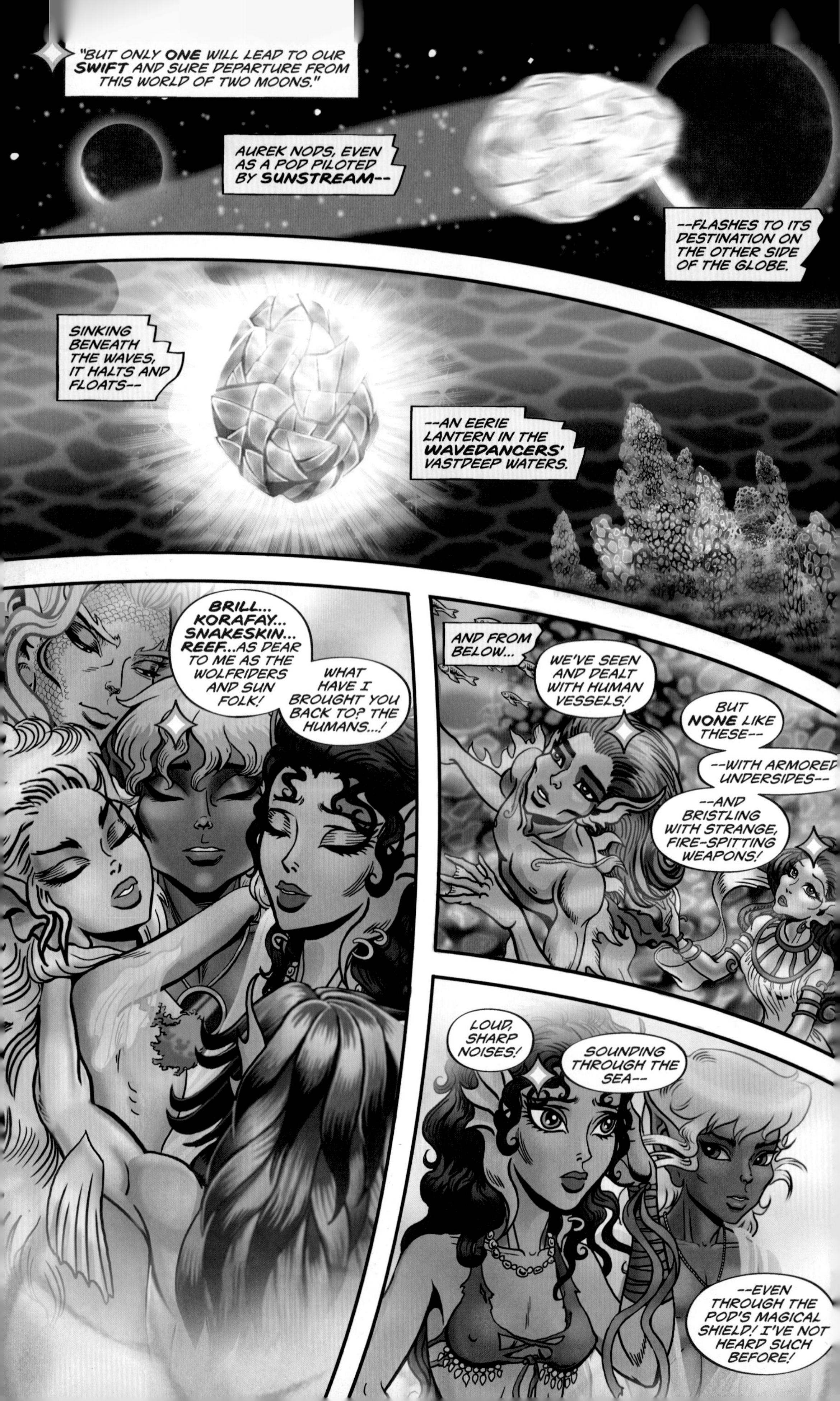
"BUT ONLY ONE WILL LEAD TO OUR SWIFT AND SURE DEPARTURE FROM THIS WORLD OF TWO MOONS."
AUREK NODS, EVEN AS A POD PILOTED BY SUNSTREAM--
--FLASHES TO ITS DESTINATION ON THE OTHER SIDE OF THE GLOBE.
SINKING BENEATH THE WAVES, IT HALTS AND FLOATS--
--AN EERIE LANTERN IN THE WAVEDANCERS' VASTDEEP WATERS.
BRILL... KORAFAY... SNAKESKIN... REEF...AS DEAR TO ME AS THE WOLFRIDERS AND SUN FOLK!
WHAT HAVE I BROUGHT YOU BACK TO? THE HUMANS...!
AND FROM BELOW...
WE'VE SEEN AND DEALT WITH HUMAN VESSELS!
BUT NONE LIKE THESE--
--WITH ARMORED UNDERSIDES--
--AND BRISTLING WITH STRANGE, FIRE-SPITTING WEAPONS!
LOUD, SHARP NOISES!
SOUNDING THROUGH THE SEA--
--EVEN THROUGH THE POD'S MAGICAL SHIELD! I'VE NOT HEARD SUCH BEFORE!

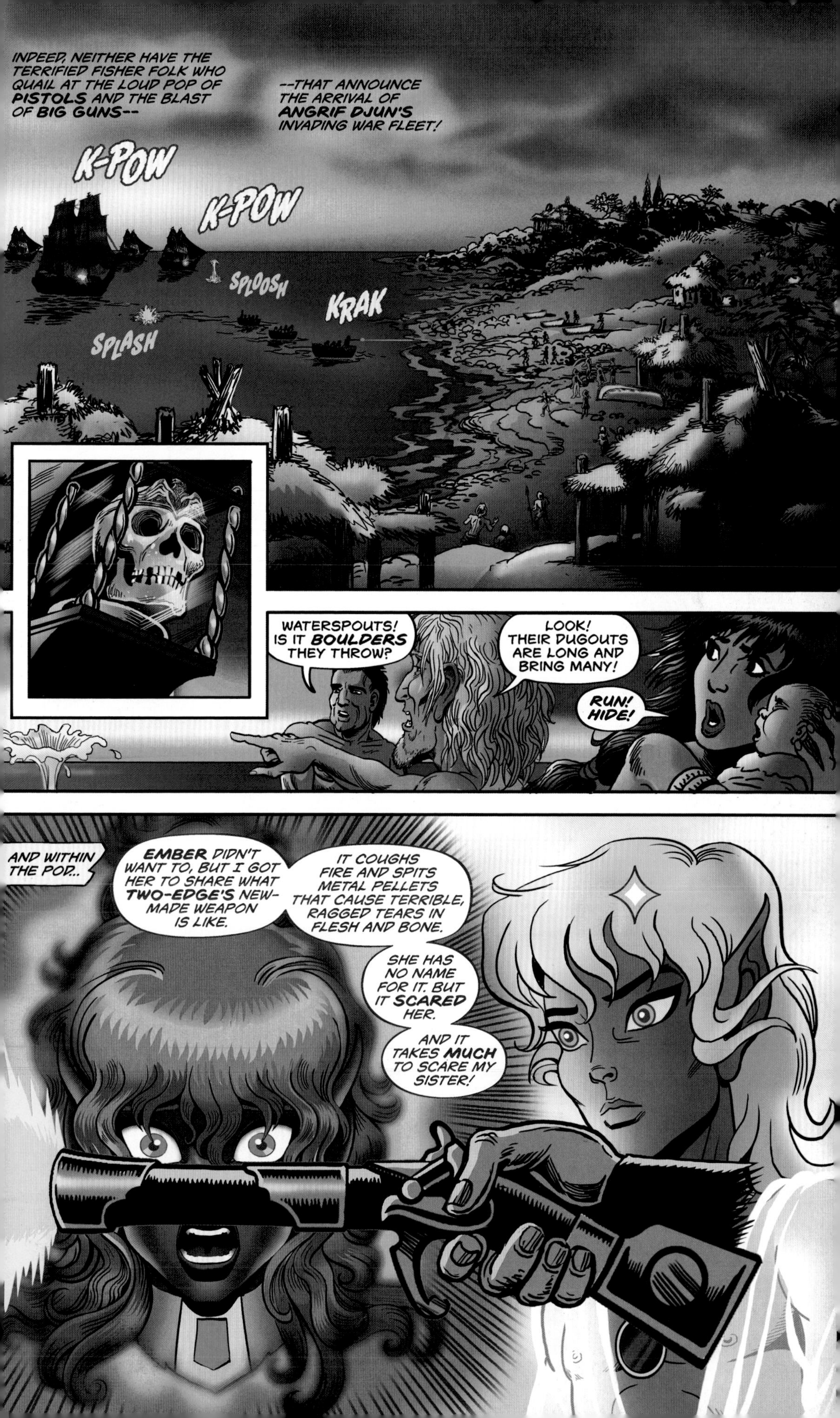
INDEED, NEITHER HAVE THE TERRIFIED FISHER FOLK WHO QUAIL AT THE LOUD POP OF PISTOLS AND THE BLAST OF BIG GUNS--
--THAT ANNOUNCE THE ARRIVAL OF ANGRIF DJUN'S INVADING WAR FLEET!
K-POW
K-POW
SPLOOSH
KRAK
SPLASH
WATERSPOUTS! IS IT BOULDERS THEY THROW?
LOOK! THEIR DUGOUTS ARE LONG AND BRING MANY!
RUN! HIDE!
AND WITHIN THE POD...
EMBER DIDN'T WANT TO, BUT I GOT HER TO SHARE WHAT TWO-EDGE'S NEW-MADE WEAPON IS LIKE.
IT COUGHS FIRE AND SPITS METAL PELLETS THAT CAUSE TERRIBLE, RAGGED TEARS IN FLESH AND BONE.
SHE HAS NO NAME FOR IT. BUT IT SCARED HER.
AND IT TAKES MUCH TO SCARE MY SISTER!

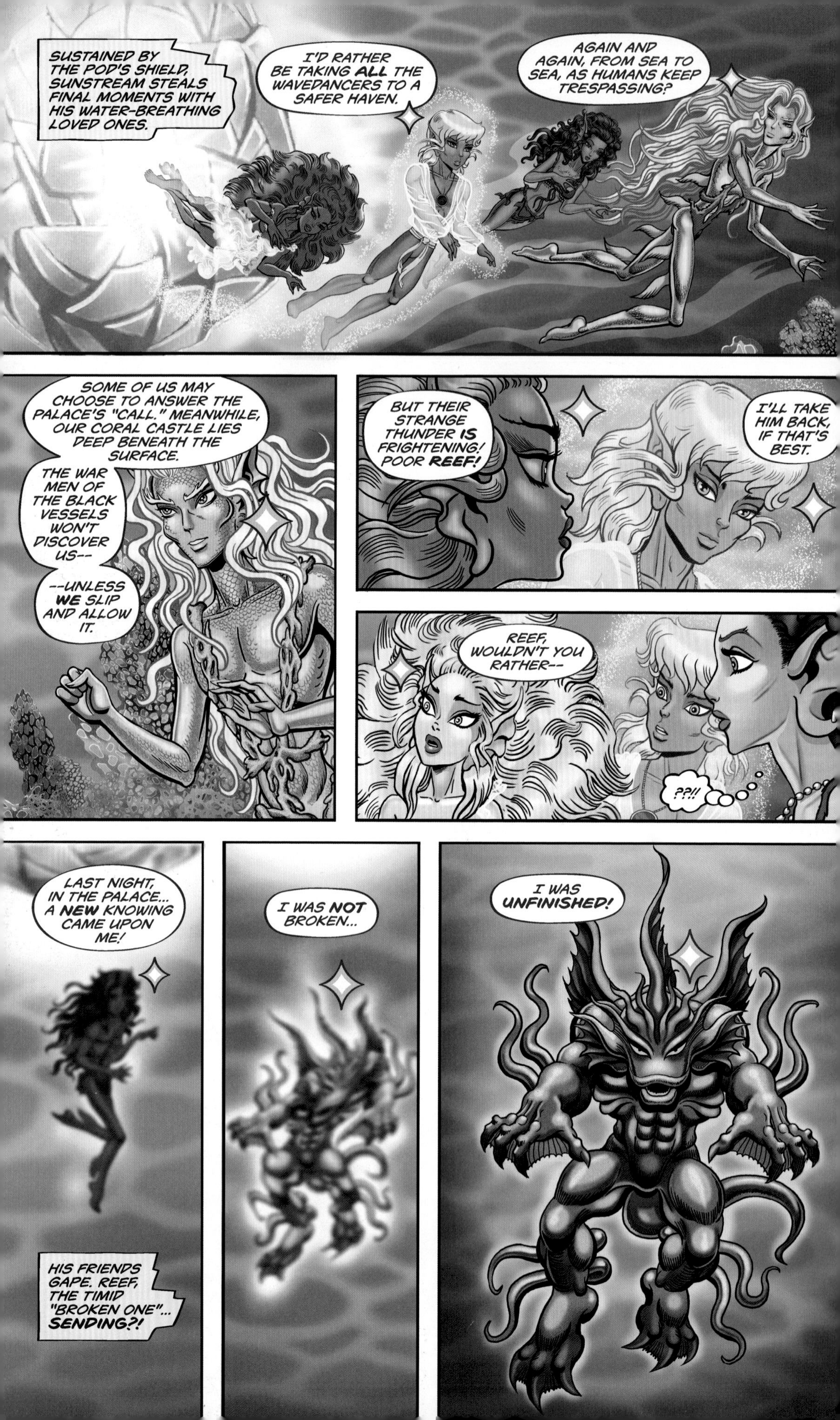
SUSTAINED BY THE POD'S SHIELD, SUNSTREAM STEALS FINAL MOMENTS WITH HIS WATER-BREATHING LOVED ONES.
I'D RATHER BE TAKING ALL THE WAVEDANCERS TO A SAFER HAVEN.
AGAIN AND AGAIN, FROM SEA TO SEA, AS HUMANS KEEP TRESPASSING?
SOME OF US MAY CHOOSE TO ANSWER THE PALACE'S "CALL." MEANWHILE, OUR CORAL CASTLE LIES DEEP BENEATH THE SURFACE.
THE WAR MEN OF THE BLACK VESSELS WON'T DISCOVER US--
--UNLESS WE SLIP AND ALLOW IT.
BUT THEIR STRANGE THUNDER IS FRIGHTENING! POOR REEF!
I'LL TAKE HIM BACK, IF THAT'S BEST.
REEF, WOULDN'T YOU RATHER--
??!!
LAST NIGHT, IN THE PALACE... A NEW KNOWING CAME UPON ME!
HIS FRIENDS GAPE. REEF, THE TIMID "BROKEN ONE"... SENDING?!
I WAS NOT BROKEN...
I WAS UNFINISHED!

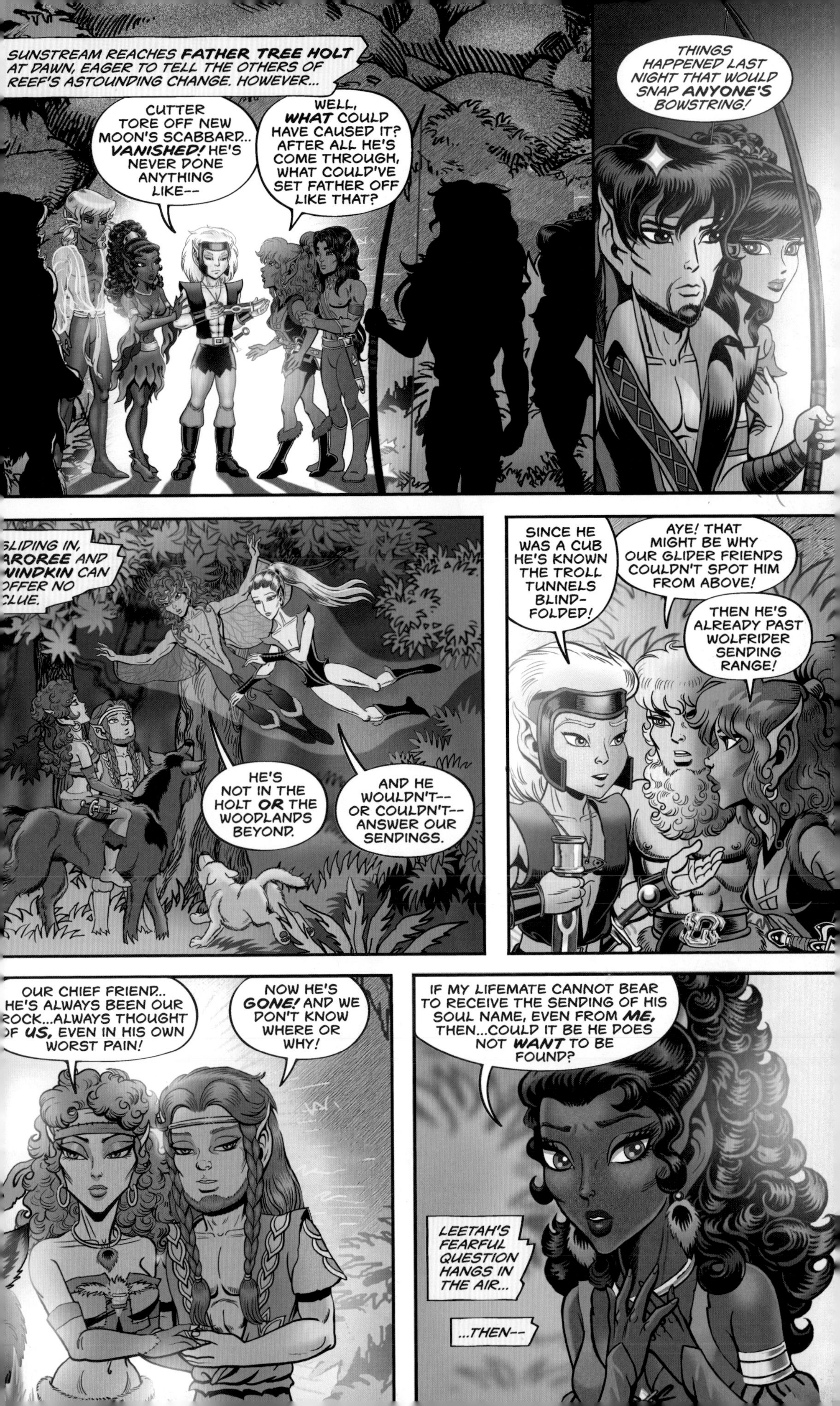

SUNSTREAM REACHES FATHER TREE HOLT AT DAWN, EAGER TO TELL THE OTHERS OF REEF'S ASTOUNDING CHANGE. HOWEVER...
CUTTER TORE OFF NEW MOON'S SCABBARD.. VANISHED! HE'S NEVER DONE ANYTHING LIKE--
WELL, WHAT COULD HAVE CAUSED IT? AFTER ALL HE'S COME THROUGH, WHAT COULD'VE SET FATHER OFF LIKE THAT?
THINGS HAPPENED LAST NIGHT THAT WOULD SNAP ANYONE'S BOWSTRING!
SLIDING IN, AROREE AND WINDKIN CAN OFFER NO CLUE.
HE'S NOT IN THE HOLT OR THE WOODLANDS BEYOND.
AND HE WOULDN'T-- OR COULDN'T-- ANSWER OUR SENDINGS.
SINCE HE WAS A CUB HE'S KNOWN THE TROLL TUNNELS BLIND-FOLDED!
AYE! THAT MIGHT BE WHY OUR GLIDER FRIENDS COULDN'T SPOT HIM FROM ABOVE!
THEN HE'S ALREADY PAST WOLFRIDER SENDING RANGE!
OUR CHIEF FRIEND.. HE'S ALWAYS BEEN OUR ROCK...ALWAYS THOUGHT OF US, EVEN IN HIS OWN WORST PAIN!
NOW HE'S GONE! AND WE DON'T KNOW WHERE OR WHY!
IF MY LIFEMATE CANNOT BEAR TO RECEIVE THE SENDING OF HIS SOUL NAME, EVEN FROM ME, THEN...COULD IT BE HE DOES NOT WANT TO BE FOUND?
LEETAH'S FEARFUL QUESTION HANGS IN THE AIR...
...THEN--

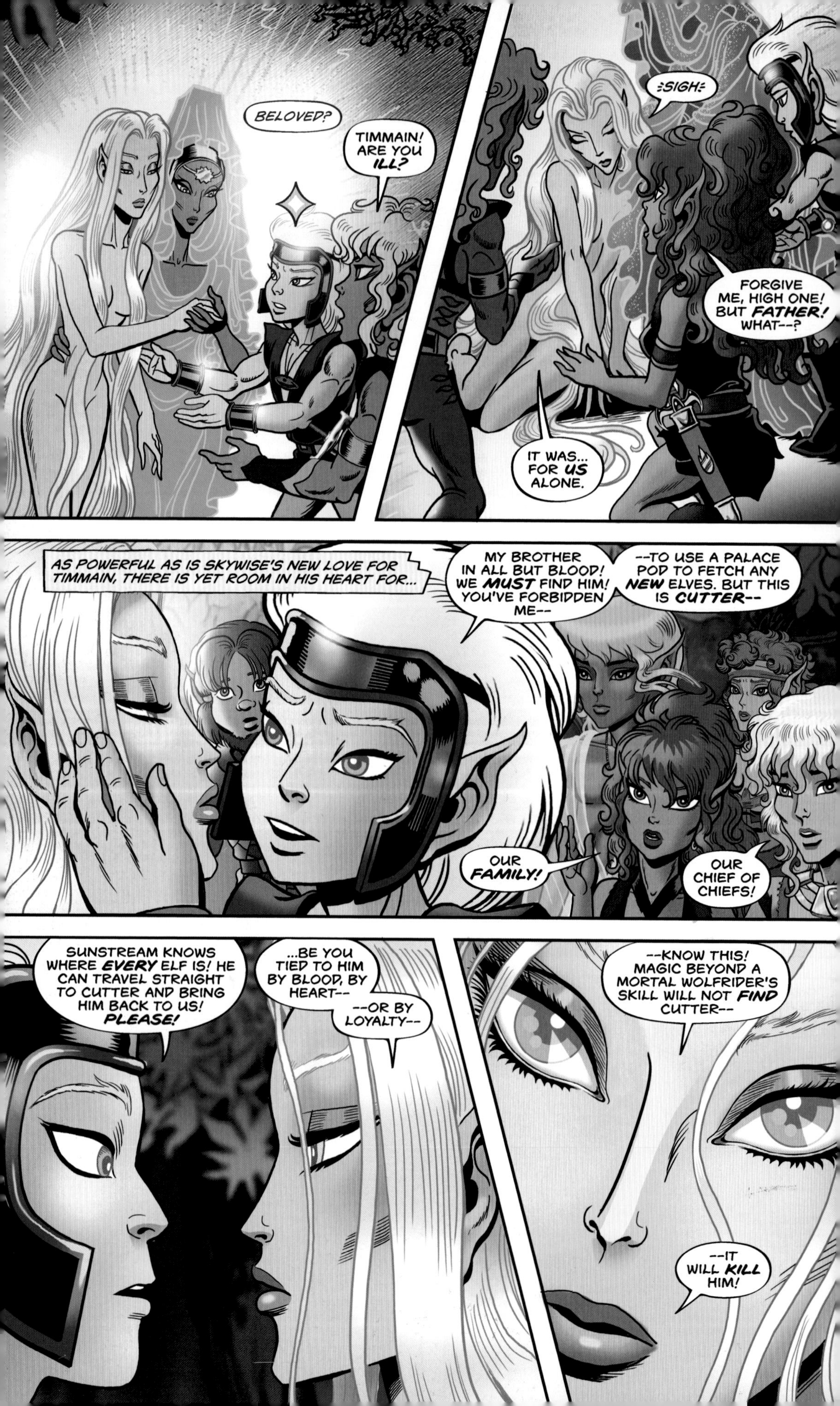
BELOVED?
TIMMAIN! ARE YOU ILL?
:SIGH:
FORGIVE ME, HIGH ONE! BUT FATHER! WHAT--?
IT WAS... FOR US ALONE.
AS POWERFUL AS IS SKYWISE'S NEW LOVE FOR TIMMAIN, THERE IS YET ROOM IN HIS HEART FOR...
MY BROTHER IN ALL BUT BLOOD! WE MUST FIND HIM! YOU'VE FORBIDDEN ME--
--TO USE A PALACE POD TO FETCH ANY NEW ELVES. BUT THIS IS CUTTER--
OUR FAMILY!
OUR CHIEF OF CHIEFS!
SUNSTREAM KNOWS WHERE EVERY ELF IS! HE CAN TRAVEL STRAIGHT TO CUTTER AND BRING HIM BACK TO US! PLEASE!
...BE YOU TIED TO HIM BY BLOOD, BY HEART--
--OR BY LOYALTY--
--KNOW THIS! MAGIC BEYOND A MORTAL WOLFRIDER'S SKILL WILL NOT FIND CUTTER--
--IT WILL KILL HIM!

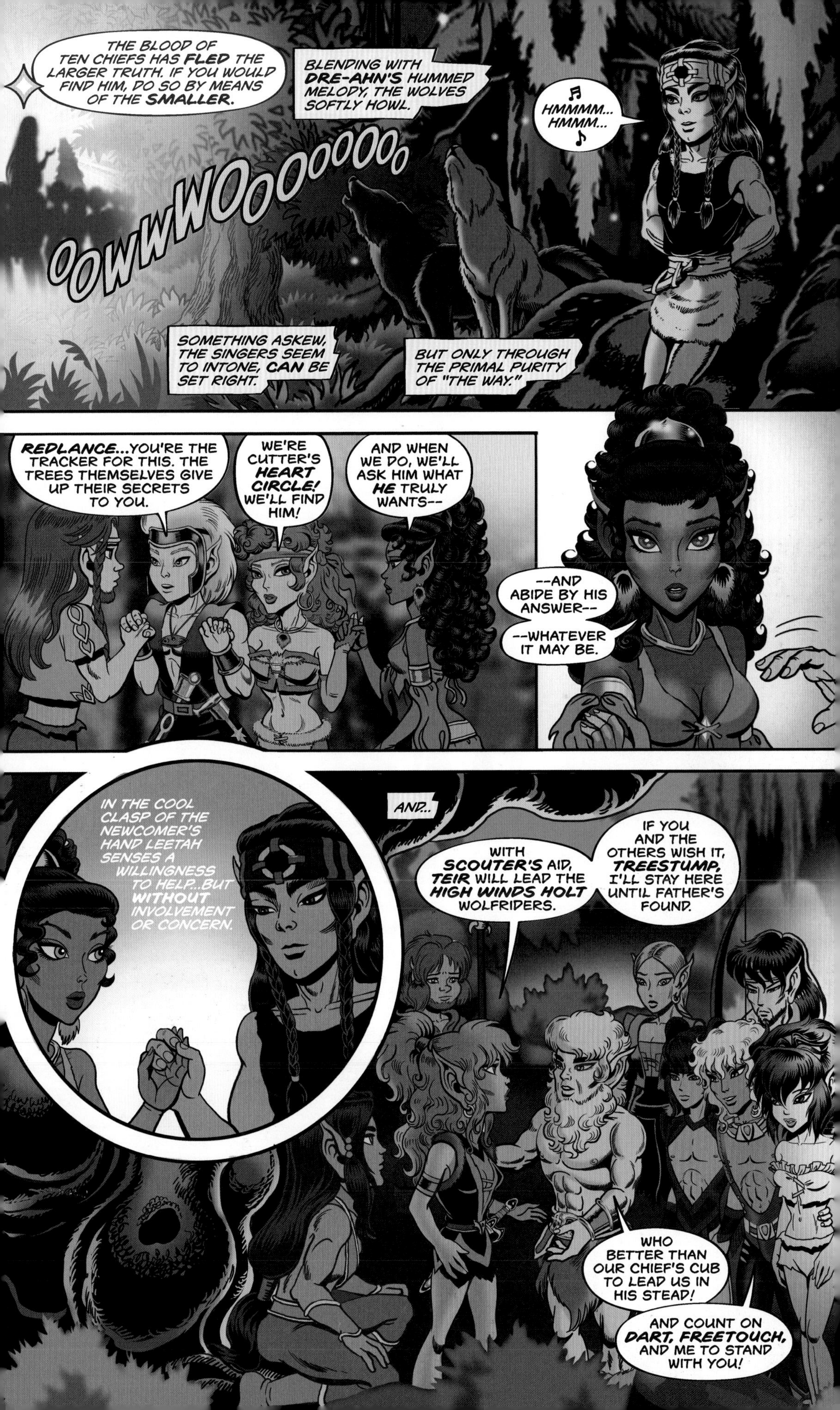
THE BLOOD OF TEN CHIEFS HAS FLED THE LARGER TRUTH. IF YOU WOULD FIND HIM, DO SO BY MEANS OF THE SMALLER.
BLENDING WITH DRE-AHN'S HUMMED MELODY, THE WOLVES SOFTLY HOWL.
HMMMM... HMMM...
OOWWWOOOOOOOO
SOMETHING ASKEW, THE SINGERS SEEM TO INTONE, CAN BE SET RIGHT.
BUT ONLY THROUGH THE PRIMAL PURITY OF "THE WAY."
REDLANCE...YOU'RE THE TRACKER FOR THIS. THE TREES THEMSELVES GIVE UP THEIR SECRETS TO YOU.
WE'RE CUTTER'S HEART CIRCLE! WE'LL FIND HIM!
AND WHEN WE DO, WE'LL ASK HIM WHAT HE TRULY WANTS--
--AND ABIDE BY HIS ANSWER--
--WHATEVER IT MAY BE.
IN THE COOL CLASP OF THE NEWCOMER'S HAND LEETAH SENSES A WILLINGNESS TO HELP...BUT WITHOUT INVOLVEMENT OR CONCERN.
AND..
WITH SCOUTER'S AID, TEIR WILL LEAD THE HIGH WINDS HOLT WOLFRIDERS.
IF YOU AND THE OTHERS WISH IT, TREESTUMP, I'LL STAY HERE UNTIL FATHER'S FOUND.
WHO BETTER THAN OUR CHIEF'S CUB TO LEAD US IN HIS STEAD!
AND COUNT ON DART, FREETOUCH, AND ME TO STAND WITH YOU!

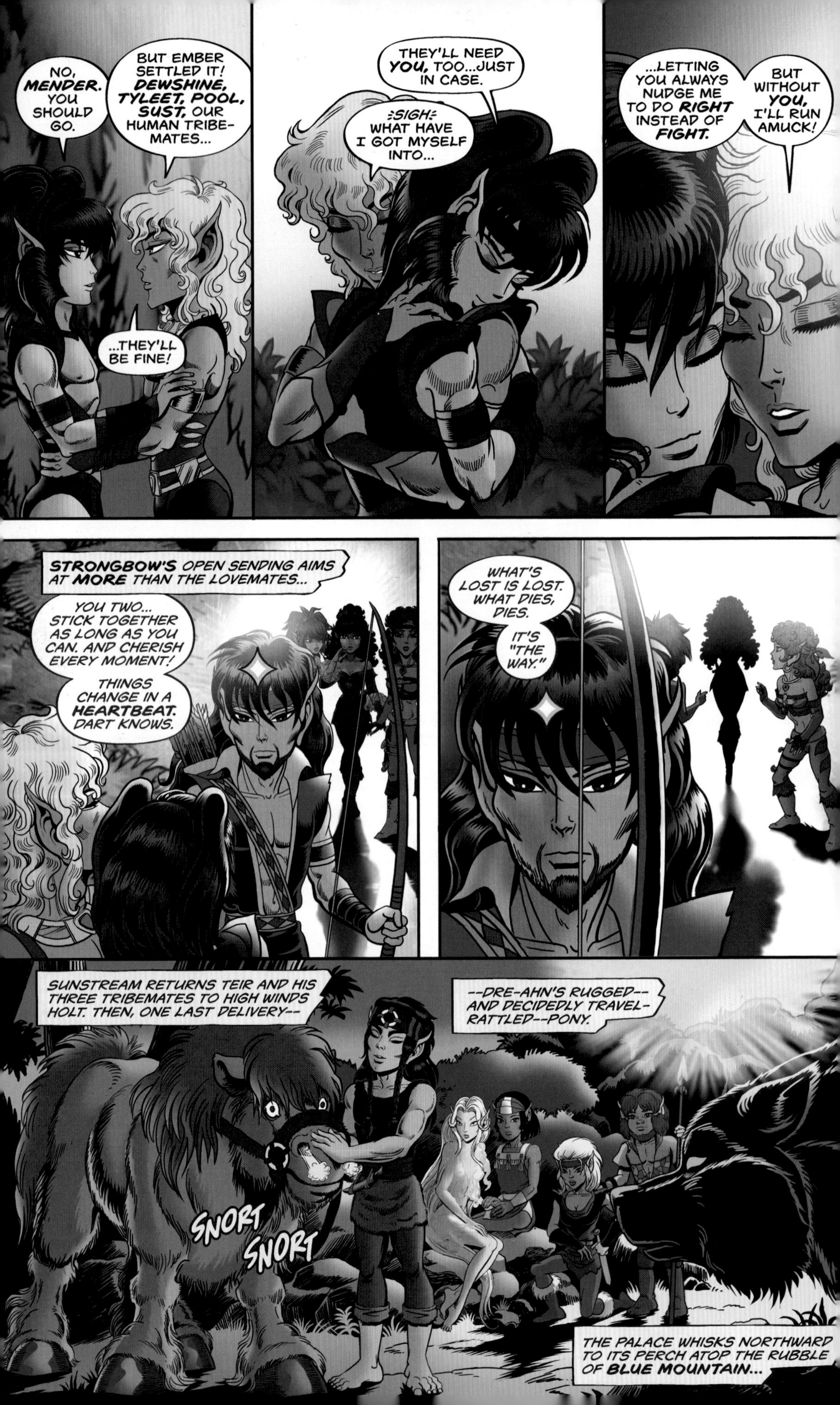

NO, MENDER. YOU SHOULD GO.
BUT EMBER SETTLED IT! DEWSHINE, TYLEET, POOL, SUST, OUR HUMAN TRIBE-MATES...
...THEY'LL BE FINE!
THEY'LL NEED YOU, TOO...JUST IN CASE.
SIGH WHAT HAVE I GOT MYSELF INTO...
...LETTING YOU ALWAYS NUDGE ME TO DO RIGHT INSTEAD OF FIGHT.
BUT WITHOUT YOU, I'LL RUN AMUCK!
STRONGBOW'S OPEN SENDING AIMS AT MORE THAN THE LOVEMATES...
YOU TWO... STICK TOGETHER AS LONG AS YOU CAN. AND CHERISH EVERY MOMENT!
THINGS CHANGE IN A HEARTBEAT. DART KNOWS.
WHAT'S LOST IS LOST. WHAT DIES, DIES.
IT'S "THE WAY."
SUNSTREAM RETURNS TEIR AND HIS THREE TRIBEMATES TO HIGH WINDS HOLT. THEN, ONE LAST DELIVERY--
--DRE-AHN'S RUGGED-- AND DECIDEDLY TRAVEL-RATTLED--PONY.
SNORT
SNORT
THE PALACE WHISKS NORTHWARD TO ITS PERCH ATOP THE RUBBLE OF BLUE MOUNTAIN...

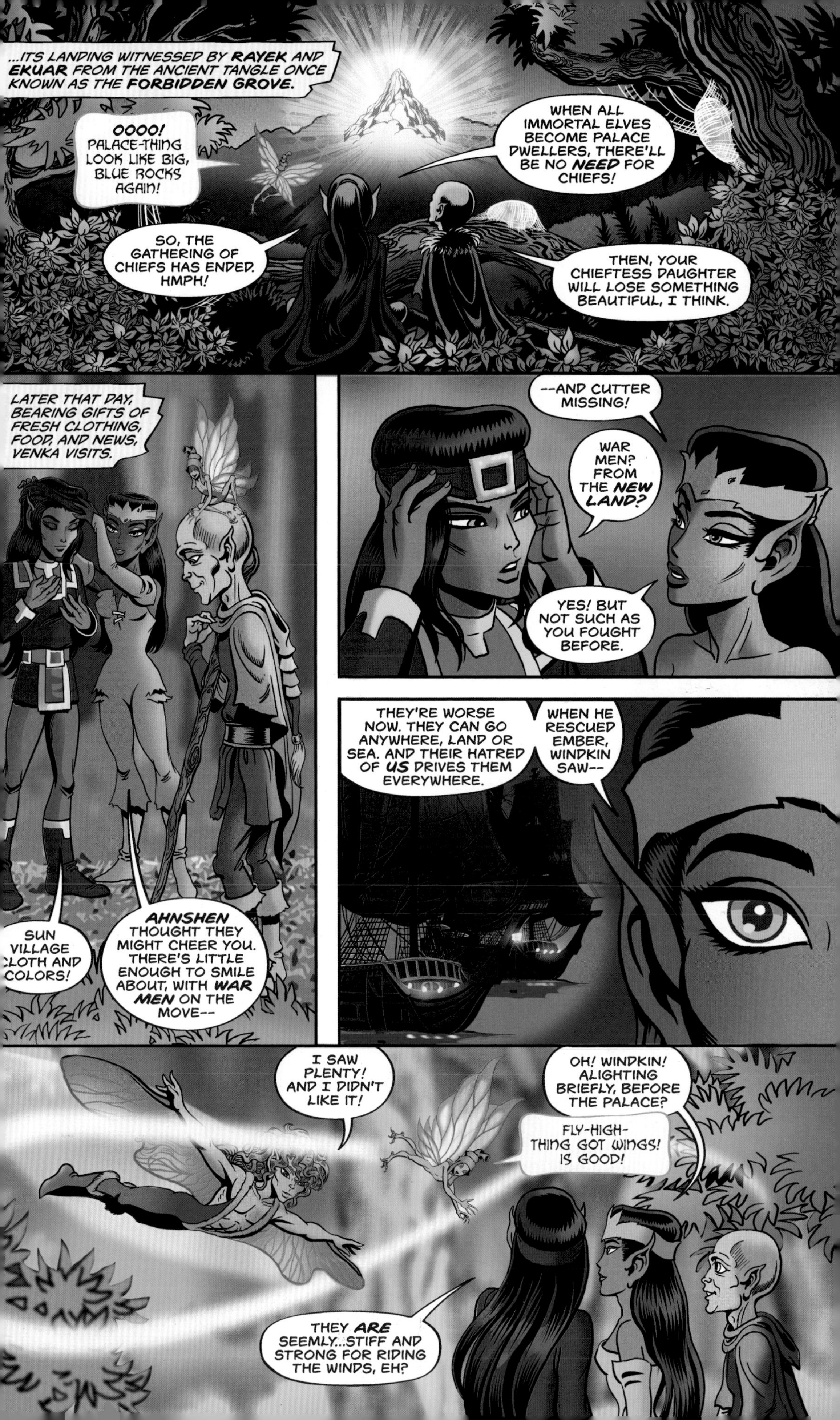
...ITS LANDING WITNESSED BY RAYEK AND EKUAR FROM THE ANCIENT TANGLE ONCE KNOWN AS THE FORBIDDEN GROVE.
OOOO! PALACE-THING LOOK LIKE BIG, BLUE ROCKS AGAIN!
WHEN ALL IMMORTAL ELVES BECOME PALACE DWELLERS, THERE'LL BE NO NEED FOR CHIEFS!
SO, THE GATHERING OF CHIEFS HAS ENDED. HMPH!
THEN, YOUR CHIEFTESS DAUGHTER WILL LOSE SOMETHING BEAUTIFUL, I THINK.
LATER THAT DAY, BEARING GIFTS OF FRESH CLOTHING, FOOD, AND NEWS, VENKA VISITS.
SUN VILLAGE CLOTH AND COLORS!
AHNSHEN THOUGHT THEY MIGHT CHEER YOU. THERE'S LITTLE ENOUGH TO SMILE ABOUT, WITH WAR MEN ON THE MOVE--
--AND CUTTER MISSING!
WAR MEN? FROM THE NEW LAND?
YES! BUT NOT SUCH AS YOU FOUGHT BEFORE.
THEY'RE WORSE NOW. THEY CAN GO ANYWHERE, LAND OR SEA. AND THEIR HATRED OF US DRIVES THEM EVERYWHERE.
WHEN HE RESCUED EMBER, WINDKIN SAW--
I SAW PLENTY! AND I DIDN'T LIKE IT!
OH! WINDKIN! ALIGHTING BRIEFLY, BEFORE THE PALACE?
FLY-HIGH-THING GOT WINGS! IS GOOD!
THEY ARE SEEMLY...STIFF AND STRONG FOR RIDING THE WINDS, EH?

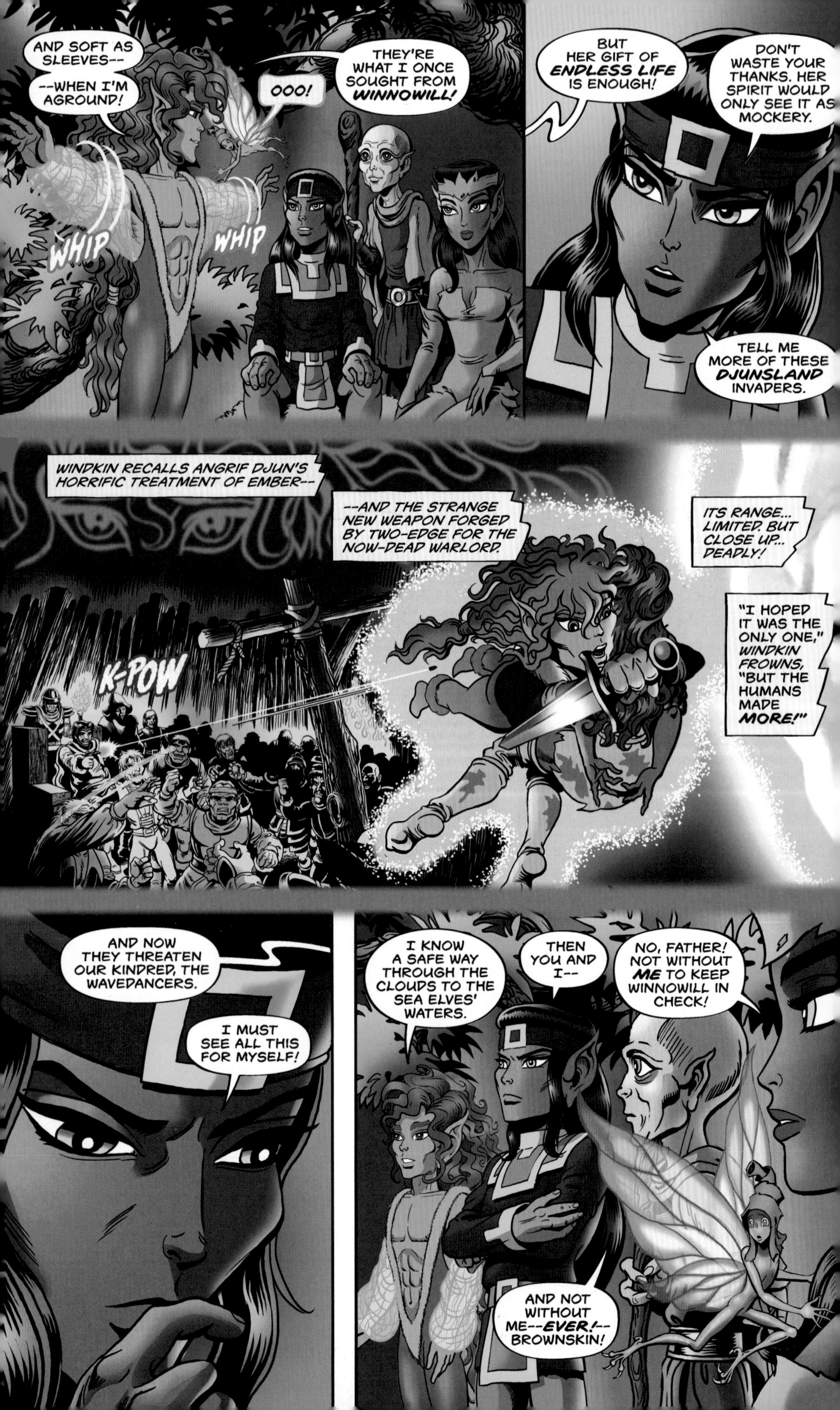
AND SOFT AS SLEEVES--
--WHEN I'M AGROUND!
OOO!
THEY'RE WHAT I ONCE SOUGHT FROM WINNOWILL!
WHIP
WHIP
BUT HER GIFT OF ENDLESS LIFE IS ENOUGH!
DON'T WASTE YOUR THANKS. HER SPIRIT WOULD ONLY SEE IT AS MOCKERY.
TELL ME MORE OF THESE DJUNSLAND INVADERS.
WINDKIN RECALLS ANGRIF DJUN'S HORRIFIC TREATMENT OF EMBER--
--AND THE STRANGE NEW WEAPON FORGED BY TWO-EDGE FOR THE NOW-DEAD WARLORD.
ITS RANGE... LIMITED. BUT CLOSE UP... DEADLY!
K-POW
"I HOPED IT WAS THE ONLY ONE," WINDKIN FROWNS, "BUT THE HUMANS MADE MORE!"
AND NOW THEY THREATEN OUR KINDRED, THE WAVEDANCERS.
I MUST SEE ALL THIS FOR MYSELF!
I KNOW A SAFE WAY THROUGH THE CLOUDS TO THE SEA ELVES' WATERS.
THEN YOU AND I--
NO, FATHER! NOT WITHOUT ME TO KEEP WINNOWILL IN CHECK!
AND NOT WITHOUT ME--EVER!--BROWNSKIN!

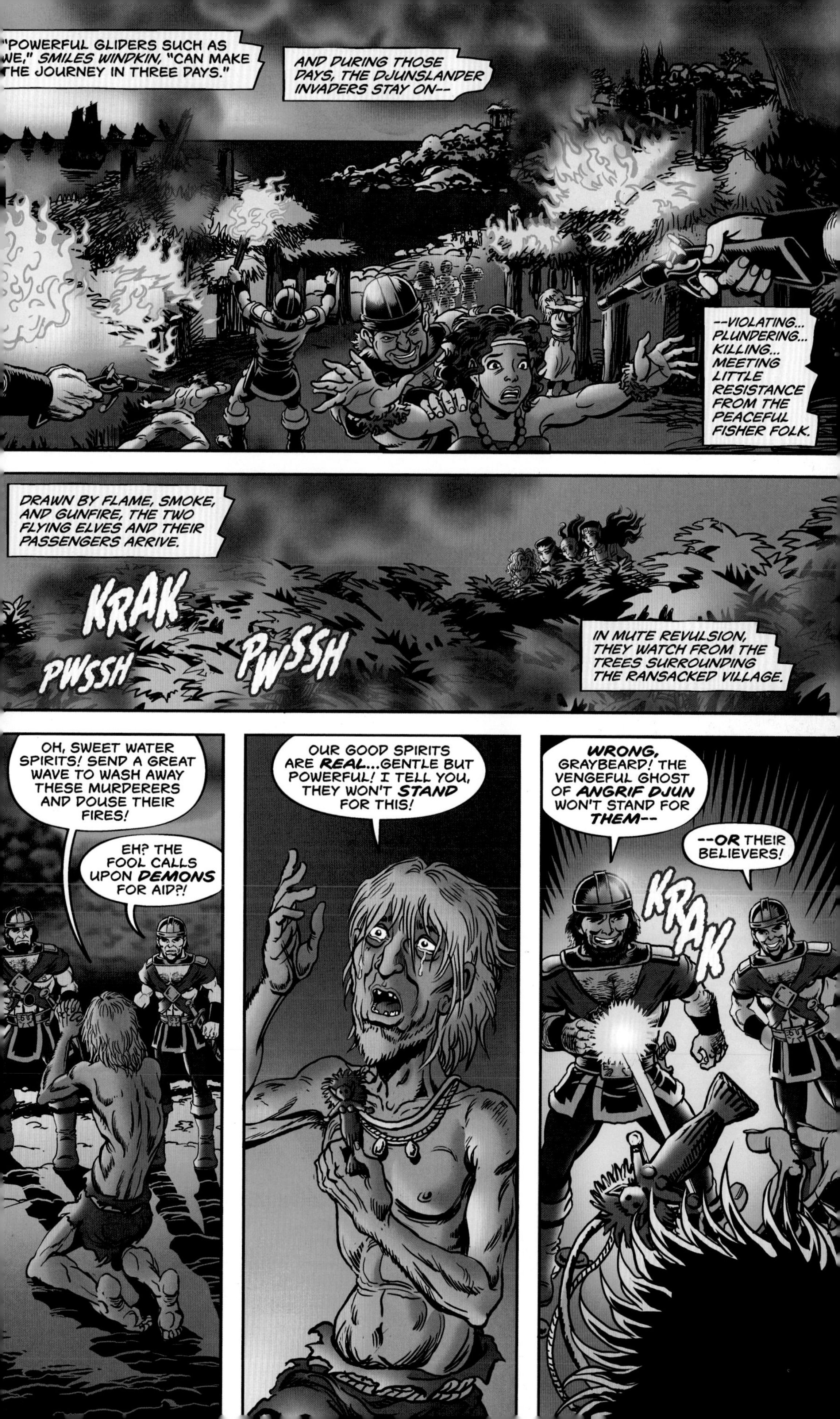
"POWERFUL GLIDERS SUCH AS WE," SMILES WINDKIN, "CAN MAKE THE JOURNEY IN THREE DAYS."
AND DURING THOSE DAYS, THE DJUNSLANDER INVADERS STAY ON--
--VIOLATING... PLUNDERING... KILLING... MEETING LITTLE RESISTANCE FROM THE PEACEFUL FISHER FOLK.
DRAWN BY FLAME, SMOKE, AND GUNFIRE, THE TWO FLYING ELVES AND THEIR PASSENGERS ARRIVE.
KRAK
PWSSH
PWSSH
IN MUTE REVULSION, THEY WATCH FROM THE TREES SURROUNDING THE RANSACKED VILLAGE.
OH, SWEET WATER SPIRITS! SEND A GREAT WAVE TO WASH AWAY THESE MURDERERS AND DOUSE THEIR FIRES!
EH? THE FOOL CALLS UPON DEMONS FOR AID?!
OUR GOOD SPIRITS ARE REAL...GENTLE BUT POWERFUL! I TELL YOU, THEY WON'T STAND FOR THIS!
WRONG, GRAYBEARD! THE VENGEFUL GHOST OF ANGRIF DJUN WON'T STAND FOR THEM--
--OR THEIR BELIEVERS!
KRAK

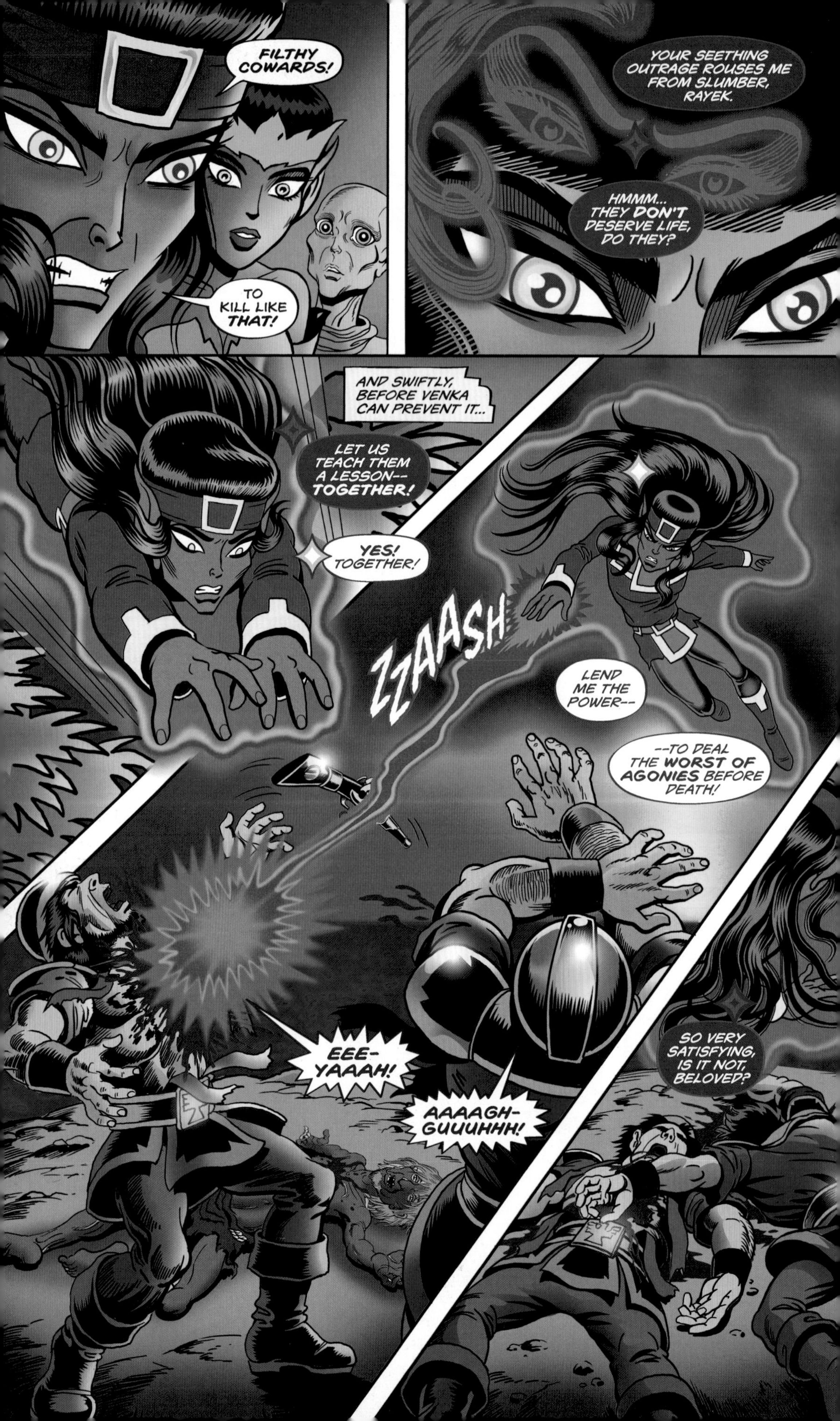
FILTHY COWARDS!
TO KILL LIKE THAT!
YOUR SEETHING OUTRAGE ROUSES ME FROM SLUMBER, RAYEK.
HMMM... THEY DON'T DESERVE LIFE, DO THEY?
AND SWIFTLY, BEFORE VENKA CAN PREVENT IT...
LET US TEACH THEM A LESSON-- TOGETHER!
YES! TOGETHER!
ZZAASH
LEND ME THE POWER--
--TO DEAL THE WORST OF AGONIES BEFORE DEATH!
EEE- YAAAH!
AAAAGH- GUUUHHH!
SO VERY SATISFYING, IS IT NOT, BELOVED?

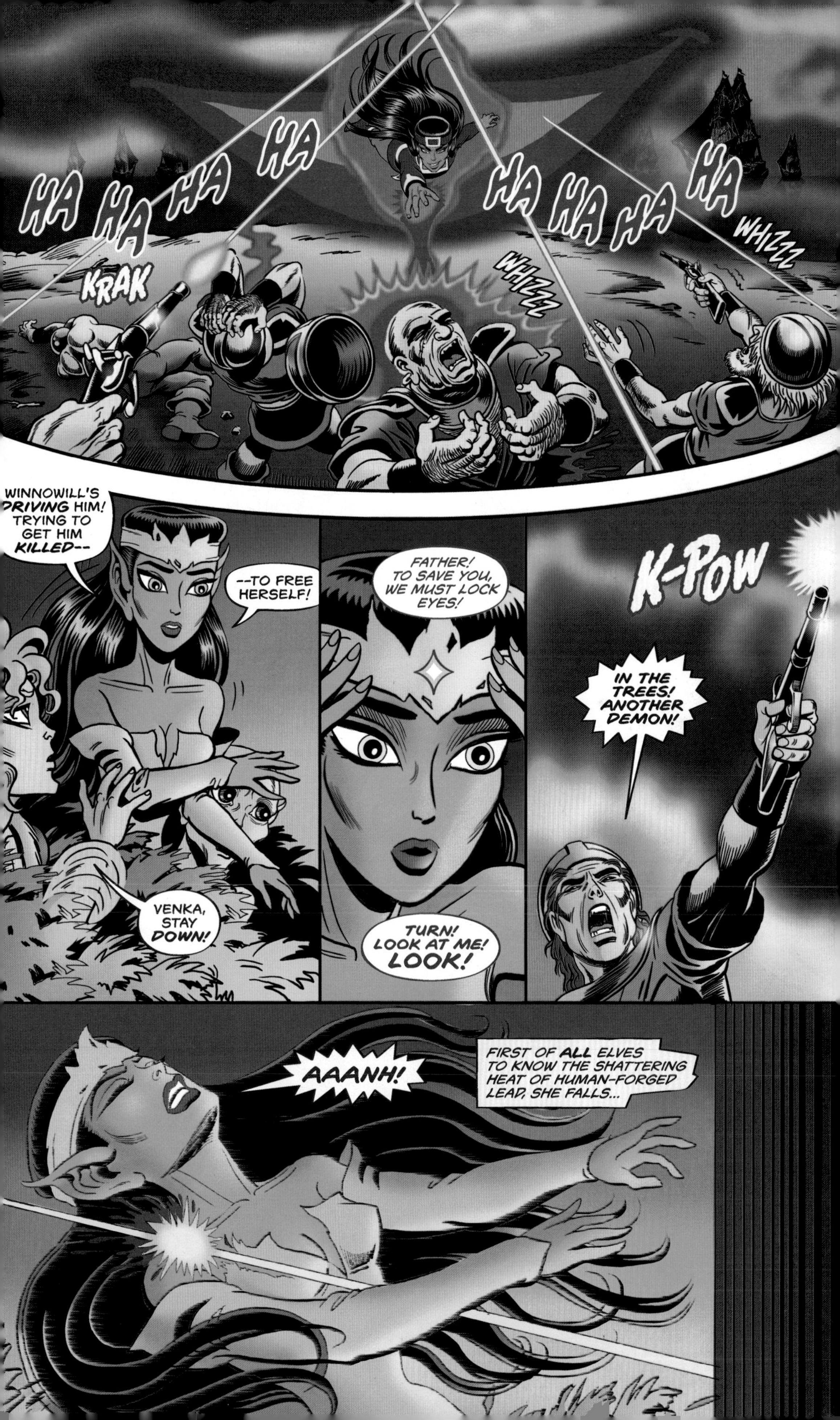
HA HA HA HA
HA HA HA HA
KRAK
WHIZZZ
WHIZZZ
WINNOWILL'S DRIVING HIM! TRYING TO GET HIM KILLED--
--TO FREE HERSELF!
VENKA, STAY DOWN!
FATHER! TO SAVE YOU, WE MUST LOCK EYES!
TURN! LOOK AT ME! LOOK!
K-POW
IN THE TREES! ANOTHER DEMON!
AAANH!
FIRST OF ALL ELVES TO KNOW THE SHATTERING HEAT OF HUMAN-FORGED LEAD, SHE FALLS...

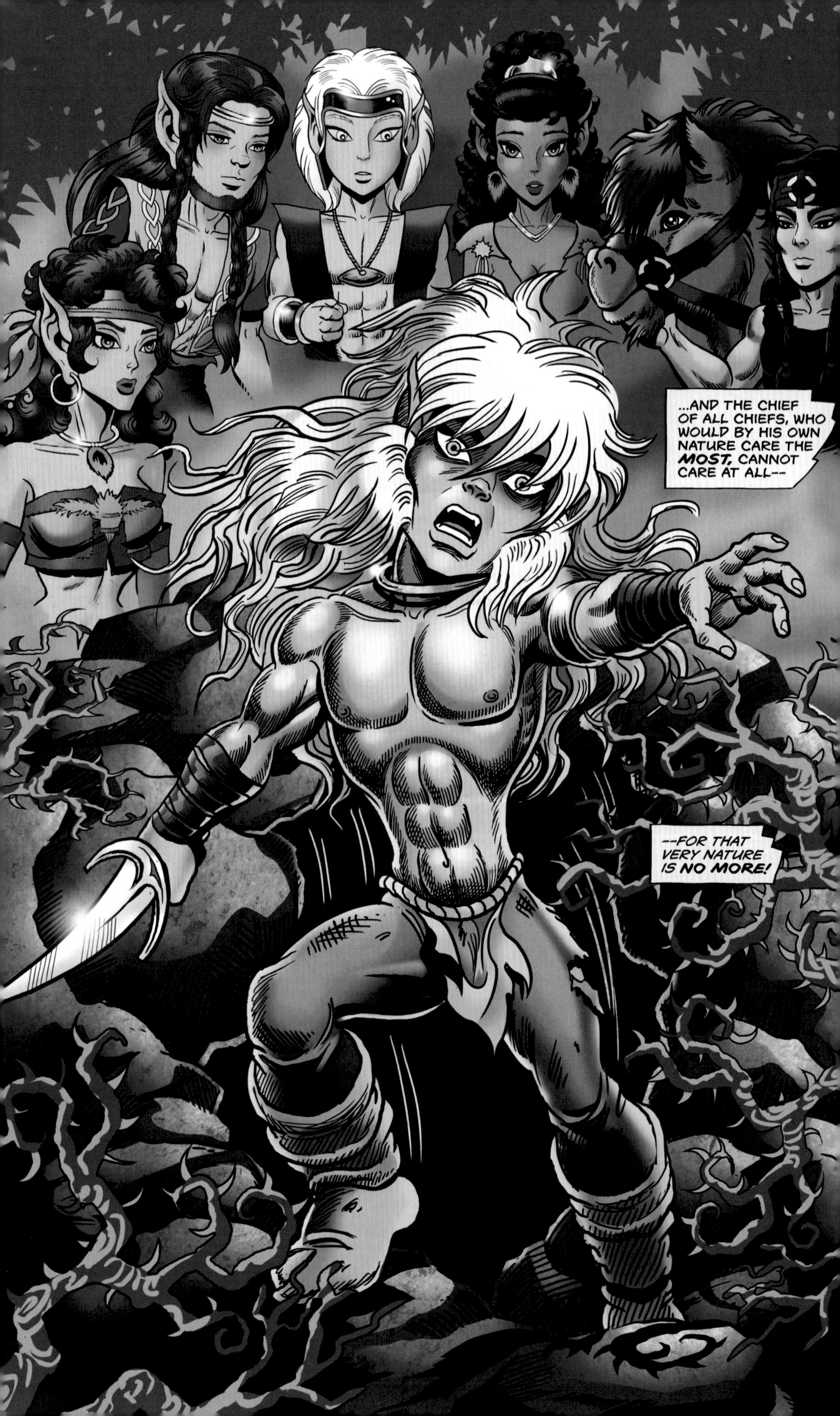
...AND THE CHIEF OF ALL CHIEFS, WHO WOULD BY HIS OWN NATURE CARE THE MOST, CANNOT CARE AT ALL--
--FOR THAT VERY NATURE IS NO MORE!

COVER GALLERY

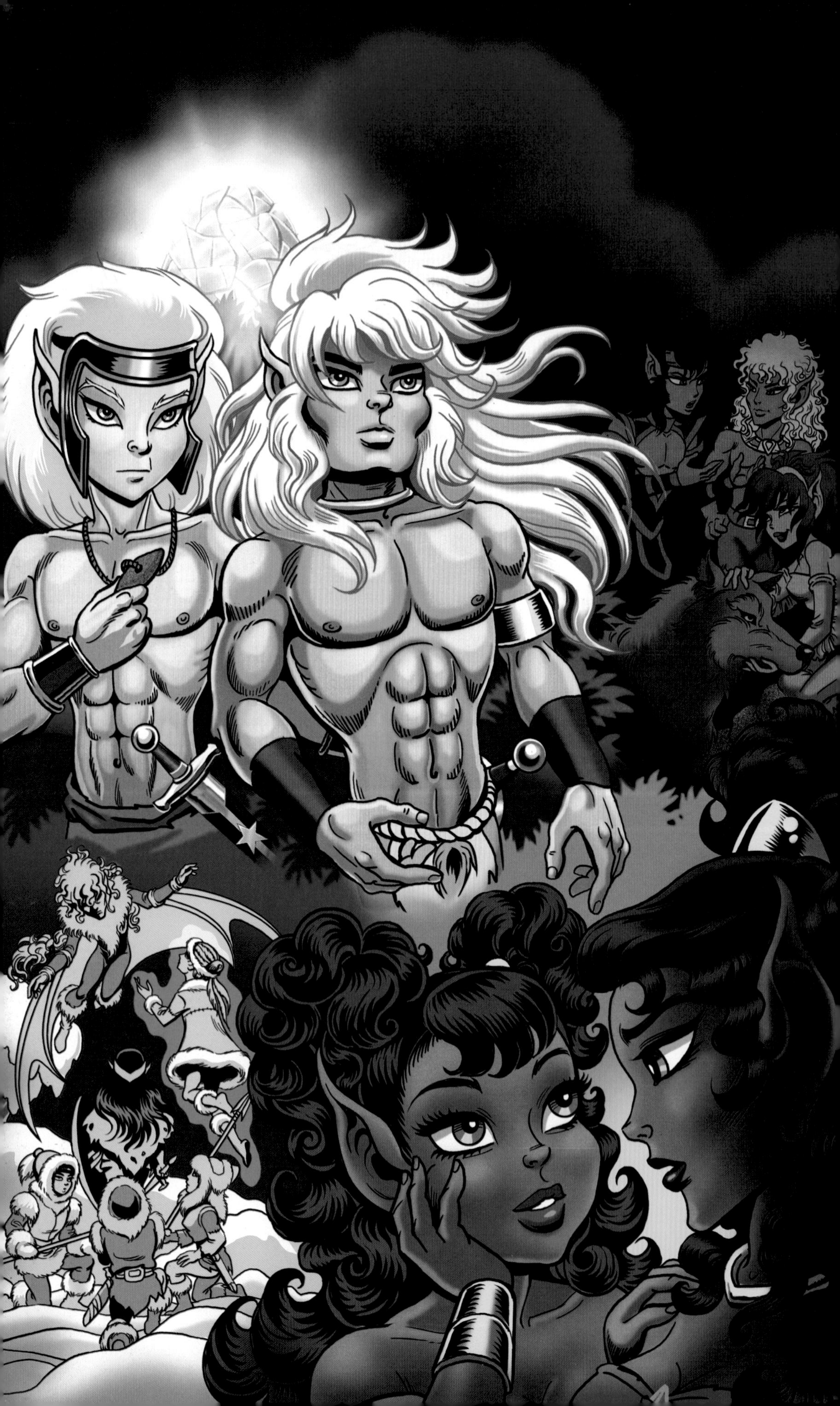

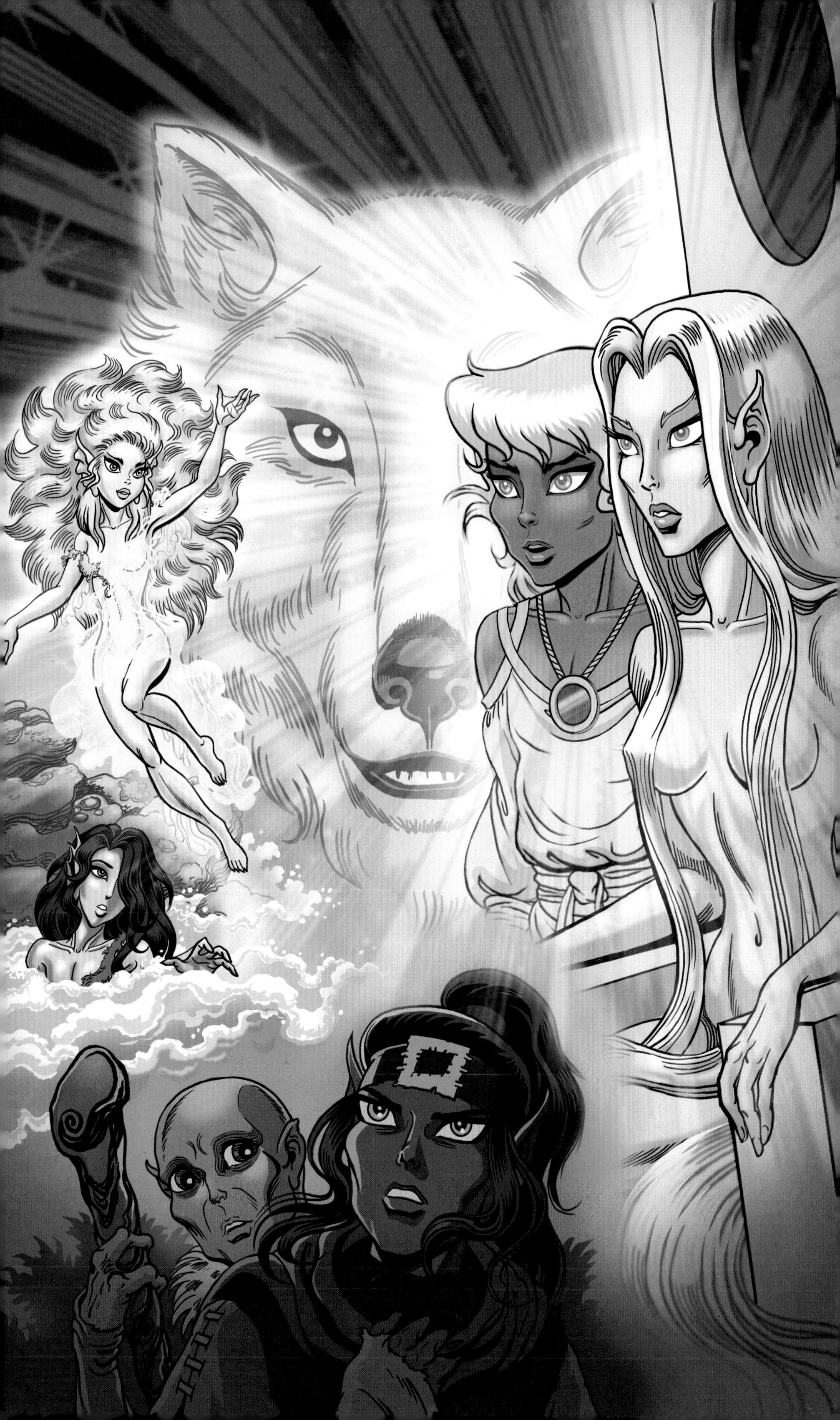

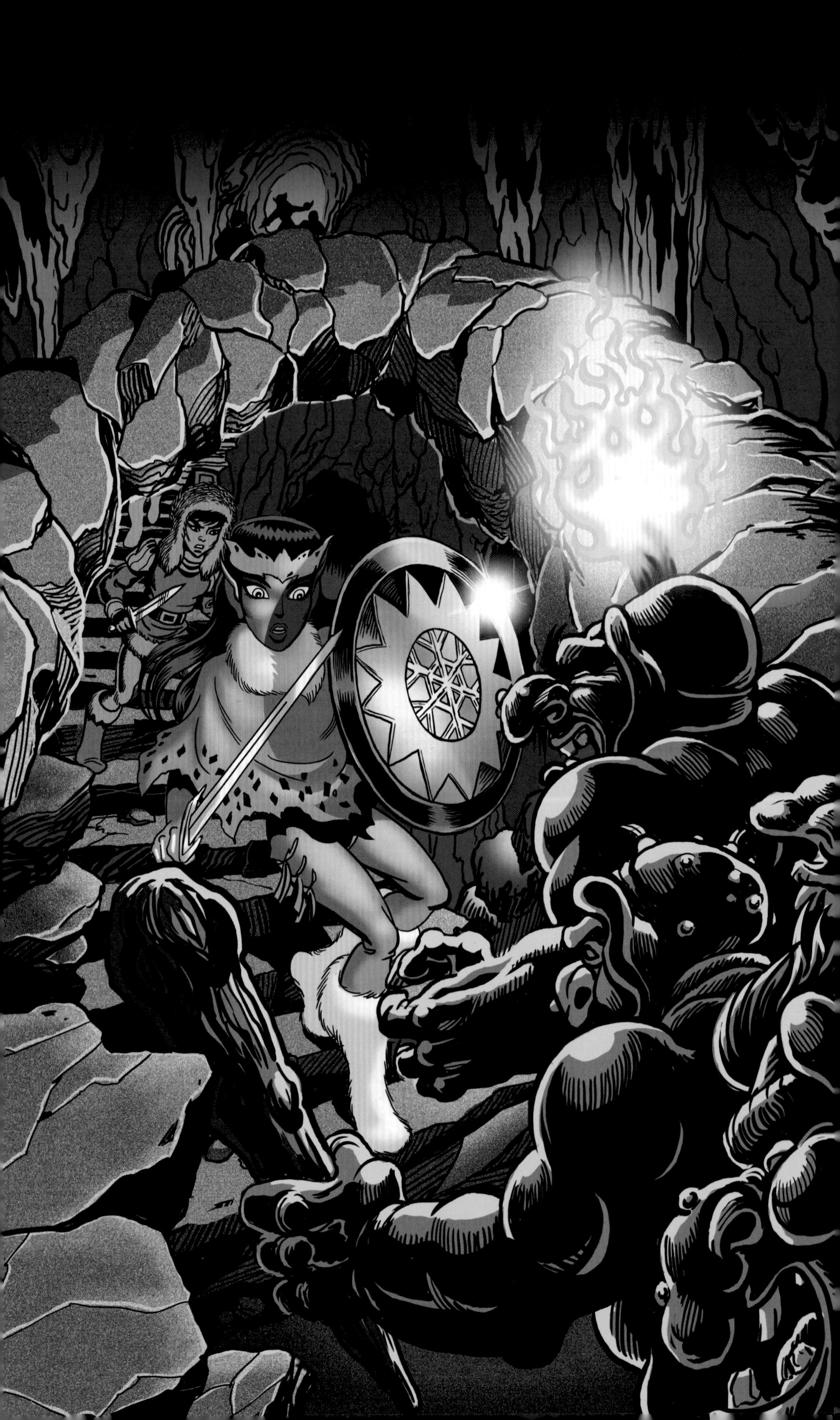

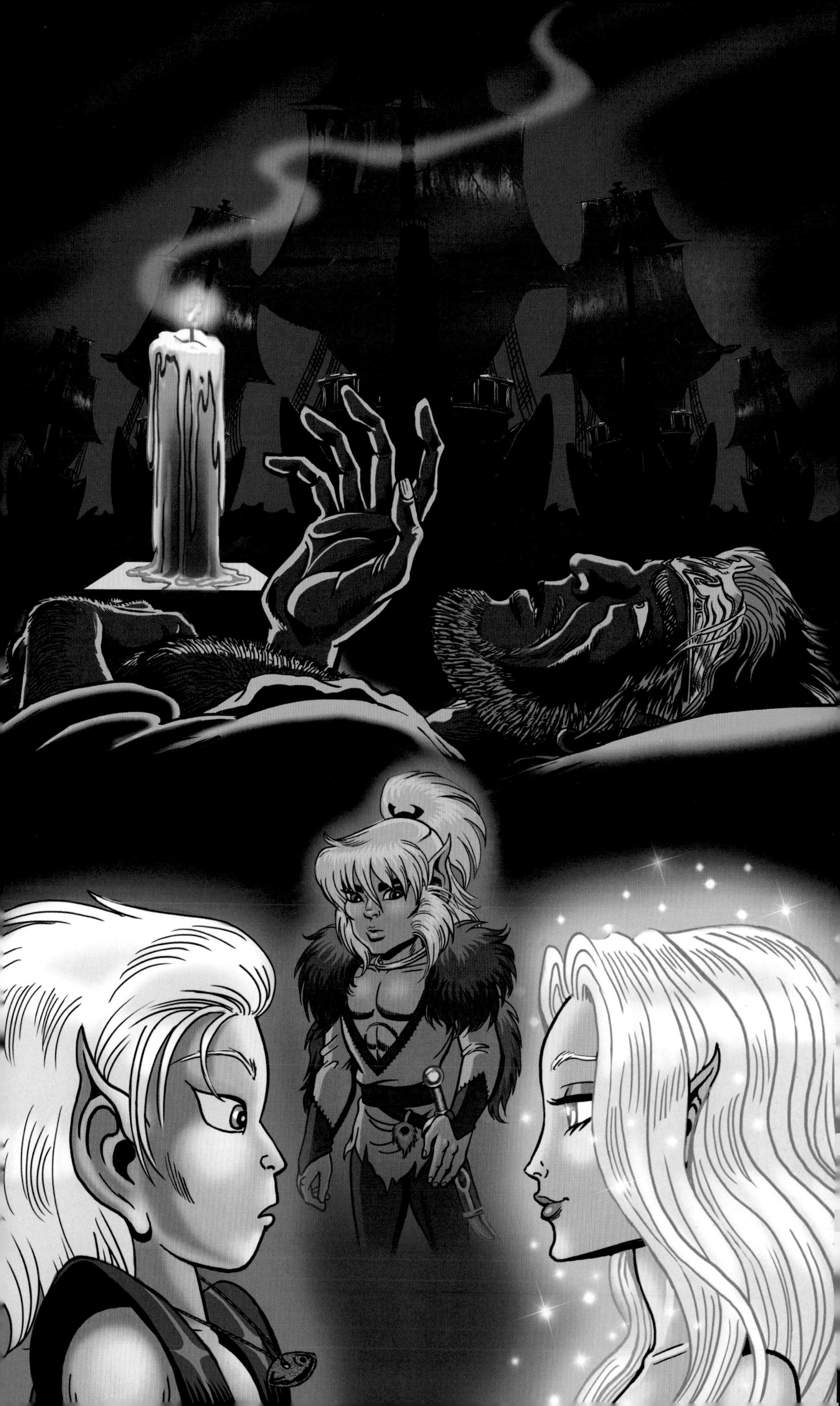

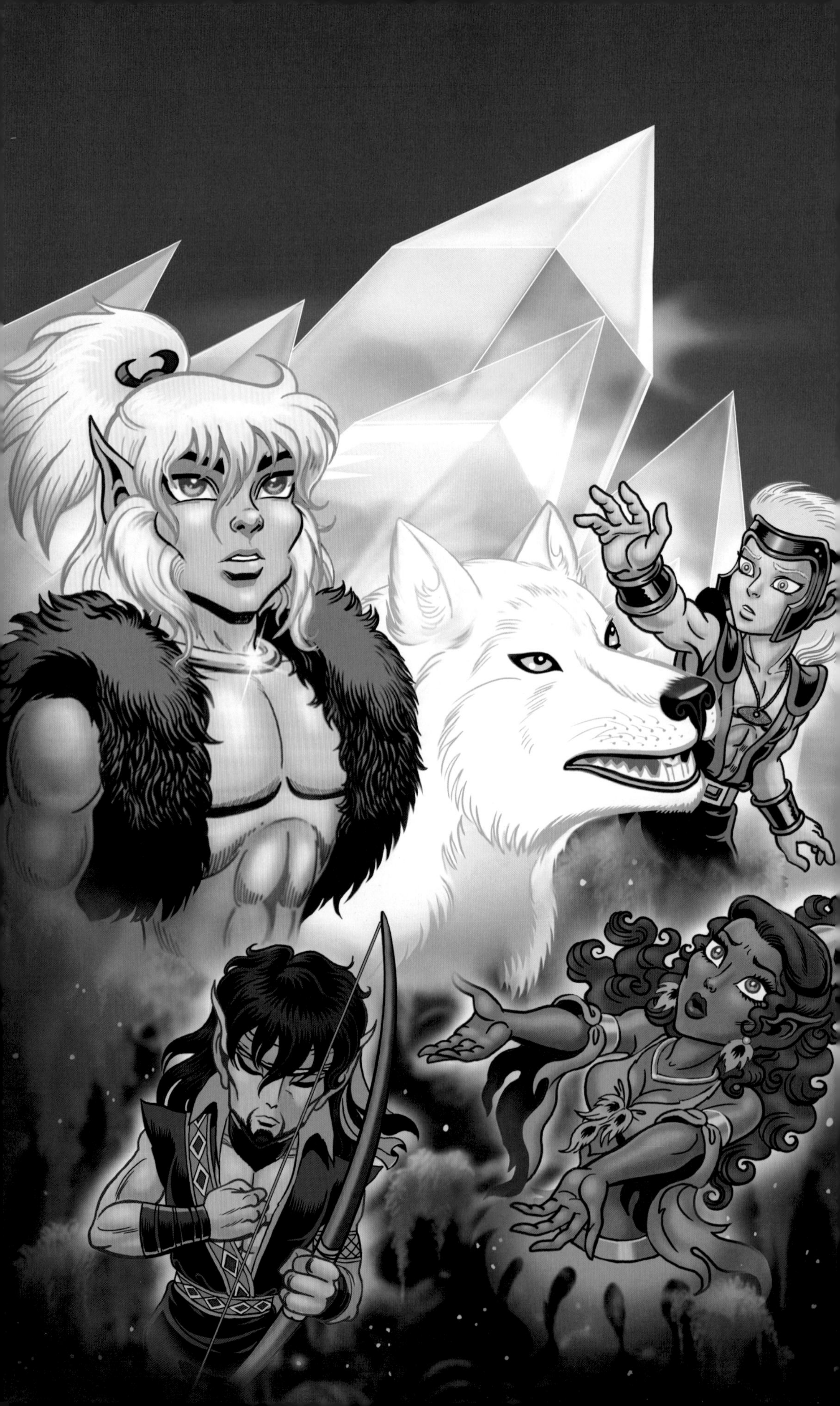

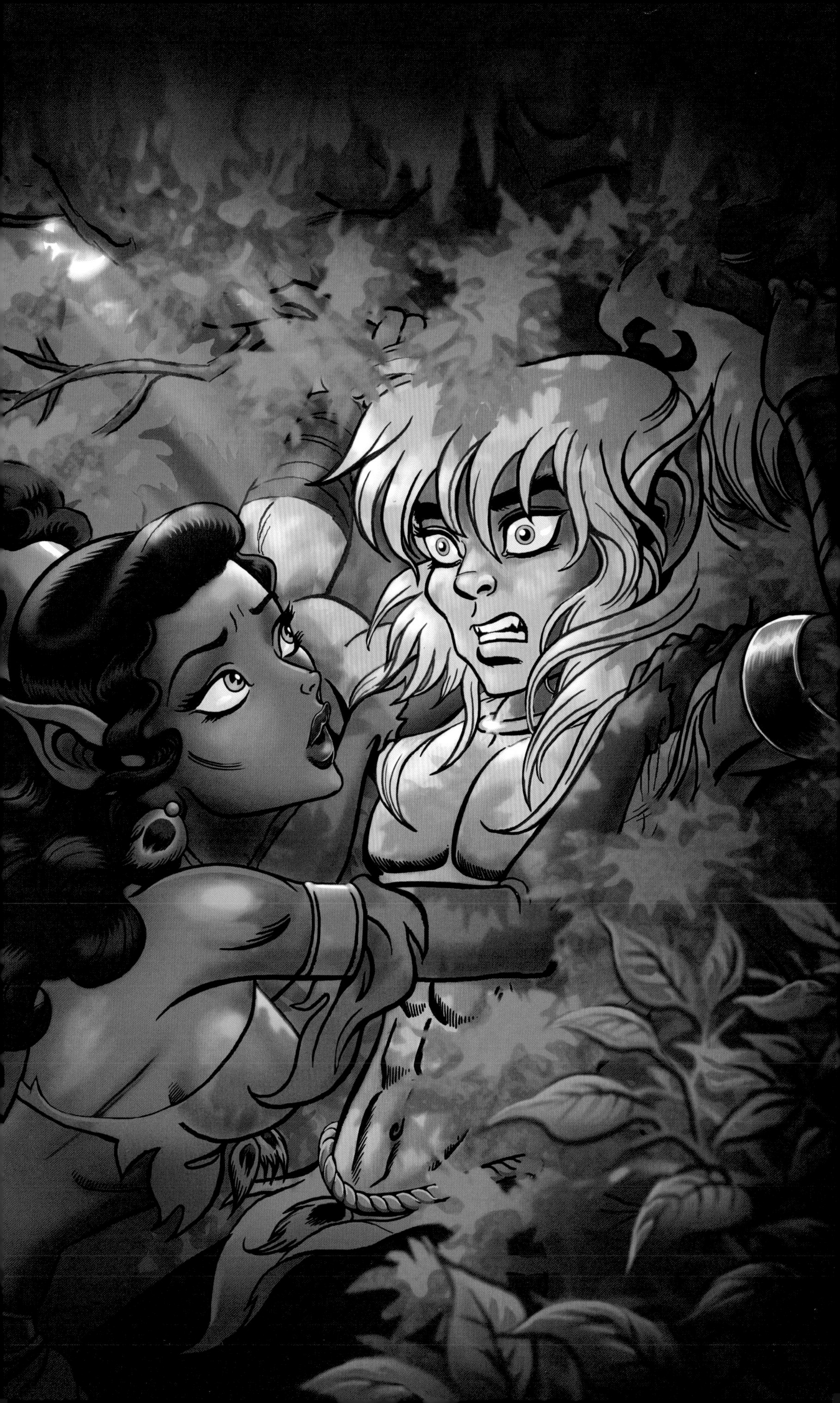

ELFQUEST®

DISCOVER THE LEGEND OF *ELFQUEST*! ALLIANCES ARE FORGED, ENEMIES DISCOVERED, AND SAVAGE BATTLES FOUGHT IN THIS EPIC FANTASY ADVENTURE, HANDSOMELY PRESENTED BY DARK HORSE BOOKS!

THE COMPLETE ELFQUEST
Volume 1: The Original Quest
978-1-61655-407-1 | $24.99

Volume 2
978-1-61655-408-8 | $24.99

ELFQUEST: THE ORIGINAL QUEST GALLERY EDITION
978-1-61655-411-8 | $125.00

ELFQUEST: THE FINAL QUEST
Volume 1
978-1-61655-409-5 | $17.99

Volume 2
978-1-61655-410-1 | $17.99

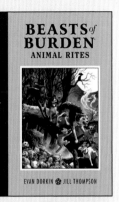

MORE YOUNG ADULT TITLES FROM

DARK HORSE BOOKS!

BEASTS of BURDEN
ANIMAL RITES
EVAN DORKIN JILL THOMPSON

BEASTS OF BURDEN: ANIMAL RITES

Written by Evan Dorkin, illustrated by Jill Thompson

Beneath its surface of green lawns and white picket fences, the picturesque little town of Burden Hill harbors dark and sinister secrets. It's up to a heroic gang of dogs—and one cat—to protect the town from the evil forces at work. Adventure, mystery, horror, and humor thrive on every page!

978-1-59582-513-1 | $19.99

REXODUS
JAMES FARR JON SOMMARIVA

REXODUS

Written by James Farr, illustrated by Jon Sommariva

The Black Blood is unleashed upon the earth again, and Amber must save her father—and the world—with the aid of the only other Black Blood survivor, Kelvin Sauridian, a dinosaur from the past. In this high-stakes adventure, can they put aside their differences long enough to save the planet they both called home?

ISBN 978-1-61655-448-4 | $12.99

Juice Squeezers
DAVID LAPHAM
WITH COLORS BY LEE LOUGHRIDGE
THE GREAT BUG ELEVATOR

JUICE SQUEEZERS: THE GREAT BUG ELEVATOR

Written and illustrated by David Lapham

Tunnels made by a legion of giant bugs crisscross the fields below the quaint California town of Weeville, and only one thing can stop them from overrunning the place: the Juice Squeezers. A covert group of scrawny tweens, the Squeezers are the only ones who can fit into the cramped subterranean battlefield and fight the insects on the frontlines!

978-1-61655-438-5 | $12.99

THE USAGI YOJIMBO SAGA
STAN SAKAI
BOOK 1
SAKAI

THE USAGI YOJIMBO SAGA

Written and illustrated by Stan Sakai

Dark Horse proudly presents Miyamoto Usagi's epic trek along the warrior's path in a new series of deluxe compilations. The rabbit *ronin*'s adventures have won multiple awards and delighted readers for thirty years!

VOLUME 1: 978-1-61655-609-9 | $24.99
VOLUME 2: 978-1-61655-610-5 | $24.99

★ *"Zodiac Starforce* is a big, bright, colorful light in the darkness." —COMICSVERSE ★

ZODIAC™ STARFORCE

BY THE POWER OF ASTRA

"*Zodiac Starforce* is everything I want in a modern magical girl story—friendship, diversity, sweet battles and enviable costumes. Kevin and Paulina have crafted a both stunningly beautiful and heartfelt adventure series."

—Kate Leth
(*Edward Scissorhands, Bravest Warriors*)

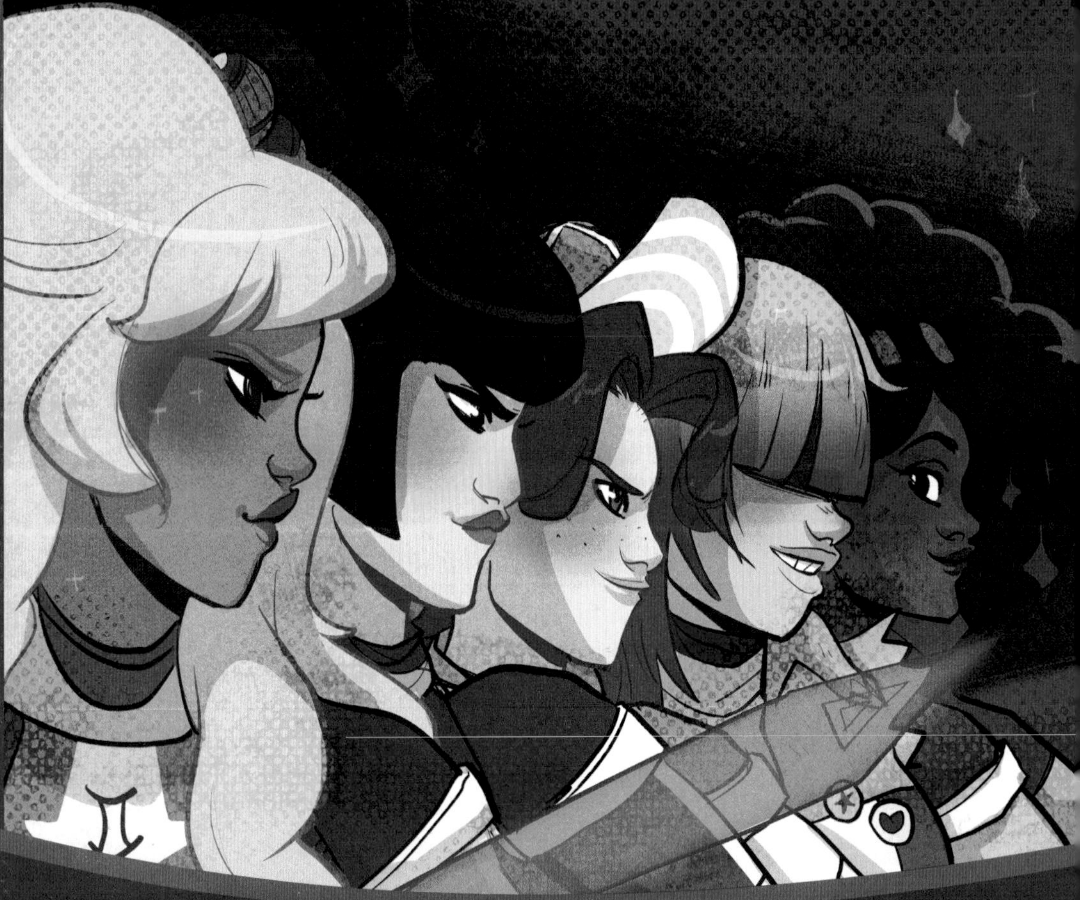

THEY'RE AN ELITE GROUP of teenage girls with magical powers who have sworn to protect our planet agains dark creatures . . . as long as they can get out of class! Known as the Zodiac Starforce, these high-schoo girls aren't just combating math tests. They're also battling monsters—not your typical afterschool activity But when an evil force from another dimension infects team leader Emma, she must work with her team o magically powered friends to save herself—and the world—from the evil Diana and her mean-girl minions

978-1-61655-913-7 • $12.99

DARK HORSE BOOKS

AVAILABLE AT YOUR LOCAL COMICS SHOP OR BOOKSTORE! • To find a comics shop in your area, call 1-888-266-4226.
For more information or to order direct visit DarkHorse.com or call 1-800-862-0052 Mon.–Fri. 9 AM to 5 PM Pacific Time. Prices and availability subject to change without notice.